The Bremo
B E A C O N

~ *Phase I — The Bremo Memo* ~

Tom Blanchard

PublishAmerica
Baltimore

First printing

PublishAmerica has allowed this work to remain exactly as the author intended, verbatim, without editorial input.

Hardcover 978-1-4512-7551-3
Softcover 978-1-4241-6731-9
PAperback 978-1-4512-5408-2
PUBLISHED BY PUBLISHAMERICA, LLLP
www.publishamerica.com
Baltimore

Printed in the United States of America

Foreword

This is an actual and factual account of an investigation that spanned exactly ninety days. Everything happened and was reported in the same chronological order as it is here presented.

This document starts off as one thing and slowly but surely turns into something altogether different. Your author was to some extent transformed and a bit radicalized by the process of composing it. Perhaps in reading it, you too will be altered in ways you least expect.

Two small notes are now made in the interest of full disclosure. Firstly, as you would soon discover, Bremo is a nickname for the city that is the focal point of this narrative, namely Bremerton, Washington.

Secondly, the secretary or administrative assistant referred to as Adrienne is actually a composite of more than one person.

I have tried to give full credit to all news sources. The newspapers read are the daily Kitsap Sun, and the weekly Bremo Patriot. Many sources were taken from the Internet and it is not possible to avoid gleaning information that has traveled from site to site to site until all references to the original source that may have been authored by name and copyrighted has been lost. Any failure to attribute any material to original sources is purely unintentional.

Case File # GW0601—WA [G File]

Transcriptions from Digital Voice Recorder #8 [OLYMPUS DW-90]

Note: Adrienne, please use this machine DVR #8 to track my on/off field billing time on the G File, but please hold all billing—see me; continue to segregate out and route both my personal and Bremo observations to my chron file and to the ongoing Bremo Background folder. I'll put the surveillance and confidential intel on DVR #3. Let's try out that Dragon Naturally-Speaking 8.1. When editing the auto type, drop in any appropriate URLs. I will register my office billing time personally. Thank you!

January 2006

01-30-06 Monday—Dropped off Vehicle #1, *Flying Cloud*: White '04 Double Cab Toyota Tundra Limited, in Navy Yard City at Long's Auto Rebuild. The Doug and Jim Singer brothers operate the place and it is a trip and a half. Wonderful to see two brothers able to function as business partners. Jim says, "Yeah…we've had our things but we got them about all ironed out." Long's was established in 1941 and I am sure there remain items here from 1941, both below and overhead resting on 12 x 8 timbers. Doug is a surfer and has done California, Mexico, and Australia among others. He has an eye on the Pacific Coast of Costa Rica. We chatted about that as I was down there last March.

Navy Yard City is rather special. I seem to recall that it is unincorporated. That is to say, a county strip or patch nestled into Bremo. This is a really tight enclave. Real estate has already doubled here in the last couple of years. Navy Yard City is no doubt considered by some to be a blighted area, but the location is excellent with some spectacular views over Sinclair Inlet across to Port Orchard, and in some cases, views down upon a berthed all-purpose nuclear aircraft carrier…at times several of them. These are very solid folk.

Puget Sound Naval Shipyard located adjacent to the city of Bremo on Sinclair Inlet was established in 1891. It was the first dry-dock and repair facility in the Pacific Northwest capable of handling the largest ships. It was named Puget Sound Naval Station until July 22, 1901 when it became Puget Sound Navy Yard. On November 30, 1945 it was renamed Puget Sound Naval Shipyard, PSNS.

Adjacent to and west of the Naval Shipyard was Naval Station Bremerton. In June 2004, nuclear SubBase Bangor merged with Naval Station Bremerton. The new command was named Naval Base Kitsap.

After the Japanese attack on Pearl Harbor of 12-07-1941, the 'day that will live in infamy', five of the six surviving battleships were brought here to the Bremo shipyard for modifications and repair: U.S.S. Tennessee, U.S.S. Maryland, U.S.S. Nevada, U.S.S. California, and U.S.S. West Virginia. These battleships were dubbed the 'Pearl Harbor Ghosts' because the Japanese had declared them sunk. Thanks to these amazing folks, the Ghosts lived on to kick some righteous butt.

During WW II, Navy Yard Puget Sound repaired twenty-six battleships…some more than once…eighteen aircraft carriers, thirteen cruisers, and seventy-nine destroyers. In addition, the

30,000-plus shipyard workers built fifty-three new vessels, including five aircraft carriers, thirteen destroyers and eight destroyer escorts. They also overhauled, repaired, or fitted out another four hundred warships. What a truly monumental accomplishment!

Bremo's Armed Forces Festival in May is the largest and longest running Armed Forces Day parade in the United States. Other events that week in 2005 included: an Armed Forces Festival Golf Tournament, an Advanced Acoustic Concepts demonstration, and a Military Culinary Arts Competition.

It starts in downtown Bremo at Fourth and Chester, goes up Warren Ave to Burwell, Burwell to Pacific, and along Pacific Avenue to Sixth Street. It began at 10:00 AM, and last year consisted of over one hundred and forty entries including bands, floats, military units and much more. Third Street was renamed Burwell Street one hundred years ago in January of 1906. It was named after Rear Admiral William Turnbull Burwell, who as Captain Burwell was Commandant of the shipyard from July 02, 1900 until August 29, 1902.

The battleship USS Missouri, site of the Japanese surrender treaty signing that ended World War II, was assigned to the Pacific Reserve Fleet at PSNS in 1955. For thirty years, she served as the city's primary tourist attraction. Hundreds of thousands of visitors walked the 'surrender deck' before the ship was recommissioned in 1985. The Mighty Mo is now proudly established in Pearl Harbor. Everyone here hated to see her go, but realize that she is now where she needs to be.

Despite this illustrious, exemplary and glorious past, Bremo fell on hard times, especially in the past few decades. Not long ago, a husband and wife team of morticians from Bainbridge Island, also a part of Kitsap County along with Bremo, somehow managed to get a permit to operate a crematorium, right here in Navy Yard City behind the beautiful West Hills Elementary School. [Kitsap County has more shoreline than any other county in the country, and a population of about 265,000. It was named after Chief Kitsap, the most powerful of all the Chiefs from 1790 to 1845. As war chief of the Suquamish Tribe he held sway over territory from what is now Olympia, Washington all the way north to the Frazier River in British Columbia. The renowned Chief Seattle was one of his sub-chiefs.]

This crematorium fiasco eventually surfaced and the general outrage was augmented by that of the school's attorney, the Bremo City Attorney, and many others. The panel that heard the Appeal at the County Seat in Port Orchard ruled that a crematorium at that location would be most illegal, inappropriate, and objectionable in a virtual myriad of ways.

The entire Olympic Peninsular is mostly under populated. Kitsap County is more wilderness, mountain, and water, than anything else. Bainbridge Island…[Adrienne please look up that reverse sexual harassment suit movie w/ Michael Douglas and Demi Moore…and plug in here. Danke!] >>> *Disclosure* (1994) <<< Michael Crichton's best selling novel was made into a movie that was directed by Barry Levinson. The movie local is Bainbridge Island / Ferry / Seattle. [Ferry: www.wsdot.wa.gov/ferries/]

Bainbridge Island… has a median home price of $500,000 and is sparsely populated. So, despite hundreds and in fact thousands of square miles of rural area, these unenlightened ones from Bainbridge Island demand to stuff a crematorium into a residential neighborhood in our City by an elementary school…and at last report, despite overwhelming and fierce opposition, were fighting on via their attorney to do just that. As if the long enduring 'real' patriots of Navy Yard City deserve any part of such an atrocity.

Bainbridge Island and East Bremo are separated only by the Port Orchard Passage, but to drive you need to go north the entire length of the island, over the Agate Pass Bridge, through Poulsbo, Keyport, and then over and south all the way past Silverdale, Tracyton, and on down to Bremo. These people would travel that far, just to burn human bodies and spew the smoke over a residential city neighborhood and elementary school. The irrationality of people never ceases to amaze me.

Of course the place would itself be cremated by the justifiably enraged local citizenry, I would suspect in rather short order, were these Bainbridge Islanders ever to be successful. The locals say that this woman looks and acts just like Olive Oyl, except that she is mean and nasty. I have no comment.

I backpack past the quietly notorious National Bar…established in 1944, Crazy Eric's Famous Burger stand, the home of Harvey's Butter Rum Batter, and the Fleet Reserve Association Branch 29—Meeting second Tuesday of every Month 18:00—NAV / USMC / USCG. One could write a book about each of the above.

14:15 ON
Took Veh#5, *Yellow Dragon*: Yellow & Black 2000 Honda Valkyrie Standard six cylinder/six carburetor motorcycle, to the Kitsap Family YMCA [www.ymca.net/] in East Bremo. The original YMCA was dedicated in Bremo on May 01, 1911. I meet with Glen Godfrey the Executive Director and cut him a personal check for $5,000. That makes $10,000 and should put me where I need to be in March when the Teen-Youth Room Expansion Project is dedicated. This is also a perfect way to rub shoulders with a Listee or two.

Amazing what you can do with an unlimited budget. Or almost unlimited…the first quarter mil is pre-approved and that should more than do it, but additional funds are certainly available if circumstances require them. I will not pad…I will not pad…I.

I have dealt with large budgets and big cases before, but nothing like this, not with all these disparate and desperate elements.

It has been raining for the past couple of months. A record rain of 18.69 inches fell in January, second only to 20.02 in 1953. Nevertheless I consider that Western Washington weather is the finest for me in the USA. Great to be back on the Valk!
14:15 OFF

February 2006

02-01-06 Wednesday—I picked up Veh#1 and managed to lose my clipped money. A few hundred tops but I had these Chilean bills that I cannot easily replace and the 'wolf' money clip was a Christmas gift from Xiao-Ping. Plus, a lucky $2 bill that I had managed to hold onto from about 1991. State Salvage on Alameda in Long Beach, California oddly enough pays everything out in $2 bills.

The $2 bill had been with me through the Whidbey Island years; the year in Maine and Western Canada in 98; all over Europe and North Africa in '02; from one end of China to the other, through the Three Gorges River Dam locks, off the coast of North Vietnam, Hong Kong, and Japan in '03; Mexico in '04; and both Central and South America in '05…but the mile or so from Navy Yard City to The Charleston Overlook apparently proved to be too much for this old boy.

Great job by Doug Singer…the Tundra looks like new. The most surprising thing was what he did with a small spot on the hood that was pebble-hit. He made it disappear w/o painting the entire hood.

13:00 ON
Stopped at the main Bremo Bank of America at Warren and 6th. Replaced the lost cash and adopted a new money clip that just happened to arrive last Christmas from Lilian in Las Vegas. I suspect there is an omen or two here that I would ignore to my own detriment.

Easy free two-hour parking everywhere downtown and no lines anywhere. I hit CJ'S, Filipino Cuisine and Café at 705 Pacific Avenue, Bremo and scarfed up a combo platter of rice, pancit, some nice pork dish but it was not adobo. No beer, but the mango nectar was perfecto. Sorry Adrienne!

Continued south on Pacific Avenue to the Admiral Theatre Box Office, 515 Pacific Avenue, Bremo, [http://www.admiraltheatre.org/]. The Admiral Theatre was constructed in 1941 and originally was to be named the Rivoli…Admiral Burwell again? It was restored at a cost of $5 million and books regional and national acts. I obtained a ticket for 20:00 this Friday, Children of Uganda, sponsored by Barb & Larry Otto. I am scheduled for the Gallery across the Avenue that evening at 17:00. Also purchased a ticket for Stand Up on Saturday, February 11.

As I leave I can't help but admire the crystalline vertical rectangular plaque:

* *

The William H. Gates Foundation

Our gift for the renovation of this theater was made in part to memorialize the contribution of Bill's family to the life of this community over many years.

His great-grandfather and grandfather established and operated the U.S. Furniture Store on the property adjacent to this theater on Pacific Avenue from 1917 to 1954.

In addition to the operation of that business, they and other members of the Gates family were enthusiastic participants in Bremo's civic and fraternal activities.

They were good for the city and the city was good for them.

Bill and Melinda Gates

* *

The Admiral Theatre Foundation Board of Directors—Joanne Haselwood, Chairman; Jerry Reid, President; Donna Gay Boyle, Vice President; Louise Cramer, Vice President; David W. Gitch, Vice President; W. Earle Smith Jr., Secretary; Kyle Kincaid, Treasurer; Ruth Enderle, Executive Director.

And...Brian Buskirk, Kyle Cruver, Klaus Golombek, Michael Huey, D.M.D., Lori Johnson, Leslie Krueger, Abraham Laners, Vickie Levi, Patricia Lund, Marilyn Mantzke, Paul McCullough, M.D., Norman McLoughlin, John Mitchell, Rodney B. Near, Judith Rammel, Tim Ryan, Gussie Schaeffer, Helen Langer Smith, and Ed Wolfe.

Adrienne: Run above against the List. Also start a second List B and put all non-hits on that one. Thank you.
14:00 OFF

I head kitty corner across the intersection to the beautifully restored downtown Bremo United Sates Post Office. In this National Historic Building the lobby boasts a WPA art project 1938 mural by Earnest Norling titled, *Northwest Logging*. It is one of those entries where you must turn either right or left to descend a few stairs to reach the main floor.

Just mentioning the era of the WPA is bringing on a rant. Our country is getting increasingly polarized. I get the distinct impression that much of the right would be happy to see the bulk of the left vanish, believing that this would be great for the nation. I get the same feeling from the left about the right.

One of our county's greatest strengths is our two-party system. A one-party arrangement is obviously inherently flawed and multi-party systems are a mess. We occasionally have a third party but it either supersedes one of the other parties and becomes a new second party, or it dies out.

Two is fundamental. We all have two sides to our brains, the right — spatial, random-access side and the left — linear, logical side. The crosscheck in our heads leads to focused action. Men and women bond in a similar faction. Classically, the woman takes the random-access side and the man the logical side although the reverse is often seen. This is the basis for all of the Mars~Venus and battle of the sexes conflict. It is when a man and a woman are in complete agreement, having approached an issue from two different directions, that they make their best joint judgments.

Our courts operate in a like fashion with a defense and a prosecution. A jury hearing these two arguments coming from opposite points of view is in the best position to render a just verdict. Would you like to stand trial where there was only a prosecutor? The point is that neither party is better than the other but that both are absolutely essential. Absolutely essential.

Speaking in the simplest of terms the Democrats are liberal, progressive, and place the emphasis on the individual. The Republicans are conservative, like the status quo, and place the emphasis on the good of the country

.

If individual interests ever got total control and voted everyone huge benefits, the whole country would collapse and that would be a terrible outcome for all. On the other hand, if all monies were plowed into development and folks had no disposable income, that would be just as bad. How could corporations prosper if no one had any disposable income?

It is the tension between these two valid forces that establishes the appropriate point of equilibrium for the particular time and place. That is what produces the proper agreements and the wonders of the United States. The historical trend over the centuries is clearly to an ever more liberal state, but tough times will cause temporary backtracking.

The best example that I can think of to illustrate what I mean is our Great Depression. If asked, most people would simply describe that era as one of the worst in our history. But let us analyze it. If you travel around the U.S. and make note of all the structures built between 1929-35 what you find is simply amazing.

You find schools in every city, often named Washington, Jefferson, or Lincoln. You also find libraries in every city. A national system of roads; many of our country's most famous major bridges like the Golden Gate; minor bridges everywhere; train stations, hospitals of all sizes including the monster Los Angeles County General, and similar ones in Chicago, New York and elsewhere; dams of all sizes everywhere including Hoover Dam; buildings everywhere including the Empire State Building; water and sewerage systems, retaining walls; tunnels both major like the Holland Tunnel and minor ones; and just about anything else that men could build.

And when they got through building everything conceivable in and between the cities and towns, they did the National Parks. Next time you are at a major National Park, look at the construction dates of those lodges, rest rooms, roads, and large rock retaining walls.
Government organizations like the WPA, CCC, and many others were designed to feed, house, and provide work to those who could not find a job. If you work for little money but food and shelter, that is the definition of slavery...except that here you had the option to quit and starve. They built just about everything except great pyramids.

And consider the background. The Great War was over. The party was on. They called it the Roaring '20s for a reason. They tried to kill the party by outlawing booze. No way, Jose. That just created the mob and Al Capone. The gals were 'flappers' and they did the Charleston, the music was fast and jazzy, the speakeasies were booming, clerks and taxi drivers were buying stocks...nothing could stop this party!

Then the boom lowered and the plug was pulled. The soup kitchens and apple lines formed up. Folks were happy to work for next to nothing. And so on. So with the above perspective, what kind of a time was the Great Depression?

Well, using the above outline, from the individuals' or Democratic view it was a terrible, terrible time. But from the country's or Republican view it was the best time ever. They built the whole damn infrastructure for the 20th Century. Paved, literally, the way for our ability to do what we did in WW II and set the stage for the prosperity that followed. This is all far from exact but you get the general idea.

It seems evident that this country will become even more divided before we come back together. People are starting to hate each other over politics. Let's try to realize that we are all essential, all mean well, all love our country, all want what is best for it, and all will make mistakes. It is just about impossible to predict how things will turn out. Good news often brings bad results and bad news often heralds a good outcome.

The first *Patriot Act* allows the FBI to look into a lot of our activity without judicial approval and without our knowledge. *Patriot Act II* as now proposed will extend that to allow them to look into our financial and also our medical records without judicial oversight or our knowledge. This is both scary, one would think unconstitutional, and would trash our Bill of Rights. The British doing that to us was a major cause of the American Revolution.

Many will simply figure that it has nothing to do with them. It will only be used against terrorists. But no sooner did they get the *Patriot Act* passed but some nut-job used it to bust a titty bar in Las Vegas. Another milestone in post 9-11 governmental action was bringing down Tommy Chong for selling bongs! Stop that chanting…Ashcroft…Ashcroft…Ashcroft.

Of course it was also clearly unconstitutional when Honest Abe suspended Habeas Corpus during the Civil War. You gotta do what you gotta do. It should get straightened out later. 9-11 was 911. We are in for some rough sledding ahead. Lets try to get through it working together.

16:30 ON
02-03-06 Friday—I arrive at the Amy Burnett Gallery, 412 Pacific Avenue. If this Bremo saga is too have a heroine, there is no doubt but that it will be Amy Burnett. Amy supplies a large portion of the heart, mind and soul of Bremo. Ms. Burnett is a local artist with a national reputation. Her work is especially prized in the Southwest, in places like Santa Fe and Sedona.

She grew up here and has operated a large and successful Art Gallery in Downtown Bremo for the past fifteen years. She was a driving force in creating the Downtown Arts District. She writes for the Bremo Patriot, 520 Burwell St., Bremo [www.bremertonpatriot.com/], has published a book of said articles as *Amy's Bremerton Window,* aids and assists all manner of local community and cultural endeavors, and is just generally a main spark plug for so much of Bremo's boosterism.

There are eighteen stops on the Art Walk that runs from 17:00 to 20:00 on the first Friday of each month. Participation is quite good for a stormy February evening. I make contact with Ms. Burnett and check out the participants.

The brochure mentions that the famous phrase, "Give em' hell, Harry!" was yelled to Harry Truman right here on Pacific Avenue. Some credit that cry with President Truman's surprising victory over Dewey in 1948.

Across the street from here, up until 1940, was the U.S. Furniture Company store operated by the grandfather of the World's

Richest Man, William Henry Gates IV. A block or two away, the William Gates Family Home on 6th St at Highland Avenue was built by the great grandfather of Microsoft founder Bill Gates at a cost of $3,000 in 1925. William H. Gates III, Bill's father, was born here in 1925.

Adrienne, I have been advised that WHG III attended a Bremo Rotary Club meeting last year, please verify. [www.bremertonrotary.org/] Or maybe it was the Central Lions [/www.bremertonlions.org/] Also please run member names and develop Lists A & B.

Highland was and remains an interesting avenue. The southern end T-bones into 6th Street. The remarkable home, presently up for lease, directly opposite this intersection has a castle-like cylindrical tower spanning both floors and ending in a conical roof. This large home was designed and built by James d'Orma 'Dorm' Braman in 1920. It is a registered historical landmark.

Dorm was elected Mayor of Seattle in 1964. Under his guidance, voters passed the largest bond issue in that city's history for public improvements. President Nixon appointed him Assistant Secretary of Transportation. The local history is endless.

In the 1980's downtown Bremo died a slow death as the merchandisers opened up in the malls in general and in the Silverdale community specifically. Silverdale now is home to a concentration of more retail outlets than anywhere else on the Olympic Peninsular and most probably anywhere in Washington State. Safeco [www.safeco.com/] was the builder of the Kitsap Mall in Silverdale.

In 1990, *Money Magazine* hailed Bremo as 'America's Most Livable City'. Several years later, *Reader's Digest* called Bremo, one of the top places to raise a family. The city's 36-hole Gold Mountain Golf Course west of town in the Bremo watershed is often included in lists of the nation's finest municipal courses. Property values have probably doubled here in the last few years, but Bremo poses one of the greatest challenges of any urban renewable project imaginable.

Bremo's population stands at 37,520 but can increase depending on which Navy ships are in port. During WW II, the city exploded to about 82,000 people as the shipyard worked around the clock to repair war-torn ships and to launch new ones. This violently rapid expansion of the town left a hodgepodge of single-family homes of every type and description. They are reflective of the various architectures, styles, and modes of construction from all parts and corners of the nation at that time. Workman simply built in whatever way they knew from wherever they came.

Building was hasty, windows were few and frills mostly nonexistent. Anything was better than living in someone's garage, a trailer or a tent. Many housing developments were Navy driven and still exist today.

Underneath it all are lovely rolling hills, spectacular water views, and a beautiful variety of flora and fauna. Most Americans think of the Pacific Northwest, or Northwet, as constantly drenched in rain and thus abundantly supplied with water. Not so. Droughts are frequent. Whidbey Island for example, the longest island in the continental U.S. has but one aquifer and is severely restricted in water resources. So are many other locales.

The Olympic Peninsular however, houses that rarity, a temperate rain forest. The main Union River Reservoir that plentifully supplies Bremo's drinking water is so clean that it requires virtually no treatment mandated by the State. Reference the Olympic National Park [www.nps.gov/olym/].

One thing about living on Whidbey Island that managed to surprise even an old cynic like me was the division between North Whidbey and South Whidbey residents. I lived on a sand spit in the southernmost bay. There was a most definite island people connection, a we are all in the same boat mentality that was beautiful and would manifest itself in numerous ways. This was most welcomed by us escapees from Los Angeles.

But I was really surprised that this feeling did not extend itself to North Whidbey. At that time in 1994, South Whidbey had no traffic signals or fast food outlets, whereas North Whidbey had a number of each. It was as if they were two separate islands. It reminded me of that cartoon, perhaps a Dr. Seuss where there were two identical sets of odd looking critters except that one group had a star on their forehead, while the other group did not. That was all it took to divide them into opposing camps.

The oldest rule in politics is to divide and conquer. It is hard not to get a kick out of how prisoners will do their damnedest to divide themselves along racial lines; while they are kept prisoners by guards of all races who are working together to keep them locked up. So many are doing time, not so much for being criminals but for being hotheaded and stupid.

Item: Yes, Long Island, NY is longer than Whidbey Island; it just isn't an island, as was determined by the U.S. Supreme Court. It is a little known fact that to be an island, the surrounding water must be of approximately the same depth. Long Island is in fact a peninsular that has a river cutting across the top of it. The depth of the river is not of the same order of magnitude as the surrounding ocean and sound.

Bremo also has a general hospital, Harrison Medical Center [www.harrisonmedical.org/]. Other popular Puget Sound islands such as Bainbridge, Vashon and further north, the San Juans, are notably lacking in this regard. Harrison is undergoing and planning major expansions over the next twenty-five years. It will draw patients not only from Kitsap County, but also from Clallam, Jefferson, and Mason Counties. The community is also home to Naval Hospital Bremo.

Both auto and passenger only ferries run between Bremo and Seattle. It is a beautiful run that takes one hour on the slower auto ferry. The ferry terminal is part of the new Bremo Transportation Center and is combined with the main local bus terminal.

Our good Mayor Cary Bozeman started his 'bringing back downtown' campaign almost immediately after taking office in 2002, cleaning up dusty streets and planting flowers. He has been on quite a roll ever since.

The adjacent area has already been developed as the Maritime Park and Memorial Plaza. This includes the Public Gardens, the Kitsap Conference Center, Hampton Inn and Suites, a marvelous fountain that goes through almost endless patterns of water including cylindrical arcs of water with amazingly distinct and sharply defined beginnings and ends, several interesting eateries, the Open Spaces area and Great Lawn, Galleries, and Anthony's HomePort Restaurant is due to open there this Spring. Another redevelopment project is a countywide Mosquito Fleet Trail. The term Mosquito Fleet requires an explanation. Before Washington State Ferries was established, private ferryboats ran all over the place and were known as the Mosquito Fleet.

The February 12th edition of the Kitsap Sun [www.kitsapsun.com/] reports that Hotel Concepts Inc. of Seattle plans to pay Bremo $930,000 for three parcels near 4th Street and Washington Avenue and including the old City Hall. This will increase downtown hotel rooms from nada in 2004 prior to the Hampton Inn and Suites, to about 280 upon completion of this new facility.

One of the biggest projects was a new regional government center on Fifth Street, a combined $72 million effort completed in 2004. The Norm Dicks Government Center was named in honor and appreciation for our Congressman for the 6th District of Washington State. [www.house.gov/dicks/]

Next come the Harborside Condominiums [www.harborsidecondominiums.com] and a new marina. Thus, one will be able to live on the new waterfront in a scintillating Harborside condo, walk on a covered walkway to the ferry terminal…and cruise in and out of downtown Seattle. That is two hours per day not fighting traffic but rather, reading a book, preparing a business presentation, studying for a class at the University of Washington, UW, or sipping a specialty coffee purchased onboard or picked up at the new Starbucks just prior to entering the terminal.

In line with this development is the hotly debated 'Tunnel Project'. The Washington State Department of Transportation, WSDOT, is designing a tunnel to separate downtown Bremo pedestrian traffic from offloading Washington State Ferry traffic. The periodic surge of ferry traffic through downtown Bremo is interfering with pedestrian and local traffic flow including access to and from the Bremo Transportation Center. This project is in partnership with the city of Bremo, Kitsap Transit, the Federal Highway Administration and the Federal Transit Administration. Other organizations have also participated in its development, including the Puget Sound Naval Shipyard and local emergency services.

A tunnel that connects the Transportation Center to Burwell Street will improve pedestrian safety and local traffic flow in downtown Bremo by removing approximately 65% of offloading ferry traffic from Washington Avenue. The final tunnel design will be completed in the spring of 2006. Right of way acquisition will be completed in the fall of 2006, with the construction contract awarded soon afterward. Such a tunnel will mesh nicely with the overall plan to make downtown Bremo a pedestrian friendly place.

The Washington State Legislature has not directly allocated funds for this project. The transportation improvement portion of this project is funded primarily by federal funds from the Federal Highway Administration, and the Federal Transit Administration. WSDOT is providing matching funds in the form of ferry toll credits issued to it by the Federal Highway Administration. City funds will only be used to cover 45% of the cost of the associated Combined Sewer Overflow Reduction project.

Moving north along the boardwalk the USS Turner Joy, a Vietnam-era destroyer, is open for tours daily throughout the summer. The USS Turner Joy played a major role in the 1964 Gulf of Tonkin Incident. Actually it was a pair of alleged attacks by North Vietnamese gunboats on two American destroyers, the USS Maddox and the USS Turner Joy in August of 1964 in the Gulf of Tonkin that sparked the full U.S. engagement in Vietnam.

The first attack was a heavy gun fired upon the USS Maddox by a North Vietnamese patrol boat. The second attack was originally thought to be perhaps eight torpedoes fired on both of the above ships. Later research, including a report released in 2005 by the National Security Agency, indicates that the second attack did not in fact actually occur at all, but consisted of misread sonar readings by nervous operators.

The USS Turner Joy can even be rented for the evening. There is nothing like having control of a U.S. Navy destroyer to make for a memorable bash!

Puget Sound Naval Shipyard, which occupies much of the Sinclair Inlet waterfront, is something of a mixed blessing, presenting an industrial facade that feeds Bremo's long-standing reputation as a funky blue-collar town.

The shipyard itself is in the midst of an upgrade that would help change its industrial exterior. It has moved historic Building 50 to an area adjacent to the ferry terminal, where it will anchor a new Maritime Park and house the Bremo Naval Museum. In its new location, the building will provide a more attractive first impression for ferry passengers, in stark contrast to the 'plate yard,' an outdoor storage area for raw steel that has been greeting arriving visitors.

The city's showcase Louis Mentor Boardwalk, actually a wide concrete walkway, is linked to the new Kitsap Conference Center and will be connected to an expanded marina to provide waterfront amenities.

Also downtown are the Kitsap Historical Museum on Fourth Street [www.kitsaphistory.org/] and The Naval Memorial Museum of the Pacific aka Bremo Naval Museum that has yet to move into Building 50 from Pacific Avenue. The downtown waterfront boardwalk is the site of summer evening concerts and the wonderful Labor Day Blackberry Festival, both sponsored by the Bremo Main Street Association.

Across the Port Washington Narrows from downtown, in East Bremo, a new ice arena opened to much fanfare last year, and has added recreational opportunities to the existing Kitsap Family YMCA, the Bremo Ice Rink, and city pool. A new skatepark is now also a reality in Eastpark.

When the WW II war work ended, Bremo's population plummeted to 27,000. It has ebbed and flowed ever since. Today, there are about 37,500 residents. That makes Bremo, Kitsap County's largest city by far. And if location, location, location, are the three most important aspects of real estate, then Bremo has it all.

But the kicker is that the entire city core is covered with these slapdash homes of every possible description. There is hardly any homogeneity to be found anywhere. Even if you do find a nice house that you like, next door may be one that hasn't been painted in over a half century; bare wood. How can this city possibly get the total upgrade that it needs and so richly deserves?

Looking at the opposites poles of this dilemma, the yin and yang of it, we have at one extreme the following. An entity buys up the whole city, bulldozers it all down and rebuilds Bremo in the finest manner commensurate with its prime location, bountiful attributes and natural resources. This would in one giant fell swoop, increase the real estate value perhaps tenfold. Who or what could finance such a huge project? Well…you really don't have to look that far away. How to do it, how to make it fly is another question. As soon as the city began to be bought up, prices would skyrocket out of practical reach.

At the other end of this spectrum, you have slowly expanding waves of demolition and rebuilding emanating out from the newly developed waterfront and the other designated centers of renewal around town. What this basically means is that these local folk, these hardworking, hardscrabble, strong, tough, talented, highly skilled, loyal and patriotic, blue-collar, shipyard workers and their families will be slowly driven out by ever increasing property taxes. This process will be excruciatingly slow and painful, and never will it result in a proper redevelopment.

Either way there are always holdouts that will never sell. I have a favorite photo, an interesting picture that I took in Beijing in 2003. It is on the grounds of a technical university, perhaps the University of Transportation or something like that. My traveling companion and translator, Xiao-Ping, lived there as a child when her father taught there. Just an outline of the foundation of her former home remains. It looks about the size of one regular sized room that was sub-divided into four tiny rooms. A fruit or nut tree that helped keep them alive during the very worst of times somehow survives.

After the Korean War her dad was sent to the Chinese Embassy in North Korea. He later became the head of the China Science and Technology Museum and brought an exhibit on tour to the U.S. and Canada. He gave me the most beautiful Commemorative piece you can imagine. It honors the 15th Anniversary of the Opening of said Museum, 1988–2003, and is a gorgeous hunk of Lucite with engravings, a clock and hydrometer, all packaged in a typically marvelous Chinese case.

At age sixteen, Xiao-Ping, during the so-called Cultural Revolution was sent on a train one thousand miles north to Siberia to work on a manual labor farm. Eventually she escaped that fate, found her way to Seattle, worked five jobs; throwing newspapers, washing dishes in a Chinese restaurant kitchen, tending an old guy, tying wire [construction rebar ~ and she is tiny], and I forget the last one; and simultaneously taught herself English. She saved twenty thousand dollars and talked her way into the University of Idaho at Moscow even though she flunked the language test. There she ended up with a Masters degree in Biochemistry and passed on a doctorate program as she was by then more than ready to enter the fray.

Many years ago this Beijing University needed to remove all of these rural-like dwellings so that it could expand into that area with high-rise buildings of learning. Ms. Zhu's family had three bedrooms so the University exchanged this humble abode for both a two bedroom and a one bedroom modern apartment. But the picture I took is of a multigenerational family that incredibly is still there. They simply refused to ever move.

A Westerner will be quick to wonder why a totalitarian government that shoots people right after sentencing and then sends the family a bill for the bullet; why such a power could not move this family…and what about eminent domain? But the property is on University grounds and there must have been some loophole in the documents. They are still right there today, with their corral and rural patch, surrounded by new modern buildings. Holdouts can holdout for amazing lengths of time.

Everywhere we went in Mainland China capitalism was rampant. People here still think in terms of Communist China or Red China. Nothing could be further from the simple truth. When you have a totalitarian government and capitalism, that is fascism…the opposite of communism. There is a Bumper Sticker that says, Ever Stop to Think…and Forget to Start Again? But really, that is not the problem; most people are just too busy and overloaded these days to find the time to stop to think about such things at all.

Like the Russians, the Chinese used communism as a means of transition from feudalism to capitalism, but the Chinese never were the true believers in the same way that the Soviets were. One more thought, most people are aware of the one child policy in China to control and reduce population, but how many realize that this means a whole huge country consisting of families that all contain an only-child…and the ramifications of that?

Getting back to the Art Walk, I eventually checked out another gallery and then slipped down around the corner, across from the Ferry Terminal to the funky Westside Burrito Connection, 208 1st Street, next to the South Pacific Sports Bar at 218. I order a huge Regular Burrito and an Alaskan Amber draft. Some fledgling musicians have taken up the vacant tables in the back but I give the pregnant food assembler two bucks and she consolidates them, and frees me up a table.

20:00 and I am at the Admiral Theatre for the Children of Uganda. It is all quite lovely. I missed my siesta and have to will my eyes open. I dig the drums, singing, and dancing and wonder if there is any way that I could possibly steal a small portion of the energy possessed by these marvelous children. **12:30 OFF**

When you come right down to it, we are all Africans, either stay-at-home African, or wandering Africans. Let me explain. Years ago during the Cold War that pitted the two super-powers against each other, the Soviet Union and the United States, it eventually occurred to me that what it really was, was a battle between the Stay-at-Home Russians, and the Wandering Russians.

When humanity moved up into the Caucuses Mountains, hence the name Caucasians, the tribe eventually became so large that it had to split in two like a giant amoeba. Roughly half stayed behind, while the other half left. I think they moved up into what is now Germany and on down into what became Greece, Italy, Spain, France and so forth.

Then about a thousand years later, the original tribe had once again grown to the point where it had to split in two. These wanderers followed the same valley pathways as before and they also descended south into Rome and elsewhere. This time they were described as the Goths, Visigoths, Vandals, and just plain nasty barbarian tribes.

Later these Caucasians set sail from Spain, Portugal, France, England, and all the rest to populate the New World, including the United States. Despite the time lags and long journeys, they are still emanating from the same original tribe; hence the Stay-At-Home Caucasians vs the Wandering Caucasians; i.e. the Russians vs. the Americans.

Back to the Africans. I sent my DNA to the National Geographic's Genographic Project and just got back the results. My Y-chromosome shows that I belong to Haplogroup R1b— M343.

This means that my ancestors left Africa in group M168 about 50,000 years ago. By 45,000 years ago they had crossed onto the Arabian Peninsular and the Middle East as M89. 40,000 years ago as M9 they passed through Northern India. Recall that Sanskrit is an ancient Hindu language from Northern India. It is a member of the Indo-European family.

Then 35,000 years ago as M45 they expanded through Central Asia and the Caucuses. 30,000 years ago, now as M173 they migrated across Northern Europe and finally as M343 they ended up in Lisbon. A bit earlier they broke off into a Great

Britain Migration, the Magdalenian Culture, the Lascaux Cave in France, and the Altamira Caves in Spain.

Interestingly to me is that when I was wandering over Europe and North Africa is 2002, I surmounted considerable difficulty in reaching the Lascaux Cave and I also found that the food that was most to my liking in Europe, was in Portugal in general and Lisbon in particular.

I have since traced my male French ancestry back to one Noel Blanchette, born circa 1608 in Saint Omer de Rosiere de Santere, Amiens, France. By the mid 1600's my antecedents had arrived in Quebec, Canada. Later they drifted down into New England to work in the mills of Massachusetts and Rhode Island.

And so, we are all either Stay-at-Home Africans or Wandering Africans, or hauled off into slavery Africans. There is only one race...the human race. Differences in skin color are merely a result in the various gradations of melanin.

Melanic pigmentation is advantageous in many ways: It is a barrier against the effects of the ultraviolet rays of sunlight. On exposure to sunlight, for example, the human epidermis undergoes gradual tanning as a result of an increase in melanin pigment. It is a mechanism for the absorption of heat from sunlight, a function that is especially important for cold-blooded animals.

It affords concealment to certain animals that become active in twilight. It limits the incidence of beams of light entering the eye and absorbs scattered light within the eyeball, allowing greater visual acuity. It provides resistance to abrasion because of the molecular structure of the pigment. Many desert-dwelling birds, for example, have black plumage as an adaptation to their abrasive habitat.

Stay-at homes seem to be generally more into the status quo and authoritarianism, while wanderers are, not surprisingly, more open and flexible. Next time you go to a high school reunion, compare those that never left the old hometown with those that moved about the country and the world.

The African Continent is a toughie. We have so many images of those emaciated starving children. To be honest, after the first sympathetic reaction, many feel that they shouldn't have babies that they can't feed and if others feed them; that will just produce even more starving babies than before. It is far from being that simple but the reaction is understandable.

Couple that with such enormous atrocities like the Rwandan Genocide, which was the slaughter of almost a million Tutsis by Hutus during a period of 100 days from April 6th through mid-July 1994. But then you read, *Left to Tell* a book by Immaculee Ilibagiza about discovering God amidst the Rwandan Holocaust, and you have to think that this beautiful young girl who survived against all odds is a living saint.

Africa is such a contrast in beauty and ugliness. The HIV/AIDS situation is another monster. Many African men for misguided reasons of so-called purity, prefer that their women be dry during intercourse. The females can accomplish this with one powder or another but this naturally leads to vaginal tearing and that is HIV's best friend. Even more grotesque is the disgustingly ignorant belief that if you have AIDS you will be cured if you have sex with a virgin. It is obvious where that leads. In addition they still have such barbaric practices as female genital excision, often called female circumcision; a procedure that is as uncalled for as it is painful and risky

Twenty-three of the poorest twenty-five countries in this world are in Africa and getting poorer all the time. Extreme poverty is killing minimally thirty thousand daily...that is one child every 2.88 seconds. The death toll of the Great Tsunami of December 2004 was around a quarter of a million people. That is about an average week's death toll from extreme poverty!

Regarding that Tsunami, can anyone actually believe that those who died were all bad people who had it coming? Or must one see all these deaths for what they were, a statistical occurrence arising from an act of nature. In this case a monstrous wave generated by a great undersea earthquake. No more and no less. True the dead were mostly Muslims and it occurred the day after Christmas...what does that mean? It means nothing, absolutely nothing.

People die when churches collapse or catch fire and Muslims have a penchant for trampling each other to death during their mass pilgrimages to Mecca. None of this is the work of a higher power; this is man making his usual mistakes.

All life on Earth collectively is known as Gaia [www.gaia.org/] and she is hurting right now. One could think of her as an aspect of Mother Nature. Can you be healthy if your body is perfect except for one leg that is terribly ill? Can our planet be healthy if one continent like Africa has such severe problems? Worldwide, eight hundred million people are living on less than a dollar per day. Meanwhile every cow in the European Union is being subsidized at $2.50 per day.

Above I mentioned Lisbon. That is what we call that city but its real name is Lisboa. This is a real pet peeve of mine. Why in this day and age do we not call and teach our children the true names of other countries and cities? Habit? The world is quite small now, and many will travel. There is no Rome, Florence, or

Venice; they are Roma, Florencia, and Venezia. Those are not that far off, but how about Vienna? If you are waiting for a train to Vienna you will have a long wait...the name is Wien. Prague...no such place, it is Praha...and so on. What sense does it make to teach the names of major world cities by deliberately misspelling them, sometimes beyond recognition?

The same thing occurs with other words like the Muslim holy book the Quran, or Qu'ran, or Quoran, why do we call it the Koran? Just to confuse ourselves? And now that it is so much in the news we are forced to start at least trying to spell it correctly. At this time I do not know which spelling is correct. Then there is the misuse of words. The absolute worst is the use of the word miracle.

In my sixty-four years I have never seen or heard of an actual miracle. But it is used more and more often in the media to describe anything and everything. Well let me correct that, all existence and life is a miracle. How about this entire world arising from nothing? Talk about a free lunch. Everything about life should be seen as the miracle that it is.

But let us say a busload of twenty-nine kids goes over an embankment and one survives. It is guaranteed that this survivor will be called a miracle. Excuse me? What about the law of averages? The above is no more a miracle than if you drop a dozen eggs and one or two don't break. If you want to pretend that some divine power personally altered reality and the laws of nature in order to save that one child...if you want to put the credit for that there, than you must lay the twenty-eight tragic deaths at that same doorstop. You can't reasonably expect to have it both ways.

Another word used a lot is decimated. It comes from deci as in decade and decimal, and it means ten. It has been said that the

Italian Military performed so poorly in WW II because they were too civilized. Well, they used to know how to do it. Decimated was the term for a brutal but effective practice of the Roman Army. When the boys really screwed the pooch they were decimated. They were formed up and every tenth man stepped forward. These men were then put to death. It didn't matter what they had done or not done, or how good or bad they had performed as soldiers. They were slaughtered. An army of 100,000 was now only 90,000; but after that demonstration they didn't hesitate to fight boldly and to work together as a team.

But now it doesn't matter what the loss is, it could be 1% or 90% or anything and the talking head newscasters will go on about how this or that was decimated. These same mindless newsreaders will also misuse language and reel off numbers that are off by orders of magnitude without batting an eye.

Adrienne, I feel another rant coming on. But if I understand your feedback correctly, you are tripping on these streams of consciousness. They certainly help me on these lonely surveillances out in the cold and dark. You know how I feel about waste and cannot even think about leaving the motor running. Besides, it would attract too much attention. Just as time can pass quickly when you are absorbed on a computer, so too with organizing thoughts and recording them. It works great and has a cathartic effect by getting this stuff off my chest.

Yes, you are right about the lack of humor. Humor is such a part of my everyday existence, and my writings are often a scream, but I too have noticed how that is lacking here. Sitting in a cold vehicle may have something to do with it, but it is more than that. Obviously I am venting but that too could be done with more humor. To tell you the truth, it is more like I am, I don't want to use a New Age word like channeling, it is more like this stuff is coming to me from a muse and that this particular muse is really pissed-off at current events and the state of humanity. My job is basically just to speak these messages out as they come to me.

I lived in the black community in Los Angels for thirty years, although the last five were spent mostly in Mexico. I have a great love and affection for black folk in general. They are a very gifted and generous people. In Africa, a hungry man with only a piece of bread to his name will often share half with you if you are in need, even though you are a total stranger. Nevertheless their grasp of public relations and introspection is often tragically lacking.

Let's take the stereotype of the lying, stealing, non-working, ghetto Black male. What is this all about? Imagine that very powerful extraterrestrials have taken over the Earth and are enslaving the human race. What would we do? Well the best of us, the strongest, bravest, and most intelligent among us would form an underground resistance movement.

At every opportunity we would steal whatever we could from these oppressors. We would habitually lie to them. We would whenever possible not work for them. In short our ideal behavior would be to lie, steal, and to not work. Once those well-justified and practical ideals became an admired facet of our culture, how long would it take to undo those aberrations once the threat was removed? It would take many generations, and then only with much introspection and great effort. Is it any wonder that the horrors and oppression of slavery in this country had the same effect on some African-Americans?

Add to that the enormous and lasting damage done by welfare systems that required the man to leave the home in order for the woman to be eligible for AFDC, Aid to Families with Dependent Children. These forces made the woman the most powerful person in the family as she controlled the purse strings. The men were damaged beyond measure.

The black community in the U.S. is comprised of so many individuals of great talent and accomplishment, doctors, lawyers, and other professionals, as well as musicians and athletes. Yet how often when the news media want a 'black perspective', do they produce some inarticulate, hostile, total ignoramus from the streets? This situation does seem to be getting better over time, but it still happens. Were the media doing this deliberately to make African-Americans look bad? It sure looks that way but then the media is supposed to be liberal leaning.

Certainly no other group would stand for it. Can you image a major news event that called for a White or Asian perspective, where the media would interview some smuck off skid row and advance this numb-nut's mutterings as gospel? Such a travesty would never be tolerated, but it happens all the time with Black Community issues.

There is also a continuous perversity by the Black Community to make cause celebs out of the worst possible material. A young girl who gets shot while stealing from a mom and pop store, a retarded axe murderer, an underage killer, a wife-murdering ex-football star, the list goes on and on. So self-defeating. The broader community could care less about such people. What about the good Black Americans who are the victims of horrible injustice? They seem to get passed right over.

And the 'n' word thing. Blacks demand that we not use that word…give me a break, anyone can say any word that they want to. It reminds me of when my little sister would demand that I not do or say a certain something or she would get very upset. Who could resist that? Even if I had no intention whatever to do or say that thing that would get such a rise out of her…I was compelled to do so. She was begging for it.

The 'n' word is used in many different ways by many different people. The range is from a term of endearment to a vicious epithet. Even at its worst use by Whites, except for a few hopelessly ignorant crackers, it refers not to Black people in general but to characterize a lazy, lying, thieving type of character. In this regard there are plenty of White people that it can be and is applied to.

Blacks have also managed to bulletproof themselves to criticism. Almost no non-Black will criticize a Black person to their face. The attitude is that if you criticize me, we will gather and protest you or boycott you or whatever reprisal is in vogue. All that accomplishes is to deny them constructive criticism…and we can all at times sure use some of that. The result is that they are often treated like dangerous children, not reasonable adults.

The same sort of thing is happening with the Great Muslim Cartoon Riots going on. They riot and demand that we not make cartoons of Mohammed. Again, anyone can draw whatever cartoons they want to. The results of the riots beyond the death and destructions is that the whole world is now transmitting Muslim cartoons in print and on the Internet. That, plus unfortunately the world now views Muslims more than ever as mindless morons. The above arose in part because Islam does not allow any physical representation of Mohammed. If you think that is strange, Orthodox Jews don't even allow the name of God to be spoken.

Respect is not something that can be demanded, it must be earned. If you demand respect in an infantile way, what you get is ridicule, hardly the desired outcome. If your religion or culture prohibits certain words or pictures, that is fine for you, just leave the rest of us out of it. You simply give away your power by allowing anyone to control your reactions to a word or a cartoon. It is also considered a really big insult if you show a Muslim the bottom of your feet or shoes. Oh really, how quaint. And do they expect the rest of the world to take note and observe this particular eccentricity?

Blacks have a great potential advantage in their skin color. New immigrants to the U.S. have traditionally spent their money within their close-knit community as much as possible. The Koreans who settled in Los Angels around Olympic Boulevard, New Seoul, are a case in point. In three short decades they have built that area up from nothing, to shopping malls and high-rises. All of this was accomplished by hard work and doing their darndest not to let their money out of that part of town.

But as time goes by, the immigrants become second, third, and beyond generations and that cohesiveness is lost as the subsequent generations join the mainstream. They no longer even recognize each other. This is where blacks would have the advantage. They can always instantly recognize each other by skin color. So if only they had the common positive trait of trading with their own, ethnically speaking, they would always have that advantage. The tragedy is that in fact, Blacks at many levels traditionally go out of their way not to give their business to other Blacks.

That is why the Black ghetto corner stores have been traditionally operated by outsiders. In Los Angeles it was first by Jews, then Koreans, and now some are from India. I mentioned a young Black girl, 15-year-old Latasha Harlins, who was shot dead by a female Korean shop owner, Soon Da Ju, for stealing a small item. There was massive Black outrage when Superior Court Judge Joyce Harlin gave probation to the shooter. The judge ended up being recalled. The actual facts are quite interesting.

Many of the Koreans who enter the New Seoul Community in Los Angeles are in fact from North Korea, not South Korea. When they escape from North Korea and arrive in the South, their extended families ship them to Los Angeles. Talk about a culture clash. If a North Korean shopkeeper shot a thief, they would probably be given a medal and a village celebration.

At the other end of this tragic event, the small shops in the ghetto overcharge so much for everything, that it is all but the shoppers duty and obligation to periodically 'pocket' some items in order to help even out the relationship. Both the young Black girl and the Korean woman thought that they were doing the right thing.

So inner city Blacks continue to eye each other suspiciously and their predators prey upon their own community. Meanwhile other groups get off the boat not knowing English, and by working together for the common good, soon sail right by some African Americans who have been here for centuries. How tragic.

I never did quite get Jesse Jackson. But he is right-on about pushing for the economic side of the problem and that the only color that really matters is green. I do know the Black community. I rode my BSA 650 Lightning Rocket from New Haven to Los Angeles in September of 1964. I had been a Repo Man in the New York Region for GMAC. I thought that I was doing really well when I quickly got a job as a bill collector in South Central with Watts as my territory. The first Watts riots were in '65.

I attended the 1967 Watts Festival featuring H. Rap Brown, Stokely Carmichael, and others, with James Brown entertaining.

I lived the civil rights movement in Los Angels, in the Black community. I was there. In fact I drove to that festival with a black coworker. Just because we were a vehicle with a Black man and a White man in it, we were pulled over by the LAPD and thrown over the hood of my car.

Another time a Black friend named Melvin had his head shaved for medical treatment. Unfortunately for him there was a militant Black group at the time called US that shaved their heads as a symbol of membership. One night Melvin was driving to work in his caddy, minding his own business when his bare head was spotted by the LAPD. They beat him so severely that he ended up in the LAC USC Medical Center on the jail ward. As the saying on the street went, "LAPD don't play."

I was originally negative on Reverend Al Sharpton but have come to respect his intellect, savvy, and good sense of humor. But why are the most talented and developed Black leaders in the public eye so few and far between? Why in 2006 do Black kids have mostly gangsta rappers and the like to idolize? Is this more fallout from the slavery experience? Children are afraid to do well in school lest they be called acting White or being oreos.

As if knowledge should be White and ignorance should be Black. This inverted sanity must be taken head-on across the board. It is all fallout from the slavery era. Bill Cosby has gone out on a limb to try to deal with it and has run into all kinds of flak. As if ignorance, stupidity, and self-defeating tactics must be preserved at all costs. Ignorance needs to be eradicated, not protected.

Minister Louis Farrakhan, the head of the Black Muslims, for all his faults has many things correct. He stresses the economic development side of the divide and the Black Muslims are known for shunning alcohol and tobacco, good personal hygiene and being well dressed. They used to sell the most healthy and delicious pies on the streets of LA, especially near the Mosque on Crenshaw Boulevard. The vendor would be all but formally attired. The last time I was in LA I scoured the ghetto looking for one of these mean bean pies, but to no avail.

Then you have Black English as a major problem. I lived long enough in the Black Community that I speak Black English. Actually I often prefer it, and it is slowly seeping into the main stream via White kids due to its expressability, but that is not the point. Unless you are going to be the one in a million that becomes a pro ball player or a rap star or the like, you are most probably going to go nowhere unless you can speak mainstream English.

The whole notion of doing well in school being White is ludicrous. Who invented basketball, baseball, football, golf, or tennis? White people did...so what? Black youths don't shun them. Black people invented jazz and blues, and rap. Do you see White people avoiding them because Blacks invented them?

There is no time to waste. Our society is spending many, many times the amount of money needed to provide splendid inner-city schools and associate support, in order to incarcerate Blacks and Hispanics. Worse yet, prisons are universities in crime and brutality. When you expect people to act like animals...you can be sure that many of them will do just that. But you can't spend the money on the schools if the students think that learning is dumb and refuse to apply themselves.

There are many signs of deep progress. Blacks in movie roles is one of them. Originally their depiction was horrible and humiliating at best. Then during the Civil Rights struggles the Blacksploitation flicks came along. As bad as they were, it was a great leap forward. Today many Black movies are being made with excellent role models. These movies are fun and entertaining while still transmitting healthy attitudes and outright wisdom to their viewers.

Decades ago I was riding the 'extra car', the RTD, the bus. I noticed an ad along the inside top row where they string them. I will always remember what it said. It was sponsored by the Los Angles Times and it read, "If the Truth Hurts...It Should".

17:00 ON
02-04-06 Saturday—I arrive again at the Amy Burnett Gallery. Judith Kay, a transplanted New Yorker via Southern California, is doing a splendid job on the piano. A raffle is underway in support of the Opera Guild. This is the staging area for the Kitsap Opera Guild's presentation of *A Night in Italy*. It starts at 19:00 across Pacific Avenue at Filippi's Pizza Grotto.

The evening begins. A buffet is laid out. The Chianti flows and the music begins. Hannah Blackburn is on this piano. Linda Mattos is the Lyric soprano and Froiedrich Konstatin Schlott the Bass-baritone. I am in a perfect groove.

At the break, the raffle tickets are drawn. Various offerings including beautiful baskets of goodies, some prepared perhaps by Amy, are won and received. Then comes the main prize, an Art Talk by Amy Burnett in your home for up to twelve guests. Topics are: Home Design, Artwork Critique, Art History, Painting, and Feng Shui.

Man do I ever need a Feng Shui. The bidding begins. I am the second bidder and the two of us go a few rounds and then I jump the bid and take the item. This goes over very well as Amy is so well liked and her Herculean efforts on behalf of Bremo very much known and appreciated. I am urged to join the Kitsap

Opera Guild. I will of course, do so. I am suddenly quire popular with these total strangers. Not as popular perhaps as the only guy with jumper cables at a Kabul wedding, but I do go over.

Adrienne: Find *A Night in Italy* program in your inbox. Run names on Lists A & B.
17:00 OFF

Super Bowl XL—What a rip. Worst officiating I have ever seen in a major game, let alone the Super Bowl with the world watching. Final score: REFS 21 HAWKS 10. I have yet to hear that the refs rigged the game…but my ear is to the ground.

02-06-06 Monday—USA Today reports that the largest U.S. long-distance carriers had cooperated with the NSA's, National Security Agency's, wiretapping of international calls without warrants, according to a published report that cited unnamed telecommunications executives and intelligence officials. MCI, Sprint and AT&T grant access to their systems without warrants or court orders, and provide call-routing information that helps physically locate the callers.

This has been going on for a long time. The old time switchboards, PBX and other equipment of AT&T and the Bell Systems were designed to enable surreptitious monitoring of telephone calls. We even spread this system around the world often without the knowledge of the receiving countries…the knowledge that we could listen in.

The Bush Administrations states that FISA, Foreign Intelligence Surveillance Act, is too outdated to handle the monitoring of all international calls to and from Al-Qaeda. This is probably true. Doubtless they are using supercomputers to filter every international call being made, looking for keywords and such, in order to home in on and give more attention to those calls that raise red flags.

To process millions of calls through a court, whether before or within seventy-two hours after the fact, would require tens of thousands of judges. Not workable. But it has to be made legal with congressional oversight. Checks and balances to unbridled power are absolutely essential.

Item: Recently it was revealed that AOL, Microsoft and Yahoo! complied with Justice Department subpoenas to turn over search data. Google has made a very high profile statement that it will not do so without a fight. Good for you Google!

I woke up this morning to find that Teddy 'The Wonder Dog' has flown the coup! Teddy, a Black Lab had promised me that if I left one of the gates ajar, he would stop dumping on my gravel walkways and trot across the road to relieve himself by the edge of the forest. This he did for about a week but now he is gonzo. I drove around looking for him, nada. On my morning walk to the post office I covered the immediate area, nada.

About noon I notice messages on the answering machine. One is from Janet with the City of Bremo. She is at the Public Works Yard up on Oyster Bay Road and so it seems is Teddy. The maintenance crew has accomplished little so far today as Teddy has been running them ragged all morning with a fetch the stick game that he has improvised. Teddy is an obsessive-compulsive ball player, but any port in a storm.

Janet has read the rabies tag number on Teddy's spiked collar, called our vet and thereby obtained my home phone number. They love Teddy but he is a distinct impediment to their mission. This is one more reason why I love Bremo. The common sense and good will in this town is viscerally palpable.

I pick up a small package of 61%, now deemed healthy, cocoa chocolate disks from the just opened *Amy's Decadent Chocolates* shop in Charleston. If you want to see my face in your establishment, just work the word decadent into your logo...and sooner or later I will be there. I gave Janet the chocolate, picked up Teddy, took him home...and gave him what for.

Muslims are still rioting, burning, and killing worldwide because they object to those cartoons published in a Danish newspaper. It is a mistake to think that these people are like us, just of a different religion, or culinary tastes, or lifestyle. I was in Morocco, in a rug shop in a souk in the Casbah in Tangier, when I was apparently too slow to make a purchase. Someone then dropped a large rolled Berber carpet down upon me from the floor above.

I sprung up with the expletive, 'Jesus Christ'. In retrospect, that may not have been the wisest utterance given the location. The merchants then attempted to inform me that getting pounded like that was 'good luck'. Yeah...good luck and good-bye! The upside was that I was sufficiently agitated that I ended up eating couscous with the most lovely Kanako Oya traveling alone from Osaka-City, Japan, at the tender age of twenty-two.

I recall a scene outside that souk in the street on a steep cobblestone hill. A very heavily laden cart was going by. The brakes for this monstrosity was a huge guy in the back wearing large thick rubber boots. He was hanging on, and dragging his feet on the roadway. I began to wonder what century these people were living in. Hard to tell but it was many many centuries ago. I keep hearing lately that they are living in the seventh century. That sounds a bit early to me, but then a

Theocracy that lops off hands and heads is way back there somewhere. Either way we are in living in different millennia.

While modern man is urged to think globally but act locally, in furtherance of the common good…These Arabs are thinking locally and acting globally, to the world's detriment and horror.

There is an item circulating on the Net regarding Muslim outrage. It lists many outrageous and horrendous acts committed by Muslims that provoked in them no outrage; from 9-11, to Muslim officials blocking the exit where schoolgirls were trying to escape a burning building because their faces were exposed, to Muslims slaughtering hundreds of children and teachers in Beslan, Russia, and so on. But when newspapers in Denmark and Norway publish cartoons depicting Mohammed…Muslims are outraged to the point of worldwide rioting and destruction! Hello?

And these very same people who are burning and killing over what are not only quite innocuous cartoons, but also accurately relevant cartoons; these same people conceive, create, and publish, practically on a daily basis…the vilest, most disgusting, and untrue cartoons depicting Jewish people that you could possibly imagine. They are even now running a worldwide contest to see who can come up with the dastardliest anti-Jewish and anti-Christian cartoons. Do they really think we will riot? Or even give a damn.

What a shame! It was Arabs that gave us Arabic numerals. Did you ever try to multiply and divide Roman numerals? The Arabic numerals along with the essential concept of the Hindu zero allow us to function as we do. They also gave us algebra, and that beautiful Moorish architecture you see in Spain and elsewhere. The word most used in the Quoran, after God, is ilm. Ilm means knowledge and was so very highly respected.

Mohammed was first motivated to act by being distressed at the treatment of women, slaves, and the down trodden. Muslims originally helped to liberate and raise women up.

What happened? In general they are in desperate financial shape. But have you ever heard of an Arab car, or boat, or train, or plane, or TV, or computer, or anything modern? Globalization is not passing them by; they have lain dormant for well over a thousand years. They often fight against progress, when everyone knows that you cannot stop progress. Whose fault is that? According to the Quoran: "God does not change the condition of a people unless they change what is in themselves." Amen to that.

Mahatma Gandhi showed the oppressed people of the world how to overcome their situation. Martin Luther King Jr. used these same techniques to successfully lead African-Americans to full citizenship. It is a shame that Osama or Usama Bin Laden didn't have the wit to follow their examples. He might well have already been successful in his mission. Instead he chose hate and death and hate and death is what he reaps.

People are basically good. Expose a grievous injustice and the world will come together to right it. If all of those suicide bombers were doing what the Buddhist Monks of Vietnam did, that is to say, if they were committing suicide publicly to protest policies that they objected to, and not killing or harming anyone else…they would probably have accomplished their goals before now and had the entire world on their side.

Adrienne, I hope all the yammering is not putting you over the edge. But with all this surveillance time and these DW-90s, what's a guy to do? I keep trying to stay off religion but now accept that I cannot.

I can tell that a lot of religion bashing is struggling to break free and come forth. Let me say right now that I am not against religion per se. If you pay attention you will see that what I will be examining is what so often happens after a beautiful spiritual movement is launched by a wonderful prophet. What happens is that the more the movement is organized into a religion, the more it becomes incorporated and bureaucratized, the more it accumulates power and feels the need to control its practitioners and to expand; the more likely it is that it will then turn into something that is not only often counterproductive but it becomes the exact opposite of what its founder would have wished for.

I realize that religion is transformative for culture and the people living within that culture. Religion has transformed primitive societies from matriarchal to patriarchal. Religion has transformed societies from polytheistic to monotheistic. All of that has probably been necessary for our development and evolution into what we are today. But I see no reason why we need all the lies and horrid practices today to reap the beneficial results of religion.

Today we may well be transitioning back to more of a matriarchal scheme of things, if in fact we really ever changed that much. Certainly we are becoming feminized in the developed western societies. Have ever you noticed that the Fundamentalist, whether Jewish, Christian, Muslim, or Mormon, that they all make a major effort to suppress their women? They are well aware of the natural power of women and fear it.

Frankly, I don't think I have ever met a married man in this country that I can recall who wasn't at a fundamental level, petrified of his wife. This is not as surprising as one might think. Men in our culture are raised by their mothers. Once grown, they marry and their new household is again ruled by a woman. Little girls are naturally bossy, at least in the U.S. They get an early start, and practice wrapping their fathers around their little fingers from about age three if not before.

When elderly men die, their wives generally live on for many years. When elderly women pass-on their husbands often join them in short order.

President Lyndon Johnson, a master intimidator if there ever was one, once said, "There are only two things you need to know about your wife. First you have to make her think that she is the boss. Second you have to realize that she is the boss." It may be a cliché that, "Behind every successful man there is a woman", but there is a lot of truth to that.

Sure some young and macho guys demand to be in charge and are very jealous and controlling. To do so they have to beat their woman until either she leaves, kills him, or he kills her or is incarcerated. Naturally there are exceptions and permutations of this but I am sure that you get the cut being made here.

If your society is polytheistic as the Greeks and Romans were, how do you control behavior? There is a God for everything. One God may have you doing something that the rulers want you to be doing but suppose you want to go up into the hills and get drunk at a wild orgy? No problema, just follow the God Bacchus and that is definitely the way to go.

But once you introduce the concept of only one God, now you have full control. One God can be extremely sexually repressive and that tremendous energy can then be sublimated and directed to the ends that the leaders want. Of course there is no free lunch. When you suppress a prime mover like the sexual urge you are going to get a lot of mental and physical fallout, illness, and crimes.

The USS Ohio has returned to service at the nearby Bangor submarine base. This sub is the first of four ballistic-missile subs now known as SSGNs, G means Guided. They now carry up to 154 mid-range guided Tomahawk missiles, and up to 102 Navy SEALs or other Special Forces. Before conversion they were SSBNs, B is for Ballistic, and carried nuclear ballistic weapons for the Cold War. Under the START II Treaty, four of our 18 SSBNs had to go. This was an alternative to scrapping them and fits in nicely with anti-terrorism plans.

The three year conversion was accomplished in Bremo at the PSNS. PSNS is also converting the USS Michigan. Both will operate in the Pacific. The USS Florida and USS Georgia are undergoing conversion on the East Coast and slated for stationing in Europe and the Middle East.

13:30 ON
02-09-06 Thursday—Veh#5—It is finally time to see Greta at Affinity Massage at 532 5th Street, just west of Pacific Avenue. Every two weeks is too long to wait. Some doctor made up a Death Calculator wherein you start with age 79 and add one year for good things that you do and you subtract a year for no-nos. Having a pet like a dog or cat gets you another year added to your lifespan. The same with a regular massage, it adds a year to your life. Greta points out that Bob Hope had a weekly massage and lived passed one hundred. That works for me.

I am in heaven for one hour. At my age this is better than sex. Greta is great. Surprisingly to me, she likes old movies like the Bob Hope ~ Bing Crosby *On the Road* stuff, black and whites. These Bremos are endlessly full of surprises, as is the whole town.

It has been said that only two strata of a society really know what is going on. One is the President, the other are the prostitutes. Well, I have found that much is also said to one's masseuse. I go to Greta for the best massages in town and someone else there for much local intel.

The building housing Affinity Massage has some interesting antiques, books and wall paintings. Just west of this building is the downtown Bremo branch of the Kitsap Regional Library system [www.krl.org/]. It was once the main library but that distinction moved to East Bremo to a new 35,000 square foot facility on Sylvan Way in 1978. This 1930s building has undergone $400,000 worth of improvements since September and will reopen in March as the Martin Luther King Branch.

I walk over to the Amy Burnett Gallery. The lady operating the adjoining Made in Bremo store advises me that Amy is only scheduled full time on Tuesdays. Her assistant, Stewart, is not on the premises. I continue on over to the Patriot newspaper office on Burwell. No one is there, and a Will Return Clock has its hands pointing to some really oddball time.

Back on the Valk, I rip over to the YMCA and drop off two XL magnetic knee tubes for Director Godfrey. These things saved me about eleven years ago. I could not walk without them. After exhausting medical treatment in Los Angeles and Seattle, including the UW Bone and Joint Clinic, a nurse at a Whidbey Island Clinic in Clinton told me, "The doctors have told us not to mention this as they say it is quackery, but many of our patients swear by magnets." They made all the difference in the world for me. I even sold them on the Net for a few years in order to share the relief.
16:30 OFF

My knees have been shot for over twenty-five years. I started running marathons at age thirty-eight. It was all the rage at the time and running in general was widely touted as the path to good health. Big mistake. That, plus arthritis and a torn meniscus pulled me to the curb. Some years back a Swedish masseuse on Whidbey Island told me to try cold-pressed peanut oil on them. Well I did once or twice, probably months apart.

Then a year ago I picked up a bottle of HAIN 100% Expeller Pressed Peanut Oil, and began using it twice a day. What a marvelous result! My knees no longer crack so badly when I bend them. I noticed an immediate increase in my stationary bike performance numbers. In 2000, before purchasing the Valk and to aid my being able to hold that big baby up, I had three shots in each knee to lubricate the cartilage. Originally the material was made from rooster combs, but by then it was synthesized and sold as SYNVISC®. It worked fairly well but only lasted about a year. In some the ways peanut oil is better.

To keep going I spend most of each and every morning exercising. It begins with yoga and weight lifting. Then a half hour on the recumbent bike, followed by a daily walk to the West Hills Post office. Cool-down periods are spent on the computer.

At noon I eat my first meal of the day. I am a confirmed contrarian. I collared over a million in the stock market with one stock that way. Every diet or nutritional plan that I have ever heard of emphasizes that the most important meal of the day is breakfast. I have found that eating breakfast is the absolute worst thing that you can do.

Maybe if you get up at three AM to start plowing the back forty you should eat a big breakfast, but not us sedentary people. Do animals get up, go to the refer and eat breakfast? I don't think so.

More likely they have to go out and work and hunt down their daily meal. With some luck they will be successful by midday. They eat then and leave a little for their supper.

I lost forty pounds in 2004, and the key was not eating before noon. That plus exercise and my special evening drink. The drink was basically, spirulina from the deep waters off the Kona Coast, flax seed from North Central Dakota, bee pollen from the Willamette Valley in Oregon, all put in a blender with apple juice and a banana.

An appetite grows when fed. The more you eat for breakfast, the hungrier you are at noon. The more you eat at noon, the more you want for supper. Eat as much as you want, but only healthy foods at noon, then in the evening a light supper. Forget breakfast…that is one major reason why this country is so obese. This advice is for adults, children are another story.

It is simply about Mother Nature. As Jack LaLanne, the fellow who swam pulling boatloads of people at age eighty-four or something like that says, "If man makes it…Don't eat it! That covers cakes, pies, cookies, candy, and a plethora of products ubiquitous in the U.S. All Mexican restaurants offer either corn or flour tortillas. The traditional corn is whole grain and healthy, the flour is usually of unhealthy bleached white flour. The status trend now in Mexico is to switch from corn to flour. How sad. A good rule of thumb is, do what the old people used to do.

Another health factor for women is their bras. Bras can lead to breast cancer, especially the ones with wire in them. They cut off the proper blood flow. Once again it is a matter of spending money to be unnatural. Trust me, I have made a very careful and extensive hands-on study of this subject!

I have lost almost all faith in the AMA and doctors in general. I say that despite the fact that I have had some wonderful doctors in my life and for my children. I have an excellent doctor that I really like right now. A few years back my blood pressure was way too high. I went to doctors in Los Angeles and Seattle. All attempted to put me on medication, i.e. pills...drugs. Drugs that later proved to be highly dangerous. None suggested that what I should do was simply improve my diet and exercise more. But that is what I did and the blood pressure problem vanished naturally.

All day long now on TV there are these terribly annoying drug commercials. They have gone beyond, if you are sick...take drugs. Now they show a healthy woman who eats properly, jogs daily, and appears to be the picture of health, but no, not quite good enough, she also should be buying and ingesting their drugs. And our children, put them on drugs whenever possible as well.

The new Medicare Drug Program is deemed necessary because so many older people can no longer afford the ten, twenty, or thirty prescription drugs that they have been put 'on'. They can't afford their hundreds or thousands of dollars a month 'nut' for drugs.

The conservative Bruce Bartlett who worked for Jack Kemp, Ronald Reagan, and George Bush 41 the Elder, has now written a book, *Imposter*, in which he rips the current President George W. Bush. The final straw for him was the Medicare Drug Program. He states that the White House deliberately withheld statistics on how much it would really cost.

The unfunded liability for Medicare Part D is now computed at eighteen trillion dollars! That is seven trillion more than Social Security's eleven trillion in unfunded liability. So even if W. had been able to accomplish his mission to 'save Social Security' completely, he would have already made the situation far worse than it was…had he done nothing.

This year, 2006 is the tipping year for Medicare; the first year in which more money will be spent then comes in. Last year the Medicare Trust Fund was predicted to last another fifteen years. This year they say it will last only another twelve years. I wonder what they will say next year?

This legislation makes the drug companies and stockholders rich, while making it so much easier for the elderly to be frightened onto a plethora of drugs. Before the War on Drugs you didn't hear about drugs all day long. People were not organizing busses to go to Canada to purchase them. If you interview people who have lived to be over one hundred years old, what do they most often say? Avoid doctors and hospitals! Work, be useful, be curious, and stay connected.

When Social Security was enacted, the life expectancy was sixty-five years for a male. On average you would draw very little before your ticket was punched. These drugs are not to prolong our potential normal lives. What could be more unnatural than filling our cells with all these foreign chemicals?

Drugs are still very crude. Someday they will be perfected and actually just solve your genetic flaws or whatever. But that is not the case today. Yes, they accomplish their main goal but create numerous deleterious side effects. So you first get on one drug and the side effects lead you to a second drug, and then the third. By now your body chemistry is so altered and screwed up that you must continue to add more and more drugs until you are a total wreck, heading for a stone wall.

I know someone whose policy is, "Just say no to drugs...unless they are recreational." At first that seems outrageous, but when you come right down to it, occasional street drugs are probably safer than daily taking all this crap that the drug companies are pushing. And pushing is indeed the right word. They push far harder than anything going on along Pusher Street in the Christiania section of Copenhagen. If you can handle the truth...follow the money. Always follow the money!

The naïve perception of what makes a medical doctor tick is often of an individual who wants to help their fellow man. I'm sure this is true in many cases, but a more realistic appraisal is often of someone who as a kid, liked to take things apart. Someone who likes to see how things work, an engineering type.

A very cranky gent in a local tavern recently advanced a rather shocking theory as follows: "The human body is comprised of trillions of living cells. Each day we lose billions of red blood cells to maintain ourselves. Do we care that they die to keep us healthy? Not really. Moving up a level, a society is comprised of living people. Do doctors care that some must die to maintain a healthy society? Not really. Well, that is the nature of things. The health of the overall community is what really counts.

The more old retired people there are who live longer and longer, the less robust and sick the overall society becomes. Cigarette smoking used to be the perfect answer. About the time one's useful working life was over, lung cancer would frequently finish you off. Recall that the AMA invested heavily in tobacco stocks until public knowledge and outrage brought that to an end. It wasn't the government that pushed the current non-smoking environment. The government happily subsidized the tobacco industry. It was public opinion in the U.S. that pushed the government. Now we export more of these coffin nails to cover the domestic loss of consumers. If we can't kill more of our own citizens, by all means let us kill more foreigners.

The only way to stop the drain on the economy, Social Security, and the health of the nation caused by the ever-expanding longevity of the senior citizenry is to bump them off. What better way then by making billions while drugging them to death?"

The above is certainly harsh, cynical, and possibly paranoid, but still he has a point. When I was a kid, the old folks would do just about anything to avoid going into a hospital. Why? Because they knew that would probably mean curtains for them. And very often it did just that. Twenty years ago while living in Mexico, it was the same situation. When an elderly citizen living in San Felipe could no longer hold off a trip to a Mexicali hospital, the family figured they had three days to plan the funeral. Just like clockwork, in about three days, back would come the corpse for the wake. No longer a productive unit...zap!

But even aside from these drug issues, in my lifetime the accepted medical advice has time and time again been through 180-degree reversals. First one was suppose to put hot packs on new injuries and later that was changed to cold packs. We were told not to eat butter but to switch to margarine. Now we are told to not eat margarine but to switch to butter. Fat was bad and carbohydrates were good. Now carbohydrates are bad and fat is actually all right.

Drinking was bad but now it is seen as healthy in moderation. Running and jogging was wonderful exercise in the 70's but now it is seen as destructive to your joints. The pyramid depiction of what constitutes the proper food groups has just been changed radically. A doctor now is telling me that the best thing to cook with is pig fat...lard! One can only conclude that despite the authoritative pronouncements that thunder forth, that they really don't know what they are talking about a great deal of the time. Better to listen to your body and do what the old people did. Doctors call what they do practice, for good reason.

We have had the War on Drugs now for decades. After years of wasting untold billions of tax dollars on this so-called war, what do we have? Illegal drugs are more plentiful, widespread, cheaper than ever before, and corruption is rampant everywhere, including politicians, the military, law enforcement, the judiciary, and elsewhere.

A few years ago, my son Tommy and I returned to our spot on Punta Estrella, Point of the Stars, below San Felipe in Baja California. It had been more than ten years since either of us had been there. Young soldiers were everywhere. Our friends told about smugglers dropping off large stacks of bails of white, shrink-wrapped marijuana, and storing them in vacant structures in the campos. It seems that the U.S. gave the Mexicans some beautiful new boats, ostensibly to interdict drug smugglers. But you guessed it, these very boats were what were being used to haul in the drugs. In fact the Mexican Army frequently violates our southern border to protect their drug traffickers.

The Mexican Drug Czar is widely known to in fact be the head trafficker. The Mexicans used to simply be paid by the Columbians to transit the cocaine and other drugs to the U.S. Eventually they woke up and realized they could make a lot more as a principal. Today it is estimated that Mexico receives about US$30 billion from Mexican workers in the U.S. sending money back to their families and about US$300 billion from the drug trade. This consists mostly of cocaine and marijuana but now also the output of super-meth labs in Mexico and both Mexican black tar and higher grade Chinese white heroin.

Combine this availability of illegal drugs, with the increasing push by Big Pharmaceuticals to start our children out on prescription drugs at an early age and it is not difficult to predict future trends. Our entire culture is now awash in harmful drugs, both prescription and otherwise.

Kids who have trouble paying attention in class are put on drugs. Having trouble paying attention in class is normal. Children want by nature to be outside running around. To sit at a desk for hours and pay attention to whatever irrelevant uninteresting material is being promulgated…that is what is not normal.

Certainly the onus is not entirely on the medical community. The thing that a doctor can legally give us that we can't get elsewhere is a prescription. We pay to see a doctor…we want a prescription. They know that…and they give us one.

In the 1970's Robert Mendelsohn, M.D., an early advocate of the natural approach to health and the author of *Confessions of a Medical Heretic,* stated in a medical speech, "When you are looking at any medical study, don't just look at what the authors want you to look at; always look at the funeral rates, too. It doesn't just matter if blood pressure or cholesterol levels went down more on the drug group than the placebo group. It also matters whether more people died in the drug group than in the placebo group. If they did, then who cares if the blood pressure or cholesterol was lower? The mortician?"

I really do not want to leave the impression that I am dumping on all medical doctors. I have needed them in the past and will probably again in the future. Many are the most splendid human beings among us. They run the gamut from a veritable saint like Doctor Albert Schweitzer to a true monster like Doctor Joseph Mengele. There are really good doctors and those that perform unnecessary operations in order to make their Mercedes' notes. We have excellent physicians and those that specialize in Medicare fraud.

The ones I am thinking of are the garden-variety doctors who took the Hippocratic Oath with the best of intentions. I had thought like many others that said that the Oath required doctors to at the very least do no harm. But I have just read the Classical version and wouldn't you know it, there is a new modern version updated by the Declaration of Geneva, and I don't see that provision in either one of them. What I did find was: Some doctors who recited the Hippocratic Oath as medical students now call it the 'Hypocritic's Oath'.

The point I am trying to make is that an awful lot of harm is being done to patients by doctors who are putting them so readily on all of these Big Pharmaceutical drug products. According to the VIOXX legal trials, that one drug alone actually doubled, that is correct it doubled the risk of having a heart attack!

It is estimated that during the five years that VIOXX was on the market, it was related to somewhere between 88,000–139,000 heart attacks and strokes! Other NSAIDS including many sold over the counter can also increase your risk. Even worse may be deaths attributable to drugs commonly used to treat Type II diabetes.

Item: Bremo's Olympic College is beginning a new era with groundbreaking on February 11, 2006, today, for a new $22 million Science and Technology building. This is part of a $75 million dollar campus overhaul. Originally designed in the '40s and '50s, it was created for easy convertibility into elementary schools in case the community college concept failed.

This is as good a time as any to touch upon the Bremer Trust. A Google search produces the following from the local Chamber of Commerce: Profile: Bremer Trust—Golden Anchor Member—no picture—no info provided—Rich McDonald, General Manager—member since 11/7/1950. Seems a bit mysterious doesn't it? Further digging reveals: 409 Pacific Avenue—Suite 301, in Bremo: bremer@telebyte.net : tel 360.377.5533 : fax 360.373.7098

The Bremer Trust's role is to annually contribute its proceeds to Olympic College. The Trust's $20 million portfolio includes nine office buildings and a three-story parking garage in downtown Bremo. In December 2005, the trust gave $300,000 to the college. Much of that came from this Burwell Parking garage.

Many failed proposals were made at redevelopment in the early '70s, including discussions of a waterfront hotel and the erection of a large canopy over the central business district. Meanwhile, most of the city's office and retail space remained in the hands of Edward Bremer, son of the city's founder William Bremer and the sole remaining heir to his wealth.

Incredibly, to receive their inheritance, William Bremer's three children were honor-bound to never marry. Bremer began to neglect his properties; never increasing decades-old lease rates, and failing to make necessary maintenance upgrades. In 1978, the Bremo City Council passed an ordinance declaring that the entire downtown was legally a blighted area!

Upon the death of Edward Bremer in 1987, the Bremer properties were placed under the complete control of The Bremer Trust, a trust held by Olympic College. Not being in the real-estate business, the college did not actively market its holdings and downtown was composed almost entirely of very large empty storefronts.

Recently the Bremer Trust hired a commercial real estate firm and an asset manager to handle the details formerly managed by a staff member. Bradley Scott Inc. was hired to manage the Trust's real estate holdings. Jim Smalley of Smith Barney was hired to manage securities. Adrienne, please see what else you can unearth on the Bremer Trust.

A big hometown welcome was in store for Bremo native, Marvin Williams. He was the number two pick in June's NBA draft. He had just played his first pro game in Seattle. His Atlanta Hawks lost to the Sonics 99-91. Locals are very proud of those who have gone on to big things. Another is jazz legend Quincy Jones who moved to Bremerton at the age of ten. As a teenager, he first met up with Ray Charles when he began frequenting the nightclubs in Seattle.

Four area school bond issues just passed by a large margin. These people are so well grounded that no doubt the local schools are well run. Bremo's Early Childhood Program was named Tops in the State. Bremo is one of only six districts in Washington State to be recognized by the League of Education Voters this year.

I am forever ruined concerning U.S. school financing after my experience in Mexico. I raised my youngest son, Tommy, in Baja California and he attended grades one through five at an Escuela Federal in San Felipe, the Professor Domingo Carballo Felix.

One year the peso had by then lost nearly half its value and thus the teachers had no choice but to go on strike. The local fishermen donated a huge amount of fish and we gave as many kilos of chicken as we could. The kicker is, that while on strike, the teachers painted the entire school and made various improvements. Can you image that ever happening in the U.S.?

The total administration consisted of a Director who was often seen building and repairing playground structures, pruning trees and doing whatever else was required. The teachers had virtually absolute authority. If a boy was acting-out she would merely have to point to the door and he was suspended. He would sit on the doorstep for days. He got back in when the teacher decided that it was time. In this way, disciplinary problems were kept at a minimum.

Some years we hauled down a truckload of paint from a Home Depot in Los Angeles. The teachers and students would paint the outside of the various buildings, the inside of the classrooms and the desks. Even the first graders would paint their own desks. Sure they ended up covered with paint, but there was such a pride of authorship that I knew of no incident there of defacement of school property by a student.

The State of Baja Norte did have oversight responsibilities. They inspected the facility once a year and provided a monthly-standardized test. This test both provided the basis for the students' monthly grade, using the European system of 1-10, and allowed for statistical monitoring by the State.

Contrast that with what we found when we left Baja to retuurn briefly to Los Angeles County. Tommy completed the sixth grade under the gargantuan beauracracy of the Los Angeles Unified School District. I got involved as there was suppossedly a major improvement project underway.

It all turned out to be an extrordianrily expensive and wasteful farce. In downtown Los Angeles there was an administrative building filled with people bent on undermining any possible changes to the system. Soon I was receiving daily mail from them. Talk about a snow job, this was a blizzard.

Oh they had elaborate meetings including one gigantic one where Willie Brown, still the major force in the California Legislature and prior to his becoming the Mayor of San Francisco, was the main speaker. But the upshot of everything was that absolutely nothing constructive ever happened.

The best thing that could possibly have happened would have been the firing of everyone at the central administrative building and then having that building razed. Meanwhile the answer to all the school problems was always the same. Throw more money at them.

The real problem was too much money supporting a bloated bureaucracy that sucked away the teacher's authority while at the same time requiring the classroom completion of ever more data sheets so that these same bureaucrats could make charts and reports to justify their own destructive existence. Charts and reports that would naturally be documenting the decline of the school system....that of course would require...more money.

Meanwhile students were so alienated and undisciplined that they were smashing brand new tennis rackets on the way to PE class, and defacing property at every opportunity. When I compared this to what the Mexican schools were doing with almost no money at all by our standards, I was absolutely disgusted.

Adrienne, please see what the requirements are for me to join the Bremerton-Olympic Peninsula Navy League.

NASCAR has become the big buzzword hereabouts. On November 30, 2005 ISC, International Speedway Corporation, released its financing proposal for a $345 million motorsports facility in Kitsap County on 950 acres near the Bremo National Airport. The plan is for an 83,000 seat stadium and luxury boxes, with a 1.2 mile oval. It would host two major and one minor race annually, along with other smaller racing and non-racing events.

While the County has not yet received a formal proposal from ISC, the Board of County Commissioners is revving up. They are sorting through what they do and do not know, formulating a list of questions and soliciting the opinions of residents and businesses in other parts of the country that have been impacted by NASCAR. NASCAR operates at thirty-two speedways, raceways and motor sports parks nationwide.

The financing plan proposes a public-private partnership where Great Western Sports will pay $166 million, or nearly half the project costs, plus any construction overruns and all costs related to the regular maintenance and operation of the facility. Kitsap, Pierce and Mason Counties will form a tri-county Public Speedway Authority, PSA, and will issue bonds to help finance track construction. The bonds will be repaid through a sales tax credit issued by the state to the PSA, and from a local tax on the facility. The remaining $13 million would come from event ticket taxes.

The biggest drawback with NASCAR is that it will create very few permanent jobs, one estimate is sixty, but have a substantial negative impact, particularly on the local highway system, at least twice a year when the racing actually comes to town. The

Pacific Northwest International Trade Alliance just approved a resolution endorsing the NASCAR project.

The USS JOHN C. STENNIS—CVN-74 is a dual nuclear reactor powered multi-purpose aircraft carrier that is home-ported to Bremo. It will be featured on a Navy sponsored Busch Series car on February 25 at the race in Fontana California. The Navy began sponsoring a NASCAR team in 2004 for a full season. The 88-Car is owned by Dale Earnhardt Jr. The name of the USS JOHN C. STENNIS will be on the hood. It is considered to be an excellent recruitment and motivational tool by the United States Navy.

The Home Builders of Kitsap County have just now also endorsed NASCAR, concluding that the economic benefits to the county would be enormous.

The racetrack would be in an area known as SKIA, South Kitsap Industrial Area. The 3,400 acres have 1,690 designated as an Urban Growth Area. 9,350 jobs have been envisioned and the purpose is to diversify the economy with less dependence on defense industry employment. Both the SKIA and NASCAR developments would put tremendous pressure on the currently inadequate local area traffic systems.

02-11-06 Saturday—I attended the Stand-up Comedy at the Admiral Theater. The second and final hour was performed by the headliner, an obese female comic named Jen Kober [www.kobercomedy.com/]. Her act revolved around a Skinny Bitch routine. She began by picking out at random a lady seated at a front row table. It turned out to be Kathryn Quade, the Mayor of the neighboring City of Poulsbo. Jen was good and funny but her Skinny Bitching the Mayor all night was hilarious.

Everyone should do stand-up at least once in his or her lifetime.

13:30 ON
02-14-06 Tuesday—I rode the bike to the Amy Burnett Gallery and spoke with Amy about five prints. Three were there. The other two should be at the new shop in Charleston at 322 Callow Avenue. The Grand Opening is Sunday, March 5th, but she will be there this Sunday, February 19th from 11:00 to 18:00. I agreed to be there.

I brought up the Art Talk in Your Home that I had taken at auction with the Opera Guild. She was a bit stunned, as she does not do Art Talks in private homes. Yikes! I have already invited my neighbors! She mentioned an upcoming Art Talk she would be giving at Olympic College. We talked it out. She knows two of my neighbors sitting Judge Anna and her husband, former City Councilman Dave. We agreed it would be fun and scheduled it for about 6:30 on Sunday, March 12, 2006.

She will come right after closing the Callow store at 18:00. She confided in me that she had just that day successfully concluded negotiations to move her downtown gallery next door where the Naval Museum now is. The museum is moving to their new home in the remodeled, with the help of $750,000 in federal funds, Historic Naval Building 50. That will become a centerpiece of Maritime Park. Once she vacates her current gallery location, it will be the new home of a major antique enterprise.
15:00 OFF

17:30 ON
02-14-06 Tuesday—Fleet Reserve Association Branch 29—Meeting second Tuesday of Month 18:00—NAV / USMC / USCG
21:30 OFF

This winter has been unseasonably warm but that ended last night when frigid Artic air came roaring in. I found an ice cover on Dragon Pond. I have a small bird sanctuary in the northeast corner of the backyard. A waterfall keeps everything moving. The goldfish that I bought as four-cent feeder fish are now humongous and hibernating out there. They love it so much outside that they have begun breeding.

The raccoons were quite the problem. They are of the bear family and a whole lot smarter than your average critter. I grew up being taught that animals can't think, that only man can reason. What rubbish…these guys did a very good job of out-thinking me! We went back and forth in an ever-escalating war over the fish. Finally I sunk a large plastic underground electrical cable box. It has a mouse hole at either end for a cable, holes that the fish can use as doorways. On top of this I piled four large round concrete and pebble stepping-stones. The combined weight makes it seem permanent. The raccoons don't realize they could possibly topple it and the goldfish know enough to take cover within.

A family of small rats insisted on living under this pond. I ended up running a four-inch flexible perforated drainage pipe from the pond over to the fence. This allows them to come and go without undue pressure from the various predators whose list they are on. This includes, cats, hawks, owls, and eagles. My splendid cat Gravity will only drink from this pond. Squirrels abound here and some will eat from my hand.

Damn! Read yesterday's paper today and saw that Black stand-up comic Dave Chappelle is to appear at the Paramount in Seattle this Sunday. Tickets went on sale at 10AM yesterday. I go online and call immediately but it is Sold Out. No surprise there. Dave Chappelle had signed a massive deal with Comedy Central that would have returned the comedian's hit the

Chappelle's Show to the network for two more seasons. Sources familiar with the deal indicate it could be worth about $50 million, vaulting the 30 year-old Chappelle into the rarefied realm of television's top earners.

The new contract is believed to mark not only a steep increase for Chappelle as star, writer, co-executive producer and co-creator of *Chappelle's Show*, but more significantly, reward him with a hefty chunk of the series' robust DVD sales. *Chappelle's Show* has become an important series for the Comedy Channel, scoring a trio of Emmy nominations last month and ranked as the highest-rated cable program for the network's demographic sweet spot, men 18-34, who comprised much of the 3.1 million total viewers that the series averaged in its second season.

Dave is brilliant, insightful, and tells it like it is. What really makes this fellow interesting is that he ended up turning down the $50 million. He felt they were trying to control him and he said that he felt like a whore. How ravenous the younger generations are for wisdom and truth. If it weren't for stand-up, where would we get the real truth? Not newspapers, not regular TV, not politicians, and not normal classes.

On the subject of schools, either the shipyard or the naval station seems to have regular whistles. One is 07:15 in the morning, one mid-day at 12:115 and another at perhaps 16:20.

Many years ago I read somewhere an analysis of the K12 school system as it has existed since the advent of the Industrial Revolution. Never since have I ever seen this 'take' repeated or mentioned...but it makes perfect sense.

This is a classic example of Marshall McLuhan's *The Medium is the Message*. The children have to get to school Monday through Friday and arrive before the final bell rings. They must obey the teacher and line up and eat lunch peacefully without fighting. They then continue on until the final bell, when they may return home. It is recorded whenever they are tardy or absent.

After years of this conditioning, the grown child then gets a job in a factory where they must show up for work Monday through Friday before the final whistle, obey the foreman and line up and eat lunch peacefully without fighting. They then continue on until the final whistle, when they may return home. It is recorded whenever they are tardy or absent.

This Pavlovian conditioning is what it is all about, most of the class content, which varies form country to country, is by and large, irrelevant. Now a Presidential Commission is considering standardized testing for college and university students. When the focus is on passing standardized tests, true learning plummets.

I was just reading an article that listed some Collage Dropouts: Bill Gates, Soichiro Honda, F Scott Fitzgerald, William Faulkner, Barry Goldwater, Rush Limbaugh, Karl Rove, Ted Turner, David Geffen—DreamWorks SKG, Steve Jobs, Steve Wozniak, Lawrence Ellison, Michael Dell, Ralph Lauren, Woody Allen, Julie Andrews, Steve Martin, Rosie O'Donnell, Ellen DeGeneres, Dan Aykroyd and the Grammy winning Kanye West, among many others.

Another thing is the repeated uproar over child labor in developing countries. Certainly there are abuses but do we not recall that England and the United States also used child labor at the beginning? The plain fact is that at the onset of industrialization, only the children will do repetitive, indoor, highly supervised, and boring work. The adults who grew up in an agrarian society, who worked outdoors, in fresh air, on their feet, and at their own pace, refuse to do these jobs.

Sure they have quotas or get paid based on their production, but within that framework, they are on their own. It is only after future generations are conditioned by the schools as above, are these programmed adults willing to work in a plant, on an assembly line.

Additionally, when the sweatshops are closed, the kids are forced into far worse situations like slavery and child prostitution. Either provide a better option or keep your nose out of it.

The cover of the January 30, Newsweek is *The Boy Crisis*. It claims that boys are falling behind at every level. A lot of material is presented. Most of it struck me as so much bullshit.

The first boxed stat is that the number of male undergraduates on college campuses is down from 58% thirty years ago to 44% now. That means simply that more girls are going to college. This is a good thing, and nothing against the boys. When my youngest son was in middle school I noticed that the girls where making major efforts to win regional sports competitions of all kinds. And they were doing much better in the rankings than the boys were.

This is to be expected, as the opportunity to participate was much newer for the girls. Like in boxing, first the champions were White, than Black, and then Latino. Just as in Los Angeles ghettos, the homes were first occupied by Whites, then Blacks, and now Latinos. No mysteries anywhere here.

After endlessly being relegated by the sports world to being cheerleaders for the boys, is it really any wonder that the girls have all this momentum to strive now that they finally have the opportunity to take to the field themselves? And now even the cheerleaders are doing ever more daring stunts and routines, to the point where injuries and even deaths are occurring in this pursuit.

The Consumer Product Safety Commission reported an estimated 4,954 hospital emergency room visits in 1980 caused by cheerleading injuries. By 1986 the number had increased to 6,911 and in 1994 the number increased to approximately 16,000. The figure I have for 2004 is about 24,000.

Does this mean boys are lazier or dumber? I don't think so. When you realize how many men today are hobbling around on bad knees and other injuries sustained in High School sports, it could well be that the boys are just getting wiser.

Another highlighted finding: "Boys love video games because when they lose, the defeat is private." That is just horseshit…pure and simple. Humans and particularly males are all about hand and eye coordination. Video games are a wonderful way to organize young minds for the new millennium and at the same time, engage in primeval slaughter that is in itself, harmless to their surroundings.

The original Atari games were compatible with my generation. A player was almost always gunning for the other guy, like our Cowboys v Indians, or Cops and Robbers…all two-player games. But when the Japanese entered the market with Nintendo, it all changed completely and became more right brain then left, more random than linear. These were highly suited to single players.

I recall back in the 70's when my kids were cadging quarters to go to the local liquor store to play the video games that were then making their appearance. It eventually dawned on me then that the end of the Cold War was in sight. Our youth were spending their own money to in effect, train themselves for future combat, while at the same time the Soviet Union not only had no such thing going on, but they were actively restricting computers as an internal security measure. Game over.

My youngest son was raised on Atari, then Coleco, followed by Nintendo, Sony Play Station, and so on. He started making web pages at age thirteen and could solve computer problems in minutes that had me baffled for hours. When I would ask him how he knew what to do, he would simply say, "I know how programmers think." Now with no formal training, he makes very good money in Los Angeles as a computer wiz.

I recall a neighbor on Whidbey Island once bragging about the great education his child was receiving at a private Waldorf School. He was particularly impressed that the school not only didn't use computers, but also forbade its students from using them at home or anywhere else. I noticed that some of these Waldorf School advocates seemed to have almost a cult or religious attitude toward these theories. Now I agree that book reading and acting in plays and classical training is a very good thing, but to keep kids away from computers during their formative years is an unredeemable disaster.

Naturally they want to do what their friends are into, like video games and computers. Totally crippling their computer literacy in this day and age is horrid and largely irreversible. It would almost be better to just cut off a finger rather than to deliberately handicap them for life. Waldorf or Steiner Schools were inspired by Rudolf Steiner. I agree with much of what he was all about but let us keep in mind that he was born in the small village of Kraljevec, Austria, now in Croatia, in 1861 and died in Dornach, Switzerland in 1925.

On the bright side, a very bright side indeed, is the development of a computer for less than one hundred dollars. Nicholas Negroponte, chairman and founder of the Massachusetts Institute of Technology Media Labs, was on Charlie Rose with a model of it. This laptop will be tough and foldable in different ways, with a hand crank for when there is no power supply. He came up with the idea for a cheap computer for all after visiting a Cambodian village.

His non-profit One Laptop Per Child group plans to have up to 15 million machines in production within a year. Children in Brazil, China, Egypt, Thailand, and South Africa will be among the first to get one. The following year, Mitt Romney, Massachusetts's Governor, plans to start buying them for all 500,000 middle and high school pupils in his State.

Professor Negroponte predicts there could be 100 million to 150 million shipped every year by 2007. It is virtually indestructible and encased in rubber. The Linux-based machines are expected to have a 500MHz processor, with flash memory, instead of a hard drive that has more delicate moving parts. They will have four USB ports, will be able to connect to the net through wireless technology, and will share data easily.

It will also have a dual-mode display so that it can still be used in varying light conditions outside. It will be a color display, but users will be able to switch easily to a monochrome mode so that it can be viewed in bright sunlight at four times normal resolution.

The project has some big-name supporters on board, including Google, which is working on a system where these machines can share programs when linked to a central server. He said that he is committed to the idea that children all over the world should be equipped with this technology so that they can tap into the educational and communication benefits of the Internet.

This marvel can also act as a light source in homes or huts without electricity. Further it functions as an electronic book. The funds saved by these updateable books alone will allow developing countries to finance them out of their normal school budgets.

Who knows what remote village will produce the next Einstein? Now he or she will have an electronic highway out of there to the world at large. Will many Muslims forego this marvelous technology and instead concentrate on teaching hate in their madrasas? I hope not.

Returning to the Newsweek article: "Middle-school boys may use their brains less efficiently than girls." The nimrod that wrote that didn't even have the conviction to state his conclusion without the weasel word 'may'. In fact there are two distinct schools of thought on the nature of intelligence.

The proponents of one general intelligence have a theory that explains the biological reasons for intelligence. Given that they see neural processing speed as the root for intelligence, their theory has an effective causal explanation. A drawback to the general intelligence school of thought is that it is heavily dependent on psychometric evaluations. Consequently, it cannot take into account the vast array of different talents that people have. As for multiple intelligences, there are many theorists who believe in that school of thought.

Sure when I was a youngster we did better on school tests, but we never even dreamed about doing things with our basketballs or bicycles that they do now, and skateboarding and snowboarding had not even been invented. All of these things require the use of one type of intelligence or another.

And video games! Every day, ghetto kids who are doing abysmally in school are reverse engineering video games, taking apart the code, line by line, and sharing and swapping the info gleaned with their buddies. It is all about relevance and desire.

For decades a constant lament has been about the younger generation's failure to read books. This is indeed unfortunate, and politically scary…what with all the mind control going on. But stop and think about how much data these kids have to process in today's world.

Books became popular after 1436 when Johannes Gutenberg came up with a press with its movable type. It remained the standard until the 20th century. Just think how primitive that is to today's digital generations. The very thought of reading War and Peace by physically running your eyeball from letter to letter, word by word, sentence by sentence, paragraph by paragraph, page by page, chapter by chapter, for hundreds and hundreds of pages; that very thought is utterly abhorrent to the average youngster. If anything they would want to watch the movie.

A movie is so much better, quicker, with much more information, and so…not so Fifteenth Century. Really, they have no choice but to generally shun books, considering the amount of data that they must process in their lives. TV and video condition them to absorb information tape to tape or digitally, so to speak. Printed words be damned.

Where do they get their news? Many get it from the Daily Show on the Comedy Channel. Why? Because it is more insightful, honest, and relevant. This may be a very good thing indeed. I used to read a major newspaper every day until about thirty-five years ago. I noticed two things, firstly that ingesting all that bad news had a negative effect on my health and secondly that the mildly toxic ink was being absorbed through my skin.

I also concluded that over time, most of the information was useless, spun, or just plain wrong. Near the end all I read were the fillers. When news stories are laid out in columns for printing, there are often gaps at the ends. These gaps must be filled, so newspapers keep available what they call fillers of various sizes. These fillers must hold true for a long time. A filler might be something that states what the projected population of Mexico City will be in 2025 and how it will rank with the largest cities at that time. So fillers have to be informative, factual, and truthful over time.

Bad news trumps good news and travels fast for a reason. It has survival value. It is in our DNA. If someone falls into a pit, the sooner the rest of the tribe found out, the less chance that the same fate would befall another. Good news is not that important or urgent. But to take in on a daily basis all the bad news occurring on the entire planet…this is way out of proportion to what our systems were ever meant to tolerate. That much bad news has a negative effect on your body chemistry. What you want to input are positive thoughts and good news.

When I became aware that the bulk of the younger generations were not reading books or newspapers, I assumed that they would fall easy prey to the spinmeisters and professional deceivers. And so I am heartened to see that they are going to the Comedy Channel and Jon Stewart, and Dave Chappelle, and the magnificent Bill Maher.

These kids are smart enough to let these geniuses digest all the news and give them the unvarnished crystalline truth. And in a time saving and wickedly humorous way. They also have ever more BLOGS as sources. BLOGS that cannot be corrupted or silenced by the powers that be. Nope…these youngsters are not as dumb as we might think that they are.

Item: My spell checker goes crazy when I read this in a WORD.doc. Take the word spinmeisters that I used in the above paragraph. The spell checker says there is no such word, but when I Google it, I get 112,000 references to it. But then according to my spell checker, there is no such thing as Google! The only thing that is not changing is change itself.

Back to the article: "A boy without a father figure is like an explorer without a map." Maybe so. Maybe not. Two of the most amazing men to become President of the United States in the Twentieth Century were Ronald Reagan and Bill Clinton. Both had alcoholic fathers who were not only habitual drunks but they were abusive to their mothers. Both rose from poverty and obscurity to become the most powerful person on Earth. Huh?

Reagan's middle name was presidential, Wilson; Clinton's was also presidential, Jefferson. So may we conclude that if you would like your son to rise to the top, your best bet is to stay drunk, beat your wife habitually, and don't forget to give the kid a presidential middle name? Now that is interesting, it might work but we do not advocate trying it at home.
Life evolves in mysterious ways. There is a Chinese folktale where what appears to be good news turns out to be bad and vice versa. Some raiding Mongols sweep into the area and take a man's daughter and both of his horses. All the villagers commiserate with his misfortune. A year later the abductor, who is the clan chief's son, returns with the daughter. He has fallen in love with her and wishes the old man's blessing for the marriage. He brings a bunch of horses and gifts.

Now the man is happy but the villagers are all beside themselves with jealousy and shun the old man and his wife. And so the story goes, back and forth, good becomes bad, bad becomes good, over and over.

02-18 Saturday — Amy calls to say that a fire in her Callow shop must cancel our appointment mañana. Some moron plugged in an antique radio and left it on causing an electrical fire. She can't touch anything until she meets the insurance adjuster there on Monday. She will take my pictures to the downtown gallery afterward and I will meet her there on Tuesday.

Item: Newsweek quotes Pittsburgh Steelers quarterback Ben Roethlisberger as saying, "I don't think I got it in." re one of the controversial calls that had ruled his run a touchdown on Super Bowl XL. The Steelers had a 3-4 point spread in their favor but the word was that the Seahawks would either beat the spread or take the game outright. A lot of late money was going on the Hawks. Not a good smell to this one at all.

02-19 Sunday — Turino, Italy — Shani Davis is the first African American man to ever win a gold medal at the Winter Olympics. He won the 1,000 meters Saturday night. The American viewing public was treated to a tape of a boorish Davis in his first interview with NBC.

Davis turned down the standard studio interview with Bob Costas as well as the usual medalist circuit like the 'Today Show'. But it was NBC's Melissa Stark's interview with him on Saturday night that had people shaking their heads in disbelief. How could anyone in that position do this to their image?

"You are the first African-American male to win a gold medal at the Winter Games," Stark said. "How proud are you of that?" "I'm pretty happy about it," replied Davis, who looked away from Stark for most of the interview. "That's it?" Stark said. "Yeah," Davis said.

After a question about his mother, Cherie, was met with a similarly abrupt reply, Stark ended the interview asking, "Are you angry, Shani?" Davis replied: "No, I'm happy. I have a loss for words right now." "All right," said Stark, clearly put off. "You sure don't look happy."

In the studio, Bob Costas and analyst Dan Hicks spoke to Davis' mood. "This is certainly not the kind of interview you're used to hearing from an Olympic gold medallist," Hicks said.

Watching this it is difficult to believe your eyes and ears. I can see millions in easy endorsement money running right down the drain. People must have gotten to him quickly because by the next day he had cleaned up his act tremendously. So much in this world is dependant on your attitude.

02-20 Monday—Somebody won a record $365 million Powerball Jackpot. That always rubs me the wrong way. Would it not be far better to have 365 people each win $1 million than to have one hayseed win all of it and probably kill himself within five years because of such a windfall? Or even better for 3,650 people to each win $100,000. Wouldn't that spread a lot of manageable joy and financial relief? Or maybe even 7,300 people each winning $50,000.

There is a cute item in the Kitsap Sun today. The Klahowya Secondary School Key Club held their fifth annual 'Senior' Prom and crowned as Queen, Louise Nystrom. Ms. Nystrom is age 100. The theme song was *Singing in the Rain*. "This has been a wonderful day!" said Louise.

Adrienne, yes, send in my application and one year individual dues for the Navy League to Rick Becker, CAOT, MSC, USN— Retired

11:30 ON
02-21-06 Tuesday—Veh#1—I drove down off Forest Ridge to Charleston at the eastern foot of the West Hills. Just a mile or so west of Bremo's downtown, you'll find the Charleston neighborhood, Bremo's original downtown and our city's new International District. The area is filled with a mix of antique, collectible, pawn and thrift shops and offers a wide range of diverse eating options. Bremo and Charleston were consolidated on December 15, 1927.

I hit Brewski's Bar and Grill or Tavern, home of the best barmaids around, and found draft Amber Bock on sale for $1.50. Had my quota and moved on down to the newly opened Paradise Cove, another Filipino eatery. Very friendly people and an all you can eat special buffet of Mexican food. The food was okay. The homemade desert was excellent.

Went on down to the Amy Burnett Gallery on Pacific Avenue. My five framed prints were set out along a wall. All are beautifully framed. Four same-sized matching frames are of Native Americans: *Chief Joseph and Chief Yellow Bull, Annie Yellow Wolf and Baby,* an *Eskimo Belle,* and a *Northern Chief.* The fifth is larger and consists of four women. It is titled *Fire Watchers.* The expression on the woman in the foreground slays me. All were painted form photographs. Annie Yellow Wolf was a wife to Chief Joseph.

Amy also gives me an unframed print that she says goes with this series. It is a woman who Amy later learned was a half-sister to Annie. She also gives me another copy of her book *Amy's Bremo Window,* to give away. I am quite fortunate to also find the last copy of a book now out of print by a local author entitled *Victory Gardens and Barrage Balloons*, a collective memoir by Frank Wetzel that centers on Bremo during WW II.

I meet Helen B Louise, Executive Director of the Kitsap County Historical Society Museum. I promise to stop by and see their current exhibit of clocks, and chat about the fabulous clock exhibit in the Forbidden City in Beijing. People talk about how the Chinese are pirating our software. A few centuries ago when Western powers were forcing their way into China, the high tech of the time was clocks. It didn't take long before the Chinese had reverse engineered these large, ornate, and complex mechanisms and began to produce their own clocks. They have been at this sort of thing for a very long time.

Ms. Burnett wraps and I load up my treasures. Amy advises that I may bring any of them back if they don't work out, but I know exactly where they are going and they are not going back anywhere.
16:00 OFF

The $365 million Powerball Jackpot was won by about eight employees of a Lincoln, Nebraska outfit. They were all very happy and it was so much better this way than if it all was going to just one person. I think they each get $22 million after taxes in a lump sum. One of them was still reporting for duty on the graveyard shift because he didn't want to put the company in a bind or inconvenience his coworkers. That is nice but it will change soon enough.

Another news item that I can hardly believe is that the game of tag has been banned from the school playgrounds in Spokane, WA. The TV also states that this is also the case in CA, NJ and elsewhere. The rationale is that tag is too dangerous as it has the potential of victimization, i.e. someone might be tagged who didn't want to be! There was also something about how they do allow football…but there is no running permitted!

This is enough to make you vomit. And they wonder why boys do not like school. They shorten recess, lengthen the year, and overload them with homework…so that even when they are out of school these kids must remain indoors doing homework.

I still remember one day when I was in the fourth grade in Rhode Island. The schoolyard was divided in half, boys to one side and girls to the other. The yard was surrounded by chain link fencing. What happened that day never happened before or since to my knowledge. Suddenly all the boys, every last one of us, formed into one large group, which then split in two. One half went over to the girls' side fence and mustered up toward the back of the yard. The girls quickly got out of the way and moved to the front of the schoolyard. The other half of the boys formed by our fence. Somehow I was the general for my half and someone else took charge of the other half.

At a spontaneous common signal, each half charged at the other. We all new it was a war. My glasses were broken in the melee. It didn't last long. We were as surprised as everyone else. The other fellow and I were hauled into the administrative office. But oh what a glorious event! The saying used to be, "Boys will be boys." Now it seems that it is becoming, "Boys must be girls."

The difference between the boys and girls was much more apparent in that Mexican School that I was associated with. Generally the girls were well behaved and worked at their studies. The boys played hard and rough and paid as little attention to their schoolwork as possible. My son Tommy was an exception and the teachers loved him for it. Tommy and I were both learning Spanish and we did his homework together each night.

I had the preconception that in third world countries, the boys got educated and the girls did not. The reality was quite different. The school days ran two shifts, one in the morning and the other in the afternoon. This was so the youngsters would have time to do their chores and also attend school. Most went to school through the sixth grade, but some dropped out to work full time.

The next level of schooling was the Secondaria, and only some went on to that. The boys mostly knew what they would be doing. San Felipe was and is a fishing town and you don't need a whole lot of book learning for that dangerous and grueling job.

It was a different story for the girls. They would be raising their children and keeping the home. This included teaching their children. There was a bookshop in town that I frequented in my pursuit of mastery of the language. I had started with comic books like *Disneylandia's Pato Donald, Mickey Raton,* and so forth. Then it was soft cover books with text and pictures. They would be on such categories as Romance, Westerns, Police, and the like. Later I went on to the Spanish Classics and eventually South American Classics.

The point is that I don't think that I ever saw a local man in that store buying a book. The clientele was all female. They had studied well in school and continued to read and learn for the rest of their lives. The oligarchy aside, it is the females and not the males, at least in rural Mexico that are self-educated.

The trend now seems to be to overprotect our boys until they are eighteen and them send them overseas to slaughter and be slaughtered. What's wrong with that picture?

You can step on a balloon but it will pop up elsewhere. You abuse the nature of these boys and push them up against a wall hard enough and long enough and what happens? They come to school armed to the teeth and begin opening fire. Isn't that a bit more dangerous then tag?

Very little is worse then overprotecting boys. Girls I am not so sure about but we do know that the sexes in this country are becoming closer in identity and that the girls are getting wilder all the time. Children must be given responsibility in order to develop a healthy and self-disciplined character.

The school that I remember with the fondest memories was the one I attended for most of the second grade. We had moved briefly to Seekonk, Massachusetts and the school was a rural one. We took a school bus to get there. The lunch period was an amazing hour and a half or more. The cooks were local mothers and the food was prepared home-style. You could have all you could eat, seconds and thirds were common.

When you finished eating you bussed your dishes and headed outside. The woods went on for many acres. You could even get out to the highway and cross it to a small store. The policing for all this was handled by designated sixth graders who wore special armbands.

13:30 ON
02-23-06 Thursday — Time for my 14:00 appointment at Affinity Massage with Greta. OMG did I ever need that!
15:30 OFF

02-24-06 Friday — Talk about synchronicity, I just now pick up the Kitsap Sun and see that yesterday a fourteen year old freshman in Roseburg, Oregon shot and wounded another student at the school.

The schools curricula have become mostly so irrelevant to our children and what is on point, like computer literacy, the students are far in advance of the teachers and have to show their instructors how to function in this information age.

Abraham Lincoln said that the aggregate of all his schooling was less than one year. Winston Churchill signed on as an officer in the 4th Hussars instead of attending university. Posted to India at age twenty-two in 1896, he had the time on his hands to pursue studies as he wished. We already mentioned some notable school dropouts above such as Bill Gates the richest man in the world. Think these are strange anomalies?

One could certainly make a case that Thomas Edison was the most successful inventor in world history. He had more than one thousand patents to his name. He attended school for a total of three months at the age of four. The teacher sent him home stating that Thomas was too 'addled' to be educated. Most of us have heard about how Albert Einstein's teachers thought so poorly of him.

Not convinced yet? This belongs under the, "No good deed goes unpunished department." Alan Turing was looked down upon by his teachers and was at the bottom of his class in many of his subjects. He was a brilliant original thinker who wrote on mathematics, physics, chemistry, biology, philosophy and psychology. He had a better understanding of computers and their potential than probably anyone else alive. His Turing Machine was a concept that anticipated many computer standard features like algorithms, compilers/interpreters, input, output, memory, and programs.

The day after WW II began Turing joined the Government Code and Cypher School and for the next three years was the key figure in the ongoing battle to decode messages encrypted by the increasingly complex German 'Enigma' machines. He took responsibility for the most difficult code-breaking task, the breaking of the German naval codes. His unlocking of those codes greatly reduced losses by our Atlantic convoys that were keeping Britain afloat.

One could argue that Alan Turing was instrumental in saving Britain and therefore Western Civilization from the Nazis in WW II, and also that he was the father of our modern computer architecture and thus our way of life. His reward? He was put on trial in March of 1952 on charges of homosexuality, which was at that time a crime in and of itself. He had never attempted to hide his sexual orientation. To avoid prison he was legally forced to submit to estrogen injections. Fearing that this persecution would never end, Alan Turing committed suicide in 1954 at the age of 41.

Schools all say that they want their students to learn not by rote but rather that they intend to teach them how to think so that they can study on their own later. Unfortunately, in practice, that is not the case. They are conformity factories. They are paid by the state to produce workers, to stamp out interchangeable units. If the state or institution has enough power, then the kids will even have to dress alike.

Life should be a joy. It is…for most happy healthy kids, at least when they are not in school or doing homework. Learning should be a joy. Learning is a joy if you are learning what you want and need to learn. Having other stuff crammed down your throat is not a joy, far from it. A person wants to first learn something that they are interested in. Once quite full of that subject, at least for a while, you then want to pursue the next area that you are lacking knowledge in and therefore have an interest for. You never really know what will come next until you get there. Your consciousness evolves bit by bit.

I have yet to meet a child that could not find joy in learning what they were interested in at the time. As soon as a school demands that all learn the same things in the same order at the same speed and at the same level, they have already lost it. What schools are excellent at is making students hate school and unfortunately the children confuse this with a distaste of learning.

Sputnik entered the scene in 1957. That spurred a great push in the U.S. towards engineering. When I graduated high school in 1960 I was steered into a very fine engineering school, Rensselaer Polytechnic Institute in Troy, New York. The problem was that I was more a poet than an engineer. Both of my SATs were in the 700's but my verbal, right brain, skills were stronger than my mathematical, left brain abilities.

It didn't take me long to realize that I would be spending six months studying six books that I had no real interest in. I stopped going to classes and began buying and devouring books. Eventually I was detected and called to the Administration. To their credit, when they knew what I was doing, they allowed me to remain and continue my self-education until the semester ended. I doubt that such an outcome would occur today.

Having discovered my great love of learning, I went home to Connecticut and began quenching an insatiable thirst for the Greek and Roman Classics, Russian authors, German authors, French writers and philosophers of the Enlightenment, and many, many others. I also dove into self-help books and anything on psychiatry and psychology. I have been and remain an avid reader and learner from many sources. What a difference between hating school curriculum and loving learning!

All children are artists, but the society does not need that many, so what happens? They start with lots of art in preschool and kindergarten. Less in first grade, very little in second grade, and then that is about it. The kids are weaned from art and then cut off. How many artists do you need in a mill anyway? The problem is that we are or should be decades past producing mostly mill workers.

Art is more of a right-brain function. The curriculum is forcing more and more away from the spatial side and into the left-brain linear processing realm. Following a line of printed words rather than taking in a video. But to be a healthy person you need to be balanced.

Our entire culture is shifting from left to right brain activity. Males are becoming increasingly feminized, not necessarily a bad thing. Baseball is a linear left-brain sport. It has been supplanted, as the most popular national sport, by football. Football provides much more random movement and is right-brained in orientation. Video games have gone from left to right. Watching movies has largely replaced reading books as a form of entertainment by the younger generations.

One thing that amazed me in China was the Chinese writing. Today they teach their children both the traditional characters and also the western alphabet. Think about that for a moment. The characters use the right-brain and the alphabet uses the left-brain! Is there any doubt who will be on top in one hundred years? They also learn English. Our kids won't even learn a second language.

To me the character language seemed so imprecise and vague and so forth, but that is what they use for virtually everything. I reviewed all manner of technical reports at a factory in Guangzhou. Everything was done in traditional characters. This was the day the famous Guangzhou Trade Fair opened and the rocket was launched that put Liwei Yang in orbit. They had the confidence to openly make that connection and broadcast the launch live. They had Henry Kissinger and Al Haig commenting on TV. The Russian Space program is moribund and the Euro Space Agency never sent up a man. The 21st Century is no question, the Century of China.

It is worth noting that China has a history of many millennia of never being aggressive outside of its own borders, in fact they built the Great Wall to keep all others out. Sure they are menacing Taiwan and took over Tibet but that is because they consider them to be part of historical China and they want all of their parts restored.

When North Vietnam was being nasty some while back, China amassed an army and went into Vietnam to teach them a lesson, but once done, they withdrew. The same thing occurred during the Korean War when Macarthur failed to heed the warnings from China and got too close to the Yalu River.

The Chinese written language employs Chinese characters h×Ö/ºº×Ö. Each symbol represents a semanteme, a meaningful unit of language. They are not just pictographs, pictures of their meanings, but are highly stylized and carry much abstract meaning. Only some characters are derived from pictographs. In 100 AD, the famed scholar Xushen in the Han Dynasty classified characters into six categories with only 4% listed as pictographs, and 82% as phonetic complexes. The latter consist of both a radical element that indicates meaning and a phonetic element.

Just image putting a man in outer space using such characters! Time and time again I have witnessed two Chinese people coming to a verbal impasse, and what do they do? They resort to the Chinese characters and very quickly arrive at a mutual understanding.

Two personal stories came to mind as I edited this. When I was about four years old, in 1946, I was attending nursery school. One day we were assigned the task of creating a picture using those big fat crayons. I diligently and enthusiastically set about my work. Just before I was quite finished the teacher ordered a cut-off. I continued to hastily finish. The next ting I knew this lady was at my side and physically pulling my paper away and ruining my work.

In frustration I hurled one of the colors in the air. I could not believe that a task would be ordered and then destroyed by the teacher. I was bound hand and foot with rope, dumped in a 'woody' and driven home to my mother. I was untied at my house. Yes…I know that this may explain a lot! But the point here is that when push comes to shove, the message is not creativity or work product, what is being inculcated is obedience.

The second situation came about because I switched from a city parochial school in Rhode Island to a rural public school in Massachusetts in the second grade. One thing I can say about those nuns is that I had been taught to write. But in Seekonk they didn't learn that until the third grade and were still printing. The teacher was a bit shocked to see me writing and made it clear that I was to print only. I had and have no problem with that. I loved that school. But it is a very minor illustration that conformity, not student development, is paramount.

It is certainly not my intention to be knocking teachers here. I could not do what they do, not with the class sizes that are considered normal. That many kids, and I would most definitely go postal on the little monsters.

The maximum span of control is usually about twelve. That is all Jesus Christ could handle and the same goes for any organization. But teachers dealing with our little savages are supposed to manage twenty, thirty, and even forty of them. This is just more built-in systemic failure.

Systemic failure like forcing young children, especially boys to sit still for hours and then forbidding them to run at recess in the playground! What loons come up with that? Is it a matter of liability? If so then pass legislation that deals with it…don't sacrifice our children who are still close enough to their nature that they know what is good and what is bad. You can't fool a dog for long…or a child. They are still in tune with the source.

A child has an inner voice. That voice is telling him to be outside with his or her bare feet on the earth, breathing fresh air, running, yelling, and playing with friends. The teacher is the outer voice telling him to wear shoes, come inside, breath dead air, sit at a desk, don't play, sit still, be quiet, and listen to her. The answer to lack of attention is not drugs. That is criminal. When I was young there was no ADD. You can't put a child on drugs for no reason so first they had to invent a name like ADD for what is normal; and then they prescribe drugs as a cure for it. Then they make billions.

Mexico doesn't have ADD. If they did, virtually every boy in school in San Felipe would be so diagnosed. Our medical people who are self-proclaimed experts on ADD have concluded that kids with ADD are more likely to grow up and become drug addicts. In other words if you take a restless five year old, tell him he has a disease whose solution is to take drugs, and you then put him on drugs for the rest of his childhood; then when he becomes an adult and has a problem…he may dose himself with drugs! I'm sorry; I regard this whole ADD fad as a criminal conspiracy.

Society does need to have its educational system produce what it needs. Societal evolution in broad terms has been described as: Nomadic or Hunter/Gatherer, Agrarian, Post Industrial Revolution, Information Age, and perhaps next will be the Age of Creativity.

It is said that the generals are always fighting the last war. The schools are no different. Our schools are still attempting to stamp out cookie cutter workers for the mills. The problem is that the mills meanwhile have long since gone overseas. The kids know its bullshit. Naturally they would rather be playing video games and allowing their brains to follow and absorb the code. That programming is one of the best things for them and will organize their minds in a very logical and highly sophisticated way. A Harvard study just out concluded that video games do not make kids violent.

So the children quite naturally and rightly rebel against wasting their valuable time on this planet, filling their head with garbage…and our response is not to upgrade our methods and make instruction and practices relevant, but to drug them into submission. These are the same folks that gave us shock treatments and lobotomies. These are our children. They are the future hope of our species. These are our children!

In fact the trend is toward ever more national and statewide standardized tests and the Feds now want to start that in higher education as well. Is it true that our kids don't match some undeveloped foreign countries on these tests? Of course it is! They are where we were fifty to one hundred years ago. The Caucasian prizefighters we produce cannot match those of Blacks or Hispanics these days. Why should they? They could have fifty to one hundred years ago. We have already been there and done that. As long as you are making progress you are moving on. The White boxers of today come from the former Soviet Union.

That's why so much manufacturing has gone overseas; it is their turn for that. We are supposed to be leading the Information and Creative Ages. That means computers and art, and that means are kids should be playing computer and video games. D'uh!

If each child has a computer that is guiding him or her through the lessons in a fun way and at the child's speed, then a teacher can move around dealing with problems as they occur. Even the order of subjects can be tailored to fit the child's needs.

I am not up on current schooling and certainly no expert, but I have been told that in many schools if a student does a report on whatever subject and they put it together by synthesizing the report from info found on the Internet, that they get in trouble for doing that and are charged with lack of personal effort and so forth.

Why? That is the only thing that now makes sense to do. That is exactly what they will do as adults and what many successful adults do now. Think for a moment. Practically all the knowledge and information on the planet is available to them on the Net, and they know that. They also know how to get it. But they are somehow expected to put on blinders and pretend that it is 1920.

Of course no society is all agrarian or all creative or whatever. The U.S. still has some hunter-gatherers out there. Just as an agrarian country has some industry, if only to make farm equipment and the like. But we need for our educational system to be leading our children forward, not dragging them, kicking and screaming back into the pre-computer, pre-digital past.

Some homework is necessary, but it should be given only out of necessity. When it is based on a certain number of hours each day, it represents what? Is it merely a means of attempting to keep the kids off the street? Why isn't the subject of the homework sometimes left for the child to pick? Maybe one kid would study an anthill, another the stars, another cook or build something, and so on and so forth. Then let each give a brief written or oral report.

That would give variety and relevance. It would also teach public speaking. And best of all, the students could study something that they were actually interested in! That is the purpose of learning. With pride of authorship, all manner of creativity could flow. Plus, each student could learn from all the others, instead of them all having done the same meaningless assignment.

But it wouldn't show up on the nationwide standards test, you may object. Well you know what they can do with that. Just like the drug war, the situation in the schools is worse every year. Bureaucrats can ruin anything. They always have when they remained unchecked for long enough. Now they are doing their best to ruin the schools.

Bear in mind that most of these kids today get their early learning of the alphabet and reading, numbers and math, animals and whatever from these colorful little handheld computer driven learning devices like those made by Fisher Price and many others. Then when they reach school age and hit the big-time, they are forced to go backward in time.

The key to running a successful and productive workforce is putting the right people in the right jobs. I have found that everyone is good for and at something. If you put the round pegs in the round holes, everything gores smoothly. Forcing square pegs in triangular holes is a fool's effort. Each child needs to find his or herself, and be developed in the way best for them. We finally now have the technology and the knowledge to actually do this for the first time. We just are not doing it very well at all.

There is a saying in the computer world, GIGO, garbage in results in garbage out. Education is no different. We fill our kids heads with irrelevant garbage and wonder why we get garbage out.

Today's world is radically different from the past and its needs are different. When Columbus landed in the New World there were hundreds of Native American tribes and many thousands of individual groups. Each group would have had an especially skillful arrow maker. That being an essential product to produce, this arrow maker probably had a protégé or two. That would have meant several thousand arrow makers in North America alone.

How many arrow makers do we need today? A few companies would be more than sufficient, even if we all used arrows. Today they would be a CAD CAM product, in other words designed by computers and aided in their manufacture by computers. Everything is going in that direction. If you are a student and number one or close to that on a national level, then you are indeed valuable and will be highly educated, at least in your specialty area.

But if you are just average, what can you really contribute? The work done by the tops in their fields will have their work or work products replicated a million-fold for the masses. What does that leave for you to do? Individual creativity will become more and more important as machines do more and more of the physical work and a gifted relative few do the heavy thinking.

Another thing that we have upside down is world travel. Instead of our geriatric cases making world tours at an age when they can barely hobble around or more often are too afraid to go at all because of health concerns; it is our young people that need and could most benefit from overseas travel. All of what they learned could be applied to the life that they have in front of them; rather than being experienced at the end of life.

I am often solicited by AARP to donate to this or that cause of the elderly. It is the young people who need the most help. Old people have usually bought their homes when they were dirt-cheap and have long since paid them off. Most young people have low paying futureless service jobs and have little chance at all to buy an exorbitantly priced home.

I didn't see any mental illness when I lived in Mexico. Basically, the people there were too busy trying to cover their necessities for that luxury, i.e. Maslow's hierarchy of needs. Despite what we would call poverty, the quality of life was in many ways far superior to our own. Families and communities were very strong. Joyous celebrations were longer. They celebrated things like Children's Day, and the Day of the Dead, that we do not. Children played necessary roles in the family's survival and had a sense of purpose rather than alienation. On Mothers Day there was not a soul to be seen anywhere as everyone had some place to go.

The pharmacist was considered far more knowledgeable about drugs than the doctors and people did not need a prescription. Don't kid yourself, that is most often true in the U.S. as well. Sure a steady stream of narcotics and marijuana traverse Mexico on the way to the U.S. but they and their children mostly shun them. Those drugs are strictly intended for the stupid gringos.

Then we would come back to the U.S. each month for supplies and family visits and see commercials for such essential medication as that needed to deal with the horrors of things like PMS. And watch ads for such vital products as pre-peeled oranges.

Item: Highland Avenue has long been primo Bremo real estate and the location of the Gates family home. Most homes were built in 1901; all but one was up before the Great depression. Located high up by the Washington Narrows, this allows views of the Manette Bridge and has been rezoned for sixty-foot tall condos. The locals are aflutter over the pending change in character of the neighborhood. They are calling for a forty-foot height limit.

In fact, in 1985 the city passed a comprehensive plan that allows for one-hundred-twenty-foot tall buildings here. The revitalization of downtown Bremo necessitates higher residential density within walking distance of the city center. Bremo will be a great place to live for those who are not looking for the burbs. Last summer Seattle Magazine ranked Manette Greater Seattle's ninth hottest neighborhood

A motion to revisit the building height limits was made at a recent City Council meeting but failed to find a second to the motion...and so it died as the five fellow councilpersons stood mute. The whole growth strategy is based upon getting many more thousands of people into these areas.

Item: Millions of acres of lush green Canadian forests are turning red and dying. The rapidly warming climate has aided the mountain pine beetle in killing more trees than either fire or logging

The Navy plans to relocate two Seawolf-class fast-attack subs here next summer. That would put all three Seawolfs in Kitsap, the USS Jimmy Carter now at Bangor and the USS Seawolf and USS Connecticut first home-ported to Bremo's Naval Station. The move is part of a strategic realignment to have sixty percent of the U.S. submarines in the Pacific. Bangor already has had three new subs added in the last few months of 2005.

Bangor is now home to eight Trident Ballistic missile subs, two guided missile subs and the Jimmy Carter. The USS San Francisco, a Los Angeles-class fast attack sub is also here awaiting repairs. This buildup is to counter the fast growth of China's military and naval forces.

There is an unusual scheme beginning to surface around Bremo, in one form or another. It has only been made possible with the recent U.S. Supreme Court's very controversial June 2005 5/4 decision to allow eminent domain for economic reasons. Lawmakers in Olympia offered several proposals to clarify Washington State's constitution's wording on the issue, but Democrats in the majority left them in committee.

The main outline of the plan being bandied about has numerous evolving variations but it generally goes something like this. Huge amounts of Bremo are condemned through eminent domain for economic reasons. But rather than simply compensating the local owners at the current market value, they would receive shares in a corporate entity that would generously reflect the greatly enhanced value that these properties would represent after major redevelopment occurs on a grand scale.

These shares could later be used to purchase new units of a greater or lesser number of bedrooms in town or sold outright, in whole or in part. The entire area would be transformed and no holdouts would be possible. This has never been done before to our knowledge. It would take tremendous effort and planning but when you consider what the people of Bremo accomplished in WW II, it is certainly not beyond their ability.

And certainly they are most deserving. Look at what the folks in New Orleans did after Hurricane Katrina. First they fail to evacuate as ordered, then they compound that by not putting sufficient water and food supplies on hand. Then they riot and loot, and even shoot at helicopters attempting to help them. Not everyone acted like that but enough did to make it a national disgrace.

On top of that, the government is remarkably corrupt, the same with the Police Department. And Mayor Ray Nagan? My mama taught me that if you can't say anything good about someone, just say nothing. So much for His Honor. Bremos on the other hand, ask for nothing, work hard, and help each other out. Man, do they ever deserve to finally receive a just reward.

A new Milken Institute ranking puts the 2005 Bremo~Silverdale area as 18th nationwide, up from 122nd in 2004, with wealthy migrants driving Kitsap County's job growth.

Item: The Philippine Army attempts to stop a coup to oust President Gloria Macapagal Arroyo. I wonder if that is fallout from her recent statement that had to be the stupidest one I have ever heard coming from a head of state concerning that horrible mudslide that left an unstable 100-acre mud field and swamp enveloping and covering the village of Guinsaugon on Leyte Island.

With widespread poverty that has many citizens eating out of landfills, President Arroyo went on TV to promise that all bodies would be unearthed for the sake of their families. The cost of this dangerous effort would be in the hundreds of millions of dollars…and all so that these victims could be what? Reburied in the very same earth!

09:30 ON
02-25-06 Saturday—I walked to VFW 239 on Dora Street in the West Hills area. Got buzzed in and hit the bar. I left a wind-ripped U.S. flag properly folded, to be forwarded to the American Legion for appropriate ceremonious destruction.
10:30 OFF

Item: 02-28-06 Warning! Financial responsibility can lead to terrorism. An article by Bob Kerr of the Rhode Island Providence Journal concerns one Walter Soehnge a retired Texas schoolteacher who decided to reduce his debt. He and his wife thought that the balance on their J C Penney MasterCard had gotten to an unhealthy level, so they sent in a check for $6,522.

The credit didn't show up. They were told, as they moved up the ladder at the call center, that the amount they had sent in was much larger than their normal monthly payment. And if the increase hits a certain percentage higher than the normal payment, Homeland Security has to be notified. Then the money doesn't move until the threat alert is lifted. Walter called television stations, the American Civil Liberties Union and Bob Kerr.

And he went on the Internet to see what he could learn. He learned about changes in something called the Bank Privacy Act. "The more I read, the scarier it gets," he said. Walter says that he holds solid, middle-of-the-road American beliefs, but worries now about rights being lost. "If it can happen to me, it can happen to others," he said.

Item: Two Washington D.C. residents have had the tiny VeriChip inserted into their bodies. The RFID chip contains medical info. The device was originally developed to track livestock, and has been implanted in over six million cats and dogs. The units last indefinitely.

My understanding of the privacy promises made when President Roosevelt signed the Social Security Act on August 14, 1935, was to the effect that the information would be sacrosanct. It was stated that the Feds would not even use this info to trace a Public Enemy Number One like John Dillinger.

Now we are asked for our social security number for just about anything. All the credit bureaus use it as their file number. I once persisted in questing this until I finally reached a high enough individual who explained to me that the credit bureau does not use the actual social security number but rather it uses another number that is identical to your social security number!

Worse yet, back in the mid 60's when I was working for local government, I was having lunch with a fellow employee who was running a computer installation for the same department. In response to some problem I was having, he offered to supply me with a computer tape of every Social Security number in Los Angeles County…to run against a tape of my accounts. I was flabbergasted. The offer was genuine.

Today we get bombarded with Privacy Policy Pamphlets from all of our creditors assuring us of the great care being taken to protect our privacy. This is concurrent with the ability of any of us to obtain private information on just about anybody on the Internet. As a licensed Private Investigator, I have long been able to access a great deal of information but now anybody can do the same and more.

This is like the War on Drugs, the longer the war, the worse the drug problem. Today we have all this privacy legislation and no privacy to be had. The damn pamphlets have so much small print that even those with OCD won't take the time to read it, not that it is understandable anyway. As the old saying goes, "What the big print giveith, the small print taketh away."

Even worse has been the SPAM situation. It used to be that I got maybe one SPAM a week and everyone would get very upset over SPAM. Then when the complaints reached a certain level, the Feds stepped in to correct the problem. What their anti-SPAM legislation in fact did was to legalize SPAM. Now I get from 20,000-30,000 SPAM each day! Bravo U.S. Congress!

OK Adrienne, about the shampoo subject that was left unfinished last night. Actually it is about more than shampoo. Have you ever noticed that the hair that goes gray first is the hair that you cut? With a man it is the hair on your head and then your beard if you shave. The body hair and eyebrows that are not cut hold their color years longer.

Since they start cutting our hair at age three or so we don't stand a chance. When hair is cut it grows longer. You pay a price for messing with Mother Nature. Now you may think that if we didn't cut our hair it would grow impossibly long. Look at a dog or cat or chimp or gorilla or any animal; they don't cut their hair. It grows to the right length and stops. The same thing happens with our body hair.

But each time you cut your hair your body gets the message that there is a hair problem and so it grows it back plus some extra length. It is the lifetime of this abuse that leads to the loss of color, and probably some longevity. If this is not the message in the story of Sampson and Delilah…what is?

I had my last haircut in 1994. Since then I have never had a bad-hair day. It takes but a few seconds to brush or comb it into a ponytail. The hair is always neatly close to the sides of my head and it stopped getting longer some time back. Each day after showering, about the same amount of hair comes out with brushing.

Shampoo just makes the situation even worse. If you remove the oil from a duck, it will sink and drown. Do we shampoo our body hair and beards? No and we have no dandruff problems there. The more we remove the oil from our hair, the more the body gets the message that more oil is needed and it goes into overproduction.

If you start using stronger, anti-dandruff shampoo, you make the problem even worse and get deeper and deeper into the trap. The way out is to back off and use milder shampoo less frequently until you need very little or none at all.

I recall as a child going through the Breakers, the Vanderbilt's mansion in Newport Rhode Island. The bathrooms were huge and had small pools in them for bathing but the guide pointed out that they got little use as the family doctor advised bathing no more than twice per year. I guess if you are rich enough you might be told the truth.

Constant showering, bathing, and shampooing doesn't make you good and clean; it makes you sick, or at the very least upsets your natural body functions, wears you down and makes you vulnerable. Naturally the beauticians are in favor of the above as they charge us to wash our hair, shampoo it, and dye it after we kill the color in it. It is said that Jackie Kennedy died from the black dye that was used on her hair. So nowadays not even wealth can save us from all the commercial forces that will do anything to us for a buck.

Deodorant is the same scam. The more you use it and interfere with nature the more you require and the sicker the area gets and the more it generates an unwanted odor. Worse yet, some companies put aluminum in their deodorant. One thing you never want to put into your body is aluminum. That doesn't stop firms from making aluminum pots and pans though.

Water is all you need. The same goes with a bath or shower, and antibacterial soap is the worst. Antibacterial soap is great for aiding bacteria to become immune to antibacterial agents...is that what we want? No soap is required or good unless you have grease or something like that to get off. Soap is like clean grease that lifts dirty grease or oil. Otherwise it is unnecessary. Your skin is the largest organ you have. What you put on it is generally absorbed. So if you wouldn't eat it, don't put it on your skin. Would you eat your lipstick and other cosmetics?

Another strange deal is toothpaste. Most assume that it has been made with the best possible compound for your teeth in mind. Guess again. The engineering problem to be solved with toothpaste is to find something that you can put into a tube that will stay in there for years without decomposing or turning color and so forth; even when many people will leave the cap off the tube. It must do that and also come easily out of the tube.

Try cleaning an enamel sink or a plate with toothpaste. Impossible, you have to use soap to get that crap off your sink, and then clean the item with the soap. So why would you use toothpaste to clean your teeth? What else could you use? Try using baking soda or salt or soap. Yes soap, it does taste a little strange the first few days but after that it seems quite normal. It does a much better job at a small fraction of the cost. You would want to use pure soap. I have been using soap for about two years now and my oral hygienist keeps remarking about how much my gums are improving. I have yet to tell her why.

A war has raged for decades over the fluoridation of water and toothpaste. The detractors' case is generally that fluoride is a poison that is a byproduct of manufacturing. Its buildup became a serious problem. The solution arrived at to neutralize and get rid of this poison was to run this stuff through the population's kidneys via the water supply.

We have been made to fear sunshine like it was nuclear fallout. Well actually that is what it is so just forget that I said that. I would not be the least bit surprised to learn that sunscreen causes cancer. We were not told to avoid sunshine until they began selling sunscreen. Sunshine does an awful lot of good for us. It creates vitamin D that helps prevent bone disease, muscle pain, MS, Types I and II diabetes, high blood pressure, and other maladies. Why do places like Minnesota and London have a higher rate of malignant melanoma than Arizona and Florida?

Once again think of what is natural and what our bodies have been used to for the longest amount of time. We have been exposed to sunshine for billions of years. We have been told to expose our skin to sunscreen, a manmade mixture of chemicals that has been around for only a few decades. I'll go with the sun. This does not mean overexposing skin that has not been used to sunshine and burning it.

We treat our animals better than ourselves. How often does the average person bath their cat or dog or farm animals? And most do not feed them junk food. Try taking some Mickey D's to the local zoo and attempt to feed it to a primate. You will be very lucky not to be arrested for endangering the animal's health.

They are considered to be very valuable. But powerful marketing forces are unleashed on us around the clock to entice us to consume that junk.

There is a movie *Super Size Me* wherein the filmmaker ate only at McDonald's for thirty days. The medical tests showed that he was ruining his health and body. He became addicted in a very short time. That is to say he would start feeling very bad until he ate more of it. The people who ate there once a week were referred to as Users by the employees; those that ate at McDonald's more than once a week were dubbed Heavy Users.

McDonald's are all over the world. I recall walking up the steps out of a train station somewhere in Europe and there was a McDonald's ad on each and every stair riser. Or being in Paris and seeing the McDonald's outlets filled with American tourists. Would you not have to be either senseless or addicted, to travel to Paris and eat at McDonald's?

Is it any wonder that the insurance companies and employers are dropping or limiting coverage whenever they can, when as a nation we are becoming sicker and sicker due to what amounts to slow bad-food poisoning? We need a better accounting and awareness of the power of the various lobbies and a way to keep track of what they are up to. For a case on point read: *Don't Drink Your Milk!—The Frightening New Medical Facts About the World's Most Overrated Nutrient* by Frank A. Oski

We are told to feed our children artificial and sugared junk that we put in a toaster. Or chocolate this or that for breakfast. The cereal that is pushed on them has artificial dyes and colors, tons of sugar, salt, and some even have candy in them. Why, so they will eat it? No, so they will get addicted to it. Kids will eat good food and like it. Do we really think they will starve rather than eat good food? Does it look like U.S. kids are starving when they waddle down the street?

The best product to sell in order to make money at any cost has always been an addictive one. Tobacco, alcohol, caffeine, dope, you name it. A century ago they had cocaine in Coca Cola and codeine, opium, and the like in all manner of remedies.

I recall decades ago when the major baby food companies were caught putting sugar in the baby food jars. The outcry at that time made them back off. I wonder if it is back in now? Hook them from birth...it doesn't get any sicker than that. Diet soda is said to be both addictive and that it makes you fat because it causes you to want to eat after drinking it.

Last night the History Channel had a program in the Modern Marvels series about harvesting. Sugar beets make up fifty percent of the sugar in the U.S. It is processed into sugar, molasses, and pulp. The first two unhealthy sugars go to people, while the good part with the fiber...it goes to dairy animals. They must be kept healthy for money to be made from them, whereas the people are for making money off of.

A culturally ingrained tradition is to reward young people for good behavior by giving them sweets. Despite myself I am also sometimes guilty of that. What a terrible signal and reinforcement both ways, of equating good performance with sugar and sugar with good performance.

Now diabetes is skyrocketing through the population. A lot of ads for blood testers and related diabetes products appear on TV. More and more youngsters are and will become diabetic at an accelerated rate. This is more great news for the drug companies.

London: Nearly half the kids in North and South America are expected to be obese by 2010, up from one third now. The European Union is projected to have childhood obesity running at 38% up from 25% at this time. This info is from the International Obesity task force.

Why would this be allowed to happen? Gee wiz, I don't know, but what I do know is that as these youngsters become diabetic, the drug companies will make billions off of them and their misery. Are human beings now the biggest cash crop on the planet yet...officially?

I was moaning about this over a meal in beautiful Vin Del Mar on the coast west and north of Santiago, Chile last year. My lunch companions were too lovely people from Bogotá, Columbia, Sergio and Claudia. He flew choppers like Blackhawks for the U.S. and she was a pediatrician. She said that this medical drug onslaught is going on everywhere.

None of this is new. Rich old men wanting ever more power and loot have been around for a long time. The Opium Wars had the British fighting to hook the Chinese on dope. Britain built itself by all manner of vile deeds.

For twenty years starting in 1713, England brought 15,000 slaves annually to America. In 1786 the English brought more than 97,000 slaves over and had more than 800 slave ships operating out of Liverpool alone. Altogether British ships transported over three million slaves.

Most of these Africans went to the West Indies to work in the sugarcane fields. There the slave ships would load up with molasses and continue on to New England where that cargo would be exchanged for rum, which by 1750 was New England's chief manufacture. The ships would carry the rum back to the Old World and exchange it for slaves; thus the profitable circle of trade fueled by human misery continued for generations.

The maritime states of New England soon joined in the slave trade. Boston, Massachusetts started in 1638, followed by Rhode Island where Newport, the chief slave port in the American colonies was located. It actually rivaled Liverpool in England. Slave trading and the export of rum became the basis of New England's economy. Thanksgiving myths aside, even the Pilgrims of Plymouth had consigned Native Americans into slavery and shipped them to the West Indies and elsewhere.

The Southern colonies were not a part of the trade, having neither ships nor molasses. In 1774, the importation of slaves was forbidden by the people of North and South Carolina. But in 1778, the new U.S. Constitution forbade Congress from banning the importation of slaves for another twenty years.

March 2006

17:30 ON
03-03-06 Friday—I arrived in downtown Bremo for another First Friday Art Walk. I walk over to where The Kitsap County Historical Society Museum has their grand opening today of a new and extensive display of historical clocks, called Changing Times—in Kitsap County.

This is a product of museum volunteers and the National Association of Watch and Clock Collectors Chapter 180, The West Coast Clock and Watch Museum in Bellingham, WA, and by members of the National Association of Watch and Clock Collectors Inc.

The Kitsap Museum turns back the clock to an era when telegraph companies and local jewelers had a monopoly on accurate time. Telegraph companies literally sold the time and jewelers gave it away to passersby. It was a time before radio and television. Kitsap County's busy commuters and trades people relied solely on large-scale public clocks owned by local jewelry stores and banks to set their watches by as they rushed to ferries or jobs supporting the Navy, schools, or other industries.

It was a time before electronics and the quartz crystal when precision timekeeping to support U.S Navy's warships, commercial business, schools, factories and domestic house-hold needs was accomplished by an almost limitless variety of well-tuned mechanical timekeeping devices. Whether purely decorative in design or singularly functional, these clocks and watches regulated the pulse of daily life and enabled ships to find their way at sea. The exhibit nods to the modern era with an atomic clock like those first placed on missile submarines in the early 1970's.

The exhibit features important clocks and watches from Kitsap County's domestic and military history. Highlights of the exhibit include a comprehensive variety of high grade and important, original and historic antique timekeeping devices brought together from local businesses, the Navy Shipyard, and from the private collections of locals in Kitsap County.

The exhibit is very interesting. It is not the Clocks and Watches Exhibit in the Forbidden City in Beijing, but it very well done and both informative and entertaining. Refreshments are served and many of those attending are folks that I am interested in chatting with.

Later my stomach forces me back to the Westside Burrito Connection across from the Ferry Landing on 1st Street. I truthfully cannot say much about the burritos but the place is enchanting, small, and always full enough that I wonder if I can find a table but always do. Alaskan Amber is on tap.

Tonight is a special treat. Six youngsters who hang out there have opened their own art gallery that very day. The walls are covered with unusual pictures, comic books, and whatnot. I locate artist Gabe Lee and purchase a T-shirt with a Buddhist Wheel of Life on the front. It is for Honey Bear, a large stuffed animal who sometimes rides with me on the Yellow Dragon. He wears my most decorated, worn, road-burned leather motorcycle jacket. HB is in fact an L- I- O- N but don't let him catch you saying that! He likes the shirt.
22:30 OFF

Item: Nations Health Status is slipping. Rankings show that twenty-eight countries enjoy a higher healthy life expectancy than the U.S., including the United Kingdom, Canada, Australia, France, Germany, and Japan…Japan being numero uno. The Japanese eat a lot of fish. We have been consuming fish for millions of years, way before land animals ever existed.

14:00 ON
03-05-06 Sunday—Attended Grand Opening of Amy Burnett's *Amy's Art and Antiques* on Callow in Charleston. This was the George Moeller's Jewelry Shop for many years until his death. Out front and in downtown Bremo near the Historical Museum are very large street clocks, perhaps twelve feet tall. They also originally had streetlights on then. They have both been beautifully restored. The shop features the original massive hand carved display cases and 1918 light fixtures.
15:00 OFF

The 78th Annual Academy Awards are on. Two new rules would be nice. One is that you cannot thank your kids and spouse and relatives by name. There are a billion people watching and we don't know these people. We do know or assume that you love your family. Second rule is that you can only thank a maximum of five entities, and family counts as one. We don't know these people either but understand that the other actors and industry folk may.

There are always such strict time constraints that they resort to having the orchestra drown the long-winded winners out and then run them off the stage. Why not use your very limited time to say something that might mean something to the billion viewers? If they had those rules, everybody could deliver some worthwhile message…without them the winners have no choice but to thank those close to them.

Jon Stewart did a fine job and everyone was cool. Stewart is such an interesting choice. He is not even a film star but he is perhaps the main source for news for the younger generations, even though his news program is on the surface, a comedy show.

Item: 03-06-06 Monday—A woman realizes that her dog has been trying to tell her something but doesn't know what. Finally the dog rams a certain spot in her breast with his nose. It hurts enough that she goes to medics who find breast cancer at that spot. The woman is treated successfully and survives. It has recently become known that dogs can detect cancer by smell.

Item: 03-07-06 Tuesday—Mohammed Reza Taheri-azar, a 22-year-old Iranian native said that he rented a Jeep Grand Cherokee because the four-wheel drive and could "run things over and keep on going." He plowed through a part of his campus known as 'The Pit', scattering students. Prosecutors charged him with nine counts of attempted murder and assault.

He said he hoped to "avenge the deaths of Muslims around the world".

Item: 03-08-06 Wednesday—There is a young girl on the Today Show. She had fallen off the top of a cheerleading routine and landed on her head, suffering a concussion, bruised lung and fracture of her spinal T1. What made her memorable was that as she was carried out on a stretcher with her neck in a brace…she continued to execute her routine with her hands and arms.

Item: AARP—Add West Virginia to the states that are trying to force Pharmaceutical Companies to disclose how much they are spending on advertising and marketing. Kevin Outterson a member of West Virginia's Pharmaceutical Cost Management Council and associate professor of law at WVU estimates that of the $3.3 billion Pharmaceutical Companies spend yearly on direct-to-consumer ads, $300 million is spent in West Virginia. The Pharmaceutical Industry has already spent over $1 million to oppose the disclosure rules being developed.

A two-year study of pharmaceutical marketing published in the Journal of the American Medical Association concluded that the gifts, junkets, consulting contracts, and the free samples that drug companies give to physicians are both eroding the integrity of medicine and hurting patients.

Item: Six people in London on a routine drug trial became swollen, turned blue, and began vomiting.

Well Adrienne, as promised, here we go on religion. It is probably a good idea as there are bound to be some people that I have yet to offend. This should encompass many more.

It should be perfectly clear that I am one hundred percent in favor of spirituality and mysticism. Everything is indeed one.

My concern comes from the effects of organized religion and the clashes of various organized religions, particularly in the modern world…the global village.

Just to break the ice, allow me to throw out some sayings: *Religion is a Dog from Hell. God Gave us the Truth; the Devil Organized it into Religions. God is in the Street; the Devil is in the Church.* Many may find the above statements outrageous, but we will develop some themes below by way of explanation as to how they came into being. I did not make them up.

Imagine how different the world would be if all of mankind lived by the Golden Rule. No, not the current one that states, 'He who has the Gold makes the Rules'. The one about treating all people as you would wish to be treated by them.

It has been said that the Ten Commandments were deemed necessary to enforce the Golden Rule; and then a million laws were enacted attempting to enforce the Ten Commandments. The Jewish Torah upped the commandment count to 613! Meanwhile lawyers work late into the night looking for loopholes through, and ways around all of the civil and criminal laws.

Who was that English King who couldn't remarry because the church wouldn't allow a divorce or grant him an annulment…so the logical solution was for him to cut off his wife's head, confess his sin, and then marry the girl who had caught his eye? Henry the VIII perhaps. There is always a way around a law.

Religion is a unifier. If the planet had one religion, it might make some sense, but still it would undoubtedly turn ugly and become a means of repression and mind control. For centuries in the West, the Roman Catholic Church had quite a monopoly and you see where that led.

Between 1500 and 1700 during the Inquisition's Witch Hunts, the Catholic Church burned one hundred thousand witches alive at the stake. This of course would be remarkable enough in its own right for an organization acting in the name of a pro-life God to do; but the fact that there is no such thing as a witch in the first place, that makes it positively astounding!

Did you ever think about that organization's practice of 'confession'? Talk about mind control! Not only were they the secular as well as the religious authority, but every week everyone was bound to go to that authority and confess to every crime in deed or thought that they had committed. Can you imagine getting by with making a Hollywood stop at a STOP sign on Tuesday…but on the following Saturday you have to go down to City Hall and confess to it! And even if you break some rule and don't confess it, your partners will anyway…or risk eternal damnation!

Human beings are herd animals. Did you ever watch a pasture of cows? They all stay in one area until the head cow decides to move, then they all follow. Same routine every day, all day. If the head cow should be removed, the second cow in line becomes the lead cow and calls the shots. You can keep removing cows until you get down to the last two…same deal. So each and every cow has the innate ability to think and to lead, but they just won't do it unless they absolutely have to.

People are the same way. That is why fashion works. It doesn't matter that fashion goes around in endless circles and cycles. Wide ties are replaced by narrow ties that are replaced by wide ties, ad infinitum. It doesn't matter that once the trendsetters have made a particular spot the 'in' place to be and everyone wants to go there…as this knowledge travels down the pecking order; it doesn't matter that the original group wouldn't be caught dead there…it just doesn't matter. It is so much easier to follow rather than to think. That is a fundamental reason why organized religions work.

I don't want to pick on the Catholic Church, but as I was raised in it, was an alter boy and all the rest, I have the most firsthand knowledge of it, and was particularly horrified by its dogma after I reached the age of reason. Also they have had the most amazing history and opportunity to take the whole control thing as far as it could be taken.

Take for example the Mass, during which everyone must alternate between sitting, kneeling, and standing, over and over in various orders, but always in unison with everyone else. So even if you attend and are thinking, man, this is like total bullshit…still you are imprinting yourself with muscle memory of it all. If not you would stand out like a sore thumb and I have never heard or witnessed that.

But it is the stories that one is told and expected to swallow…simply amazing! Just to name one let's take and oldie but goodie, Noah's Ark. We are told with a straight face that four thousand years ago, some dude built a boat in his backyard, put a male and female of every species on Earth into it, and then tooled around for over a month as the entire Earth filled up with water…and so on.

Now the simple and totally obvious fact is that if today one utilized every single boat on the planet, every aircraft carrier, every battleship, every everything, there is no way, on Earth, that anyone, or indeed everyone could put two of every living thing on board, using everything that floats. For one thing not all species have even been seen and identified yet.

Two is not nearly enough to propagate any species anyway; it takes an awful lot more. But good old Noah supposedly built this ark and put on board two elephants, two tigers, two lions, two deer, two sheep, two…whoa wouldn't they fight? What would they eat? Where would all this water come from? Why wouldn't the added weight alter the Earth's orbit? No need to go on, as the whole thing is really more preposterous a story that any deadhead stoner, blasted out of his mind, could possibly come up with.

Yet no less a scientific person than astronaut James Irwin, who walked on the Moon in August of 1971, spent years searching for Noah's Ark. Irwin retired from the astronaut corps in 1972. After years of fund-raising and planning, Irwin set out for Ararat or Aghri Dagh, a 17,000-foot mountain in Turkey near the border with the former Soviet Union. This peak, he believed, was where Noah had landed in his ark, as related in Genesis 8:4.

Irwin set out in 1982 expecting to face bears, leopards and poisonous snakes but it was gravity that proved his undoing. That August he was knocked unconscious when he fell a hundred feet down the mountainside. He returned to Turkey the following month but Turkish officials would not grant him permission to scale the peak. In 1983 he again visited Ararat and a guide accompanying him reported spotting some wood protruding from the snow. A blizzard forced them off the mountain before they could reach it. A year later Irwin reached the wood. It was an old pair of skis.

What is both frightening and revealing of the power of mass delusion is that a Newsweek Poll of December 2004 showed that fully 60% of Americans believe that this Noah story is literally true! School didn't do much for their ability to think. The same poll shows a literal belief by 61% in the six day Creation and 64% in God's personally parting the Red Sea for Moses. There was an interesting TV documentary made that scientifically examined the possibility of natural causes parting the Red Sea and it made a positive finding and conclusion, with no Divine intervention required.

Why does the so-called Holy Bible cause seemingly sane men to act so insanely? This is a serious question. Visit any large psychiatric hospital in the U.S. and don't be surprised if the majority of adults there will have been driven insane by studying the Bible. First they get all wrapped up in it, then they try to live their modern life by literally following this several thousand year old compilation of primitive Middle Eastern nomadic tribal thought.

Finally when their brain overloads on the endless inherent contradictions, they begin hearing voices. When they start following the voices...they get locked up. The Bible has caused more people to go off their rockers than all of the other books ever written, combined. Think about that...and it is the only book that they place free in all hotel rooms! Why would anyone want to label a book that drives people bonkers the Word of God? The numbers of humans who believe that they have heard God talking to them are legion. Anyone can join their ranks. All you have to do is to hallucinate.

And hallucinate is exactly what untold numbers have done. The Biblical God is hardly pro-life. The Bible is full of examples where God advocates or condones murder, rape, incest, child murder, infanticide, child abuse, abortion, slavery, and you name it. There are websites dedicated to referencing all of that by chapter and verse.

According to this Holy Book, God even asked Abraham to kill his own son! Then when the deed was about to take place, God said in effect, "April Fools!" But God was still in enough of a bloodthirsty mood that he had Abraham burn a ram instead. According to this, God just loves the smell of burning flesh. Is that how we want to instruct our citizens? If you hallucinate and think that you hear God telling you to murder somebody…that you had better do it? Are we all daft?

David Berkowitz the serial killer known as 'Son of Sam' began hearing his neighbor's dog telling him to kill. He believed that this neighbor was Satan. Or how about that beautiful, sweet, innocent Mormon girl Elizabeth Smart. Some polygamous Looney Tune took one look at her and immediately God dialed him up with, "Yo Mitchell, go grab you some of that!"

This fellow Brian David Mitchell roamed the streets of Salt Lake City as an itinerant preacher. He was known as 'God Be With Us' and his wife as 'God Adorn Us'. He had changed his name to Emmanuel and authored, *The Book of Emmanuel David Isaiah*, twenty-seven pages of densely packed rambling religious crap.

He was competent enough to pull off burglary, kidnapping, rape, and elude detection and capture with the whole world watching. When an innocent man was arrested in error for his crimes, he didn't utter a peep. In fact that innocent man died due to the stress of it all while incarcerated.

None of these actions would pass any kind of ethics test but for Mr. Mitchell, a man with his own private chat room with God, none of it was a problem. Mitchell has never been tried because since his arrest he has been able to present himself to the authorities as one of those individuals where the wheel is spinning but the hamster is dead. Do we really want to preprogram these madmen with a Biblical imperative to obey auditory hallucinations no matter what they tell you to do?
Two long-term observations regarding psychiatric hospitals, firstly that it is often difficult to distinguish between the staff and

the patients, birds of a feather flock together; secondly that it is very often not the crazy person in the family that is institutionalized but the weakest family member who was driven there by the one who is both deranged and mentally tough.

The Catholic Church teaches all the children the Ten Commandments. Commandment number two states: "Thou shalt not make unto thee any graven image, or any likeness of any thing that is in heaven above, or that is in the earth beneath, or that is in the water under the earth. Thou shalt not bow down thyself to them, nor serve them: for I the LORD thy God am a jealous God, visiting the iniquity of the fathers upon the children unto the third and fourth generation of them that hate me. And showing mercy unto thousands of them that love me, and keep my commandments."

Scholars generally agree that the first nine words are original and the rest represents spin that was piled on later at various times. At the very same time the Roman Church is teaching the Ten Commandments, it is chock full of graven images of every sort and description, and at all the 'holy places' they are for sale by the thousands. Hello? Is anybody home?

The business of God's punishing down four generations is significant. Can you imagine that if you robbed a bank, your great great granddaughter would be punished for your crime? Does this make any sense whatsoever? Well yes, in fact it did make perfect sense to nomads in the Middle East millennia ago. That is the whole point of this rant. All this hash meant something to the illiterate unlearned tribal nomads of the Middle East millennia ago. But to be followed literally by a rational person today is far beyond just plain stupid. It is not sane.

The Bible justifies slavery more than once. In Abraham's covenant with God, he is not told to free his slaves but rather to circumcise them. In another passage with Paul and a runaway slave, Paul doesn't consider helping the poor slave to escape but instead he tells the escaped slave to return to his master. That was then…this is now.

Another noteworthy clash of the ethics of those ancient times as compared with our modern world is to be found in the Biblical injunction against incest. The Good Book goes on at some length and detail as to exactly what relationships constituted incest…and guess what? A man having sex with his own daughter or daughters is not on the forbidden list. It was not considered at that time to be incest! That was then folks…this is now.

We have all seen maps that were made at the time of Columbus and know how inaccurate they were. They did the best that they could but their knowledge and tools were so limited. Today we have satellites that map everything down to an amazing level of perfect accuracy.

Who in their right mind would attempt to navigate today with a map that was thousands of years old? Nobody that was rational. Is attempting to guide your life by the Bible any different?

Punishment was extreme in past times because it had to be. How do you catch lawbreakers when you have no DNA, no fingerprints, no telephone or instant communication, no photographs, and no anything except eyewitnesses? That is why any unfortunate stranger in town would take the rap. If you wanted to do wrong, you just waited for a stranger to show up and then you did your evil deed.

Suppose Noah's original plans were unearthed, would any reasonable person think that is how we should build our ships today? Of course not, but to lead our life by their lights? Oh yes, with a closed mind, a dead heart, no soul, and a blind eye. I ask you, what good can possibly come from acting such a fool?

The same thing applies to the Biblical imperative to be fruitful and multiply. Genesis 1:28 made perfect sense for Adam and Eve…but now? When I was born in 1942 there were about two billion people. Now there are well over six billion people. Ponder that, a tripling in my lifetime. That can never happen again, not even a doubling, unless of course we come close to total annihilation of our species. More people were born during my lifetime than had ever existed on the Earth since the beginning of time.

Now the fisheries are all severely threatened, the reefs are dying, the rainforests are being slashed and burned, species are going extinct daily, icecaps are melting, and thirty to forty thousand children die needlessly each and every day! When an organism is reproducing out of control and threatening the host; that, my friends is the definition of cancer. Man has become a cancer upon the Earth and still these mouthpieces for the devil exhort us to be fruitful and multiply; that abortion is murder, and that even birth control is wrong.

Imagine what our Earth would be like if there were still only two billion people today. The Chinese actually did something rational about the situation by limiting families to one child and what does the world do? It condemns them for it! Our right wing whackos do all they can to undermine family planning everywhere in the world today.

Why do they do that? Many are just the followers who know not what they do but their leaders do it because they want more followers in their camp, whether that is a religion or political party or tribe or whatever. The more people under you, the richer and more powerful you can become. Rich old men consumed by insatiable greed and endlessly lusting for power will be a recurrent theme as this document progresses.

In 1800 the world's population hit one billion. You can see how long it took to go from one billion to two billion. Now we are adding another billion in ten years. We are burdening our Mother Earth with the equivalent of a large city every few days. In Brazil they are called favelas. The people swarm in from the countryside, squat en-mass on some land and throw up a city. No legal basis, no building codes, no nothing, just another instant city. They start off living in cardboard boxes and work on up from there. These favelas are everywhere, often right next to the highest priced real estate around.

Brasilia was a great idea. Rio was the capital city. They then planned Brasilia as a more centrally located capital city to be made from scratch and perfectly planned. So far so good.
They planned perfectly for a dream city for 700,000 people. They cut the ribbon and five million people moved in! Instant nightmare.
It doesn't take much math to project future population growth. Why weren't we being warned? If the church could allocate significant resources for such patent insanity as trying to determine how many angels could dance on the head of a pin, why could they not take a look at man's over-running the planet? Isn't there something in the Bible about man being a good steward of the Earth?

Try this one on. Let us say that it is the year 1475 and that Satan decides to manifest himself on Earth. So he comes and possesses the body and mind of the Pope. He now has more power and wealth than any other man on Earth, and is naturally also diabolical. What is the worst he could possible do?

He is supposed to be God's representative on Earth. He is supposed to be the Great Shepard who looks after, cares for, and tends his flock…herd animals. He is supposed to set an example of holiness, charity, and mercy. So what does he do?

He fornicates promiscuously and sires many children. He surrounds himself with idols and gold and wields golden implements and wears golden clothes. He sells absolution for sins and rakes in the lucre while thus promoting sin, at least for those that can bear the toll. He establishes the Spanish Inquisition and for centuries he tortures innocent good people and burns them alive in the town squares. He suppresses true knowledge at every opportunity and persecutes people who state the simplest of truths like that the Earth revolves around the sun.

But wait…isn't that exactly what did happen? It sure is my friends. That is exactly what happened. If it swims like a duck, waddles like a duck, and quacks like a duck…it is a duck. *God is in the Street; the Devil is in the Church.*

If God were into making Divine interventions, wouldn't you expect him to have taken some strong action at this juncture? Hurl a few lightning bolts at El Papa at the very least?

That was a long time ago you may say. True, they have lost that secular power. They can't torture or burn alive today, here in the U.S. No, certainly not, but they can be filing bankruptcy all over the U.S. because of the payouts they are being forced to make for all of the wretched pedophilia that has been going on and covered up by the top authorities for decades and decades. Magical mumbo jumbo will take its toll.

11:00 ON
03-12-06 Sunday—I ran down to Amy Burnett's *Amy's Art and Antiques* on Callow in Charleston, figuring that she had probably forgotten about the Art Talk that she is scheduled to give tonight in my home, as she doesn't really keep a calendar. She was there, so was her husband Earl, cool guy, and their dog Spare. Yup, she had no idea that the Art Talk was today. The deal was put back on the rails and I found some real treasures in the shop in the form of old printing stamps that had been used in newspaper ads for the likes of Bremers Department Store, Hudson Photographic Artistry, KBRO, Bremo Lumber Company, Lyons Club, PSNS, SHELL gasoline, and more.

I spent the rest of the day in preparation for the party. Fortunately my next-door neighbors Dawn and Donna bore the brunt of the work of pulling my crib together that they had started two days earlier and they also catered the event. Everyone invited showed, including a couple just returning that day from the Grand Canyon. They had gone south to get warm and ended up driving through a foot of snow and raced to stay ahead of a snowstorm much of the way back. Everyone showed. All are wonderful people. If I don't have the best neighbors ever, I don't know who does.

Amy and Earl arrived with their dog Spare who went into the yard with Teddy. They got along beautifully and that helped because Teddy was somewhat bent out of shape after having been unceremoniously booted out of the Ping Pong Room...to make way for the event's food serving area.

Everything went perfectly. This would be perhaps a bit scary but the gods have been behind this project from the beginning, as many, many signs and omens continue to show.
23:00 OFF

Item: A Seattle corporation, Shoush Holdings, that is family owned by Mansour Samadpour, that had earlier bought two downtown Port Orchard buildings, is now buying two restaurants and another retail space in the city center. I may be mistaken but I think that Bremo was originally called Port Orchard. Port Orchard now is right across Sinclair Inlet from Bremo and a ferry runs frequently between the two.

11:00 ON
03-14-06 Tuesday—I gained access to SubBase Bangor via the Navy League and attended the monthly luncheon. A scheduled talk was given by the captain of the Ohio the first sub converted from an SSBN to a SSGN. Also the son of a member, a Marine Sergeant recently back from a fourth tour in Iraq gave a talk with slides. All in all a very interesting and rewarding time. One excellent contact was established. I do not want to push it.
14:30 OFF

Why do rational people come off their trolley regarding matters of religion? Recall the Heaven's Gate bunch back in March 29, 1997. California, Rancho Santa Fe investigators said that they had identified 30 of the 39 members of a millenarian cult who had committed mass suicide in a hillside mansion. The bodies of the group were scattered on their backs on cots and mattresses. All but two had purple shrouds over their heads and shoulders.

Most had died of suffocation. Plastic bags had been placed over their heads after they had ingested a mixture of alcohol and Phenobarbital. Investigators revealed that a half-dozen of the eighteen male members of the cult had previously been surgically castrated. This including Marshall Herff Applewhite, the 65-year-old leader of the group whose body was found among the dead. The group demanded celibacy of its members and avoided any suggestion of sensuality.

The group had lived quietly, almost unnoticed in this upscale community, with members spending much of their time designing computer programs for various commercial clients. On tape, Applewhite attempted to explain why he and the others were about to take their own lives. He said that human bodies were just temporary earthly parking places for the soul and that suicide would free the soul to make a rendezvous on a higher plane of existence with an Unidentified Flying Object that was trailing the Hale-Bopp Comet, currently on a swing past the Earth.

A farewell videotape made by cult members suggested that they had gone to their deaths quite willingly, some even joyfully. "We couldn't be happier about what we're going to do," one woman said, her voice choking a bit but her face anything but sad. Another woman, smiling, added, "We are all happy to be doing what we are doing."

The tape was especially strikingly for its upbeat tone, considering what lay ahead for those speaking and peering into the camera. On it, one cult member said that his death would bring him "just the happiest day of my life. I've been looking forward for this for so long," he added. A woman who appeared to be in her twenties looked intently into the camera and said, grinning broadly, "We are all choosing of our own free will to go to the next level." Another woman said, "We just wish you could all be here and be doing what we are doing." "We have no hesitation to leave this place, to leave the bodies that we have," said another.

.

A document, found by detectives was titled *The Routine*. It outlined how the cult members were to go about killing themselves. First, it said, fifteen of the thirty-nine cult members, called 'classmates' would kill themselves with help from eight 'assistants'. Then fifteen more 'classmates' and eight more 'assistants' would repeat the process. It was unclear how the final nine cult members were to go about killing themselves. To bring on death, the cult members were to ingest, in order, a dosage of Dramamine followed by tea and toast, followed an hour later by alcohol and sedatives.

Now this Applewhite character had a lifelong history of being a complete and total crackpot. The cult members made a living as computer programmers, so they had to be intelligent, educated, knowledgeable and up on technology. So how could they possible be so abysmally stupid as to follow this chowder head to their early deaths?

Or go back to James Warren 'Jim' Jones and The People's Temple. Reverend Jones held degrees from Indiana University and Butler University. He was not a Fundamentalist pastor, but belonged to a mainline Christian denomination, having been ordained in the Christian Church...The Disciples of Christ.

On November 18, 1978 the whole fandango ended in Jonestown, Guyana when the group's leadership reached a consensus to commit group suicide. A total of 914 people died, 638 adults and 276 children. Most appear to have committed suicide by drinking a grape drink laced with cyanide and a number of sedatives, including liquid Valium, Penegram and chloral hydrate. Some sources say it was Kool-Aid. Other victims appear to have been murdered by the injection of poison. The Guyana's coroner said that hundreds of bodies showed needle marks, indicating foul play. Still other victims were shot. A very few, came to their senses, managed to flee into the jungle, and survived.

Not all of these whack-jobs are suicidal. Aum Shinrikyo, Supreme Truth, is a Japanese religious cult obsessed with the

Apocalypse. This previously obscure group became infamous in 1995 when they released deadly sarin nerve gas into the Tokyo subway system, killing twelve people and sending more than 5,000 others to area hospitals. The attack came at the peak of the Monday morning rush hour in one of the busiest commuter systems in the world. Witnesses said that subway entrances resembled battlefields as injured commuters lay gasping on the ground with blood gushing from their noses or mouths.

After the 1995 subway attack, Japanese police discovered that Aum Shinrikyo had accumulated hundreds of tons of chemicals in order to make enough sarin gas to kill millions of people. According to the authorities the cult had also acquired a Russian military helicopter that could have been used to distribute the gas.

Based on the testimony of several cult members convicted in the 1995 attack, Aum Shinrikyo had also experimented with biological warfare, including numerous attempts to spread anthrax and botulism. A 1998 inquiry by the New York Times found that the cult had carried out at least nine biological attacks but that all had failed.

Aum Shinrikyo is a doomsday cult whose teachings are based on tenets borrowed from Hinduism and Buddhism. Its more benign activities include yoga, meditation, and breathing exercises. But at the center of the group's belief is reverence for Aum Shinrikyo's founder, Shoko Asahara, who teaches that the end of the world is near. The police have portrayed the nerve gas attack as the cult's way of hastening the Apocalypse.

In the book *Under the Banner of Heaven* by Jon Krakauer, he relates that in 1984, Ron and Dan Lafferty murdered the wife and infant daughter of their younger brother Allen i.e. their sister-in law and their own little niece. The crimes were noteworthy not merely for their brutality but for the brothers' claim that they were acting on direct orders from God. They had been studying their Holy Books intently for many months.

Krakauer tells the story of the killers and their crime but also explores the shadowy world of Mormon Fundamentalism from which the two emerged. The Mormon Church was founded, in part, on the idea that true believers could speak directly with God. But while the mainstream church attempted to be more palatable to the general public by rejecting the controversial tenet of polygamy, Fundamentalist splinter groups saw this as apostasy and took to the hills to live what they believed to be a righteous life.

When their beliefs are challenged or their patriarchal, cult-like order defied, these still-active groups, according to Krakauer, are capable of fighting back with tremendous violence. While Krakauer's research into the history of the church is admirably extensive, the real power of the book comes from present-day information, notably jailhouse interviews with Dan Lafferty.

Far from being the brooding maniac one might expect, Lafferty is chillingly coherent, still insisting that his motive was merely to obey God's commands. Krakauer's accounts of the actual murders are graphic and disturbing, but such detail makes the brothers' claim of Divine instruction all the more horrifying.

In an age where Westerners have trouble comprehending what drives Islamic Fundamentalists to kill, Jon Krakauer advises us to look within America's own borders.

Or go back with the Mormons to the year 1857 when they deceived and attacked a group of one hundred and thirty seven pioneers. Their wagon train was traveling from Arkansas, through Utah, and on to California. The Mountain Meadows Massacre stands without parallel amongst the crimes that stain the pages of American history.

It was a crime committed without cause or justification of any kind to relieve it of its monstrous character. When nearly exhausted from fatigue and thirst, the men of the wagon train were approached by white men, with a flag of truce, and induced to surrender their arms, under the most solemn promises of protection. They were then all slaughtered in cold blood.

Item: Since members of the LDS cult must perform two years of missionary work after graduating high school, they have three qualities the CIA wants, foreign language ability, experience in a foreign country, and former residence in a foreign country. Utah and particularly BYU has been one of the prime recruiting grounds for the CIA. A disproportionate number of Mormons achieve high levels within the CIA, FBI, Military Intelligence, and nearly all levels of city, state, and federal governments. The Senate, Congress, Cabinet, and the White House staff are full of Mormons.

It is said that Utah houses one of the largest U.S. Government's foreign language translation operations in the country. The Mormons are highly fluent, high security classification eligible and very disciplined.

Item: Fully automatic, high quality text-to-text MT, Machine Translation, across vastly different knowledge domains is very challenging. When you throw in a scarcity of training data and speech-enabled front and back ends, then the ideal symbolized by the Universal Translator concept becomes unachievable, even with today's best technology. Due to overly optimistic expectations and a subsequent collapse of government funding, research into MT survives in only a few institutions that can afford going it alone, such as IBM and guess who else, non other than…the Mormon Church.

Returning to religious horrors, how about recent events in Indonesia where Muslim mobs raped young children while shouting, "Allahu Akbar!" i.e. "God is Great!"

Belfast, Ireland…Roman Christians and Reform Christians until recently had been killing each other for many decades. Israelis and Palestinians, both of whom trace their ancestry to Abraham, and thus are brothers and sisters, apparently take such a fancy to the Cain slew Abel story…that they just can't get off that page. Sunnis hate Shiites and Shiites hate Sunnis, how can people embrace religion and miss the point of it so completely?

One could go on for days. The point is, what is it about religion that makes apparently normal people act like the criminally insane? Why are the most heinous and vilest acts known to man committed in the name of religion and God? Why?

I certainly don't know. Humans have a semi-brainy spine and atop that our reptile brain, then around and above that is our mammalian brain, and finally our frontal lobes and higher human brain. The despicable acts above must originate from our reptile brain…the one that says, either mate or kill. Religion must penetrate to our core. Truthful or not, it must satisfy some very basic needs.

If you went to bed one night and awoke in a boat out at sea, what would you be focused on? Where am I? How did I get here? Why am I here? Who put me here? What am I supposed to do?

We have all found ourselves on Earth. The fundamental questions are the same as those posed in the last paragraph.

Where am I? How did I get here? Why am I here? Who put me here? What am I supposed to do? The funny thing is, that with all of our knowledge, our knowledge that keeps doubling every few years at an ever-increasing rate…we have not a single answer to any one of those fundamental questions. Not a one. No one really knows.

Oh you can turn on your TV any day of the week and there are men and women who profess to know these answers. They will go into great detail, a snow job on these subjects and another thing that they will surely do is to ask you to send them money. Stealing in the name of the Lord. What is that, the third oldest profession?

People as herd animals are mostly followers in varying degrees. There is always that two percent who go the opposite way of the rest of us. This is important for the survival of the human race. This two percent is almost always wrong but on those rare occasions when the group gets it wrong, those misfits are our salvation.

People are also lazy, especially when it comes to thinking. They say to be happy you have to live in the present. Probably true, but deceptive. True I am happiest and most joyful when riding the *Yellow Dragon* and one must remain in the now to survive on a bike. But everyone I know that lives in the present is broke. Those that exercise foresight, i.e. living in the future are well off. Maybe you should become financially independent first…then live in the present.

Thinking requires living in both the past and the future, and mentally running trends, comparisons, and whatnot. Much simpler to just follow the leaders and let them do all that mental stuff. Okay, but when we have a President who thinks that so-called Intelligent Design should be taught in the science classrooms…we are in very deep trouble and heading for a Theocracy. Theocracy means oppression, repression, brainwashing and mind-control.

I'll tell you a secret, I voted for George W. Why? The Muslims hit us on 9-11 with their Islamic Fundamental fanatics. I felt that turn-around was fair play. Let them get a good taste of our Christian Fundamental fanatics, and see what they are capable of. Make then think twice before hitting us again. Actually it wasn't so much W. that I voted for as the machine behind him, his dad's old crew. People wonder how he could just sit there in a kiddy school after being informed of 9-11 and do nothing. Simple, he knew that Dick Cheney was running the country; he just sat there pondering how it would all play itself out.

Good old George W, a self-proclaimed Uniter not a Divider. The first thing he did was to split the entire country right square down the middle. Clean in two like it was a diamond. I mean the election was so close that they were pulling chads off of single votes. They had to go to the U.S. Supreme Court, who violated their own States Rights principles, to hand him the election. It was clearly 'wrong' yet I agreed with that decision.

I should say here that politics aside, President Bush has grown remarkably into that job since his first election. When he became President the man could hardly talk. Now he delivers excellent speeches and seems ever more comfortable in front of the Press. That office will really work wonders on any individual. One of his greatest strengths in politics has always been the way people continually underestimate him and what he is capable of.

Item: Bremo is a city of renters. The rental population is as high as sixty percent. A good deal of which could be described as semi-slum housing. What a shame. It needs to be corrected, comprehensively. Yet this negative situation makes a master makeover much easier to pull-off.

Item: The second Tacoma Narrows Bridge is eighty percent completed. This is the main access to the Olympic Peninsular. The traffic increases each year as the area continues to be discovered by retiring Americans in general and those from California in particular. The enjoyment of the seasons, mild winters, almost endless shoreline and natural beauty being the main attractions, but there are many others.

They say that God sleeps in the rocks, awakens in the plants, walks in the animals, and is conscious in man. I like that. That jibes with the teaching that God is omnipotent, omnipresent, and omniscient i.e. all-powerful, everywhere, and all knowing. I can buy into that.

The conclusions of the greatest ancient thinkers of India now agree perfectly with the latest knowledge developed by modern physics. To understand this concept of God one must drop the childish concept of a man sitting on a throne in Heaven. Or as Bill Maher puts it, "The Invisible Friend in the Sky for Adults." If God is everywhere, that means a shovel full of dog poop is a shovel full of God. God is the energy field of pure potentiality that everything is comprised of.

God's laws are the laws of mathematics and physics. Gravity is one of God's laws. You can easily tell a law of God's from one of man. Man's laws change a lot, God's do not. I remember being shocked a long time ago when I learned of a time in a South American country when due to a war, the number of young men eligible to marry had dropped off to the point that the Catholic Church's membership was dropping off and would continue to drop significantly for a very long time.

The response of the Vatican, of the Pope, was to issue a special temporary dispensation that allowed the remaining men to impregnate the abundance of women without a mate. Now this made perfect sense if the true goal of that religion was to perpetuate itself and to grow. But the very idea that the same exact behavior that was previously deemed to be a mortal sin that would result in your burning throughout eternity in hellfire, that this same behavior was now okay with the wave of a magic wand…it was a real eye-opener to be sure. Such are the laws of man.

Back to gravity, this is really hard to believe but in 1719, thirty-seven years after Sir Isaac Newton published his *Principia*, a cement-head named John Hutchinson, a highly placed British theologian, published a work entitled *Moses' Principia* whose intent was to actually refute gravity! There is simply no known limit to the extent that religion can destroy basic brain function.

All who believe in a Creator agree that God expects us to use our God-given fingers and toes, our arms and legs, the organs of our body, but then why would so many believe that we are not supposed to use our brains to think but rather to follow other men who talk nonsense and ask us for money? Does that compute?

It is our brains that make us human. The head of anything, whether it is the head of government, the head of state, corporate headquarters, a military HQ, you name it and the head of whatever it is, is housed in the most splendor and is the best cared for. If we go through life without thinking, are we living as humans?

The evidence of Creation is clear that this Universe has been evolving for about sixteen billion years, at least in this cycle since the last Big Bang. The Earth has been evolving for about the past four billion years. So what a slap in the face it is to God to go around preaching such nonsense that God made the world in six days and that it was all done only six thousand years ago!

Imagine having labored with love for over sixteen billion years on something; and just because some illiterate, uneducated nomad with virtually no access to knowledge many centuries ago suggests that all it took you was six days; that even today the beings that have evolved as a result of your sixteen billion years of effort, that these very beings will continue to blindly cling to this stupid primitive notion of a six-day creation, while ignoring all the overwhelming evidence of your great handiwork!

It is God's Universe that has the Earth traveling around the sun. It was the Pope's ignorance or worse that arrested and silenced Galileo for saying so.

It was in the year 1650 when some lunkhead named James Ussher, an Anglo-Irish Archbishop declared that Creation occurred on the evening before October 23, 4004 B.C. Well now, how could we possible question an utterance like that?

Do you really believe that evolution is just an unproven theory? In my lifetime I have seen the evolution of resistant strains of bacteria that require ever-new antibiotics to combat them. Flu viruses mutate and evolve every two years or so. If one had been able to look at their own development in their mothers womb they would have seen themselves pass through the stages of evolution, of having a tail and so forth, prior to their own birth.

Trust me, one visit to the 'Monster Ward' at LAC USC Medical Center would convince most people of evolution. TB has evolved into antibiotic-resistant strains. Why do you think the world is holding its collective breath watching to see if this Bird Flu will mutate itself away from us or into us?

What about the dinosaurs that became extinct sixty-five million years ago? How do you slam them into your silly, infantile notion of a six thousand year old Universe? Have billions been spent on such telescopes as the VLT at Paranal Observatory in Chile, the Keck Observatory, the Hubble Space Telescope and VLA, or the proposed OWL, TMT, GMT, and JWST, have these billions been spent to study the Universe back many billions of years if the world was created six thousand years ago? The Egyptian and Chinese Civilizations go back further than that!

Item: Looking back in time nearly nine billion years, an international team of astronomers found mature galaxies in a young universe. The galaxies are members of a cluster of galaxies that existed when the universe was only five billion years old.

This compelling evidence that galaxies must have started forming just after the big bang was bolstered by observations made by the same team of astronomers when they peered even farther back in time. The team found embryonic galaxies a mere 1.5 billion years after the birth of the cosmos. The 'baby galaxies' reside in a still-developing cluster, the most distant proto-cluster ever found.

Adrienne—Please schedule me for the YMCA Grand Opening on Monday March 27 at 1:30 PM.

Item: A new upscale six-story hotel and six-story condominium complex is to be located on the Bremo waterfront. Kitsap County Consolidated Housing Authority announced a partnership with developer Alan Laurie to build the six-story hotel where the Sinclair Building now stands on Washington Avenue. The concierge services may be made available to the neighboring Harborside Condominiums currently under construction.

Item: Westpark to be redeveloped by Marathon Development. Westpark is about six hundred units that were originally built as temporary housing for the Navy during WW II. It is now owned by the Bremo Housing Authority. Westpark is slated to become a mix of commercial and residential properties, some of which will be low-income, but not all. Current residents that are unable to stay will either relocate on their own or with the help of BHA.

Item: 03-16-06—Charlie Rose Show: A Discussion About the Diabetes Epidemic with: Marc Santora, The New York Times; Dr. Mitchell lazar, Director, The Institute for Diabetes, Obesity and Metabolism, The University of Pennsylvania; Dr. Richard Bernstein Author, *Diabetes Solution: The Complete Guide to Achieving Normal Blood Sugars*, and Martin Silink President-Elect, International Diabetes Federation / Professor of Pediatric Endocrinology, University of Sydney

This is truly horrifying, I had no idea it was this bad. The U.S. is now running 800,000 new cases yearly. More veterans had amputations last year from diabetes than in the Vietnam War! I am not completely positive of all these statistics, according to my notes there are 94 million cases worldwide with 6 million new cases per year. The U.S. born child of a Latino or African-American now has a one in two chance of becoming a diabetic! When you go to Harlem and see people in wheelchairs due to amputations, don't assume it was due to an accident...a likely cause is diabetes.

New York is the epicenter of the epidemic in the U.S. and the worldwide epicenter is in the India—China—Pakistan region. Children have historically had Type I and adults Type II but kids are now getting as much Type II as Type I.

Prevention is not covered by insurance…amputation is. The answer is more exercise and fewer calories, especially carbohydrates, and particularly those from refined sugars and starches. But the Feds are subsidizing corn, as in High Fructose Corn Syrup…the very fattening sweetener that is popping up everywhere, and gym classes are declining by all measures.

Fruits and veggies are carbs but mostly cellulose and good for you. Soda is practically diabetes in a can and the junk food you get in the packages are major culprits. Every morning I hear the Little Debbie commercials; the ones that say to give this stuff to your kids and 'Unwrap a Smile'. Yeah…and help your child get diabetes.

I believe this is a New York Times excerpt, author unknown: "May Chen is slender and healthy, a lively little girl whose parents left their rural Chinese village just a decade ago in search of a better life. But at age 9, still in pigtails, she is already coming face to face with the forces that many say are making America fat and diabetic.

When May watches cartoons in her family's apartment in Flushing, Queens, the commercials tell her that junk food is good food…the latest message from an industry that spends $10 billion per year marketing junk food to children.

When she strolls down Main Street, she walks a growing gantlet of fast-food restaurants, many of them built with the help of government loans.

At her public school, the City sells sugary Snapple in vending machines to raise money. But it does not pay for a full physical education program, so May's fourth-grade class has gym just once a week, in violation of State law.

And when she and her friends gather for snacks, she basks in their approval as she produces the high-calorie American-style treats, from chips to sweets, that are rapidly replacing traditional foods in the local markets."

Richard Bernstein learned that he had diabetes at age twelve. He is now age seventy-two and appears to be in good health. He was fortunate in learning about and buying a machine decades ago that allowed him to monitor his blood sugar level around the clock. This is what enabled him to self-treat his illness so successfully.

He was so excited when he realized that he had found the answer to his diabetic condition that he contacted the AMA, his doctor, and others. The response was that the AMA would have nothing to do with him and his own doctor accused him of trying to put him out of business!

They are now developing inhalers for insulin delivery for those who don't like needles but they are twelve times as crude at delivering accurate dosages and the absorption rate is only 6-10%.

Remember Popeye and his spinach? In those days the commercial intent was to have a popular cartoon help moms to get their kids to eat something that was very good for them, namely spinach. And moms all across the country did just that, using Popeye's power to cajole their offspring into eating spinach. Look just how far have we have sunk since then!

Even the likes of John Dillinger had some good intentions. According to a survey of the applause at movie newsreels, FDR was the most popular man in America, Lindberg was number two and Dillinger was number three. Not bad for being Public

Enemy #1. It was a time when 25% were out of work. The time of the dust bowl and massive numbers of family farm foreclosures by banks. These people hated the banks but were powerless. Dillinger was a robber hero who liberated money from these banks and did help numerous people with his ill-gotten gains.

Interesting observation, Adrienne! Actually this anti-religious diatribe is not the main thrust of where this is all going. This approach has more to do with the ocean of lies and bullshit that we are all forced to swim in these days. The world-destroying force of human overpopulation...that is what is coming down the pike. This analysis of religion is a means to get a handle on our long history of being deceived by those in power who profess to be helping us. Religion has a long and sordid history of being adverse to the dissemination of the truth to average people. Thus it seems a good place to start.

If we are as sick as our secrets, then we are getting sicker every day. George Orwell may not have gotten the year and the details exactly correct but it is his future world that we are now living in. Could somebody tell me what is 'friendly' about being killed by your own men?

Item: The parents of U.S. Army Ranger and former professional football player Pat Tillman have reacted angrily to new revelations surrounding the circumstances of their son's death last year in Afghanistan.

The 27-year-old Tillman, who abandoned celebrity and a multimillion-dollar contract with the Arizona Cardinals after the 9-11 terror attacks to join up with the Rangers, died in a 'friendly-fire' attack in Afghanistan on April 22, 2004. A May 4th article by the Washington Post's Josh White reported that soldiers on the scene knew that they had mistakenly shot and killed Tillman along with an Afghan soldier working with the

Rangers, in a bungled operation and immediately reported this to their superiors.

The military responded to Tillman's death with deception and a cover-up. Authorities withheld information from family members in a cynical effort to promote the former football standout as a hero who died at the hands of the enemy in the 'War on Terror'.

There is an entire book written as a dictionary of military newspeak and doublespeak called *Battlebabble* by Thomas Lee. The book is far left in orientation but it is quite an amazing compilation of newly created words whose purpose is to soften the horrors of the original old words. Such things as 'collateral damage', rather than 'innocent civilians of all ages horribly killed and maimed'. Almost no one objects to this misuse of language. As the one-liner goes, why do we drive on the parkway and park on the driveway?

Item Governor Gregoire hails visit by Chinese President Hu Jintao on April 18-19. The usual tours of Microsoft and Boeing will be followed by a State Dinner at the home of Bill and Melinda Gates in Medina.

Item: 03-17-06 Friday — HBO's Real Time with Bill Maher — This fellow Bill Maher has the distinction to me as being the only person in my lifetime that I have ever felt was attempting to tell me the truth about religion and everything else as he sees it. A living oracle of truth. Such a scarcity of truth-tellers alone is extremely remarkable.

But then it was comedian Lenny Bruce who was the first to begin speaking the plain unvarnished truth about all sorts of things in his act. What happened to him? He was repeatedly thrown in jail…and finally broken and destroyed. Despite the First

Amendment, they had a list of words that he was not allowed to say in a nightclub. Words that everyone in the nightclub was obviously familiar with, or else what would be the point. Words that are now in most of the movies that are made today.

The likes of the great Richard Pryor and the marvelous Chris Rock have carried on that torch. Could it be that the authorities hate truth speakers for fear they will awaken people to think? Once awakened, who knows where the public's thinking could lead?

If you can fool all the people some of the time, and some of the people all the time, what would happen if you could never fool any of the people any of the time?

Another great show except for that nut-job Richard Belser being on the panel. Maher played a current Big Pharm commercial for some junk medicine and right after reciting a bunch of horrid side effects, a little bee whispers, "A wise choice!"

There was some talk about how the corporations now totally dominate the political process and the government. Ralph Nader has long been warning about the political system's degeneration into being a broker between large corporations and politicians. A poll shows that only 32% of the people approve of their politicians yet 99% get reelected!

Remember when we used to laugh about how in the Soviet Union or Iraq, how the politicians would win with 99% of the vote? Now between these guys gerrymandering their districts and the amount of money it takes to win an election…we have the same situation here.

Some of the most evil corporations seem to be Big Pharm. The junk food being pushed on us makes us sick, then Big Pharm pushes all these junk remedies that make us even sicker, and encourage us to continue the ill behavior that is harming us to begin with. The simple fact is that there is no money to be made from healthy citizens. And if something is beneficial but not patentable, they try to get it banned.

03-18-06 Saturday—Found the following email in my inbox from my physician and friend on Whidbey Island:

> *Greetings from Dr. Weeks:*
> *This is a broadcast email calling you to action.*
>
> *Big Pharmaceutical is upset with the trend towards people using natural 'bio-identical' hormones and is using a $300 million budget to try and close down the compounding pharmacists.*
>
> *This is a very important issue for you to understand and to take simple action on. If 20,000 people do NOT send word to the FDA by March 31st, then safe alternatives to synthetic hormones will be taken off the market.*
>
> *Shame on Big Pharma in general, and on Wyeth, makers of the disgraced drugs Premarin and PremPro in particular.*
>
> *Take the necessary time to READ the following information and to print out and send or fax in your letter.*
>
> *Kind regards,*
>
> *Bradford S. Weeks, M.D.*

Item: The nations most popular sleep drug Ambien is causing some people to sleepwalk and sleep-eat huge amounts of food. The next day they know noting about it. Others are sleep-driving to work the next morning after insufficient sleep. This is relatively rare but prevalent enough that they are being called DUIa…for Driving Under the Influence of Ambien. In 2005, there were 226.6 million prescriptions written for Ambien in the United States alone.

Item: Today's paper has an article titled, Religion and Science Can They Be Compatible? What a shame that in 2006 we still have to debate something as basic as that. Of course they are compatible, or should be. Why would science and ethics not be compatible, as long as both are approached rationally?

03-19-06 Sunday—It is a gorgeous morning about 9:45 AM as I enter SR3, a beautiful four lane divided highway, to go north a few exits in *Flying Cloud* to pick up some supplies from Costco in Silverdale.

The speed limit is 60 mph but the vehicle was cold so I was going as slow as I safely could, about 50-55 mph. After the first exit on Kitsap Way the engine had warmed up and I began traveling with the flow of traffic that was between 60-65 mph. Virtually all the automakers now set the odometers to run fast in order to shorten your warranty period and this causes the speed to register higher than it actually is. Conditions were perfect and the traffic was light to medium.

I was in the back of two lanes of vehicles and in the right hand, slow lane. Suddenly the truck in front of me began oscillating in his lane. My gut reaction was that he was drunk and as he jogged right, I pulled left and decked it to pass him rapidly.

As I did so I noticed up ahead on the right shoulder a bunch of vehicles of which about half were WSP, Washington State Patrol, cars. I now realized that this was what had caused the truck to move erratically, and as I was now past him, I immediately pulled back into the right hand lane and returned my speed to 60 mph.

There were four white WA State Patrol cars working this stretch of northbound SR 3. An hour and a half later, when I returned by there, they were still at it, pulling vehicles over left and right, all in a short stretch of road where I have never seen them operate before. They do work this highway extremely heavily, however.

I was now back in behind these two lanes of traffic, except that now that one truck that I had passed was behind me. I continued on and past the WA State Patrol cars and their detainees. No sooner did I do so but a WA State Patrol unit pulled out with lights on and pulled me over.

A truly gorgeous little young female trooper had detained me. Was this my lucky day or what? She was so young and naive that no matter what I laid on her she was going to cite me for a radar reading of 74 in a 60.

She also somehow managed to pull over another white truck behind her. He started to leave and she ordered him to stay put. But she later allowed him to leave without a citation.

The ticket is for $122. I have the best traffic lawyer in WA State, Jeannie Mucklestone, Esquire. She charges me $500 for the Seattle side of Western WA and $750 over here on the Olympic Peninsular. My driving record is as clean as the proverbial hound's tooth.

I do believe that this young State Patrol trooper felt that what she was doing was a legitimate effort to slow down traffic. Every year, law enforcement gets more chicken-shit. All over the country they are out citing drivers in order to raise money. It has been scientifically studied and a determination has been made as to what is the safest speed to post.

Basically you monitor to see what speed the normal flow of traffic is and then you go +/- 10 mph. The divided highway that I was on has a normal traffic flow of 65. It would be higher but for the extreme level of law enforcement. Thus the optimum acceptable speeds in the interest of safety would be 55-75. Even my peak passing speed of 74 would fall within those parameters.

In fact, my short burst of speed was a reaction to the unsafe conditions brought about by the WSP and this four-way kill-zone that they had established. They were shooting fish in a barrel with radar on a quite Sunday morning. Their goal was to issue as many citations as possible and probably had a competition going on amongst themselves.

Had the goal been to slow down traffic, they could have simply spaced themselves out and driven at the speed limit. Or just parked and saved the taxpayers and the environment the gasoline expenditure. Certainly no one would pass them or speed in their presence. The way they were functioning tends to allow vehicles to go faster than normal once they are past the kill-zone, as they are confident that the highway ahead is not being patrolled at all.

The more chicken-shit the law enforcement the less respect the folks have for police authority. The anger and financial burdens created by exorbitant tickets serve to increase distrust of the police. Certainly dangerous drivers need to be pulled to the curb and in some cases taken off our roads. But the only legitimate role for policing our driving is public safety. That is the basis for all traffic laws. Setting up chicken-shit stings in trick locations does nothing to further that and making people irate only increases the pressure on them and makes them more of a hazard.

There is nothing more chicken-shit than radar and lasers. It used to be that they had to clock you for a quarter of a mile. That was the accepted standard. If you were speeding for more than a quarter mile and a cop followed you, you were busted for speeding. A moment's burst of speed to avoid hitting a dog or to pass a tractor, or whatever was expected. To their credit I think that law enforcement generally resisted radar for that very reason but the bean counters prevailed, as they always seem to do.

We citizens are being targeted and preyed upon by just about everyone these days as a means of making money. Junk medicine, junk food, scammers and telemarketers operating out of 'boiler rooms' preying particularly on the elderly and the ignorant, professional politicians that remain in office forever, and cynically misapplied law enforcement.

And then there are the Insurance Companies, the corporate Dr. Jekyll and Mr. Hydes. The Agents' half of these organizations, those who take your money, are nice, polite, friendly, and courteous. The Claims' half, those who are supposed to pay money to you, are a bunch of vicious, nasty, underhanded chiselers. Ahhhhh, I feel much better now!

Item: Batavia, Ohio—A sixty-six year old man killed a neighbor's fifteen year old boy for walking on his grass, by shot-gunning him in the chest. According to the neighbors, the man was really devoted to his meticulously kept lawn.

This is as good a time as any for me to bring in Fox News's Bill O'Reilly of *The O'Reilly Factor*, the so-called 'No Spin Zone'. I must confess that I do watch that show regularly. I cannot stomach his substitute hosts or that fellow Sean Hannity who follows him on *Hannity and Combs*, but I do watch Bill. I did talk about the yin and yang presentation at a trial as a good way to get at the truth but it is just too much for me to get my news from two people spouting opposite extreme viewpoints.

That is why we used to venerate such newscasters as Walter Cronkite; someone you could trust whom you knew had the experience, knowledge, and integrity to give you a reasonable cut on the day's events. Now we have mindless talking heads on networks owned by mega-corporations that will read whatever is put on the teleprompter.

Every once in a while I hear a startlingly real item of news on a 24-hour news channel, and then it is censored out and you never hear it again. It slips through in the endless quest to be first with the news but then a higher up becomes aware of it and kills it. This doesn't happen that often but often enough that it is quite real.

I watch Bill O'Reilly. Not that he never irritates me, like how he spins his fair and balanced image each and every night by reading one or two emails that say he is too far right, along with one or two emails stating that he is too far left. As if we are supposed to be so mentally challenged that such a rendering would convince us that he must be dead center. Now if he gave us the true stats of an objective poll wherein 91% said that he was too far to the right and 9% felt that he was too far to the left, now something like that would actually have some meaning.

Then there is how he browbeats the living hell out many of his guests and calls anyone and everyone who chooses not to go on his show a coward. That is way beyond the pale. And those guys who substitute for Bill O'Reilly, one in particular I cannot hack at all. As soon as their faces come up, I am gone.

But O'Reilly truly seems to mean well and he tries to be fair. His understanding of the Black Community is rare and his willingness to confront Blacks with honest constructive criticism is practically unheard of these days. That comes through without question. His Catholic Church upbringing seems to have left him fairly well brainwashed despite his obvious intellectual abilities and experience.

To his credit, he did speak strongly against the pedophilia and called for Boston's Cardinal Law to resign. But once the Catholic Church gets a hold of a young mind, they do a very thorough job indeed. Bill constantly jumps on the theme of a major cultural battle being waged in the U.S. with the secularist progressives pitted against the traditional religious groups. He is of course all in favor of the religious crowd.

I wonder though how much is really that, or is it more a matter of the perception that the younger generation is going to hell in a hand-basket, a generational recurrent theme if there ever was one. Looked at this way, the older generations that were brought up on school prayer and Judeo-Christian ethics were a much milder and nicer crop them what we now seem to be raising.

I can agree with that to some extent, but does that mean it is necessary to immerse these kids in a barrel of lies and absurd stories? Is that really the only and the best way? What about teaching the Golden Rule daily? Perhaps even starting and ending every class with the Golden Rule? How about teaching ethics classes frequently? You know…like Jesus Christ did? Is that too far fetched? Might that approach be less divisive, truthful and thus more effective than attempting to stuff a bunch of nonsense into their savvy little heads?

How about all that lynching of Black people in the South by Whites. Do you think those Whites were atheists or do you think they were regular church going Christians? We know what they were. The only people they hated worse than Blacks and Jews were atheists. There is no way you could have an ethics class that said it was okay to string-up people of a different skin shade...but religion didn't seem to have an insurmountable problem with the morality of that.

These Christians also didn't have a problem on September 15, 1963 when they bombed the Christian Sixteenth Street Baptist Church in Birmingham, Alabama. This act was one of the most abhorrent crimes of the civil rights movement. Four young girls attending Sunday school, Denise McNair, Cynthia Wesley, Carole Robertson, and Addie Mae Collins, ages 11 to 14 were murdered and twenty others were injured.

The whole notion that one has to be religious to be moral is a crock of you know what. I have sent some of my children to Catholic school and my youngest I took to church once in San Felipe when we were living in Mexico. I asked him what he thought of the church service. He said that he appreciated me having taken him but that once was enough. To be honest, two rows in front of me was an elderly lady with a startlingly beautiful granddaughter that I became fixated on. She is all that I can remember about that service.

One thing that we did do was become masters at extricating vehicles from the sand. Though we lived on an isolated point, on holidays and weekends both Mexicans and Gringos would show up for recreation. The Gringos with their new four wheelers would manage to get all four wheels buried in the sand. Sometimes they would even lose their vehicles altogether to the second largest tidal swings in the world after the Bay of

Fundy. They would drive out onto sandbars at low tide and later get stranded out there when the tide came in.

Using our ATVs, nylon straps, and an assortment of modified jacks, we never found a vehicle that we could not free from the sand. We did this for anyone who asked and never accepted payment for the rescue. This boy is the most moral young man that I know.

Here is an interesting note on the difference in attitude between the Mexicans and the Gringos. When an American got stuck they would tend to freak out. They would apply power and make matters worse. They would be totally frustrated and in denial. Then they would run around like the world was coming to an end. On the other hand, when the Mexican family got stuck, they would all pile out, look the situation over, have a long discussion, breakout some food, have a picnic, and generally make an enjoyable day out of being caught in the sand.

Who said, "Good people do good things, bad people do bad things; but it takes religion or government or both to make good people do bad things."?

How can one not advocate being progressive in a world that is changing and evolving so very rapidly? And we have these Christian Fundamentalist who have the nerve, the unmitigated arrogance and gall to appear on mainstream TV programs like Larry King and O'Reilly and state that Christianity is the only way to Heaven and that all other belief systems and religions are demonic. That all the people who subscribe to them, no matter how good these people are, or how exemplary their lives, that all these people will go to Hell and burn for all eternity.

Just talking like that is close to being a hate crime. Can you imagine how Jesus Christ would respond to such ignorant ill-willed cretins of that ilk? It is enough to make you puke. And these people are occupying leadership roles in their communities and filling children's heads with this vile garbage…just as some Muslims are teaching hatred of Jews and Christians in some of their madrasas. These rabid nincompoops need to be shunned if not removed from decent society. *Religion is a Dog from Hell.*

That last paragraph is a bit rough, deserved, but rough. I should strive to be more politic. One must remember to hate the sin and not the sinner. The people who think like those mentioned above would have us believe that if we allowed then to dunk us in a river and believe as they do, that we would be saved.

The thing that we need to be saved from is them and those like them. Well, they should know that if they would stop reading millennia old conflicted texts, come to their senses, get in touch with reality, and follow the Golden Rule, that then they could really be saved…from themselves. This would occur whether they took a bath or not. Real truth needs no rituals or mumbo jumbo. Actual truth can stand on its own.

Years ago when I owned rental units in the Los Angeles Black ghetto, I would occasionally get a potential renter who would make a point of informing me that they were a Christian. This was odd in and of itself as to my knowledge everyone who ever applied was a Christian. It didn't take me long to understand that these people who played the 'Christian card' like that were in fact nothing but trouble and the last people that I wanted in any of my units.

They wielded their so-called Christianity as a weapon. There is something, probably an inferiority complex, that makes people want to feel superior to their fellow man, and religion is often the means that allows them to labor under that delusion.

Item: 03-20-06—Newsweek Page 72—Books: *A Contrarian's Christ—Making a Case for Jesus as the Enemy of Religion.* The book is *What Jesus Meant,* by Garry Wills. Wills also wrote *Papal Sin: Structures of Deceit,* in 2000.

Well, it looks like this guy Wills is attempting to tell the truth also. It is an interesting thought, Jesus as the enemy of religion. It makes perfect sense. His assault on the temple and attempt to throw out the moneychangers certainly speaks to that theory. There is no evidence that he ever built buildings for places of worship. It is well known that Jesus hung out with the lowly and the social outcasts while shunning the high and the mighty. He preached equality and foresaw a revolution after which the last would be first and the first would be last.

He preached many beautiful concepts, like judge not lest you be judged. Recall the story of how he stopped a woman from being stoned to death, still a Muslim practice, by stating, "Let him who is without sin cast the first stone." How far is that from the Christian Church's practice of judging people left and right, torturing them, and burning them alive? *God Gave us the Truth; the Devil Organized it into Religions.*

Item: The Olympic Soccer and Sports Stadium in Bremo is currently serving 240 teams with 100 more waiting. The expansion goal is to build another regulation-size indoor soccer field.

I must get off this religion theme for a bit before I blow a gasket or something. How about geography, that sounds harmless enough, or at least non-controversial. North v South is an interesting place to start. Whenever the North fights the South, the North invariably wins. Our Civil War is but one example out of a great many.

But before we go there, note that virtually all the news that we get concerns the Northern Hemisphere. Some of this is due to the fact that so many of the people in the U.S. had ancestors that came from Europe. But Australia has a white population from Great Britain and still you hear very little from down there.

Wars that take place in the Southern Hemisphere would favor the side from the South i.e. the colder clime toward the South Pole. People near the equator have year round warm temperatures and it is relatively easy to find food. The colder the climate, the more it is necessary to store food up for the winter, and in that winter, one has the time to ponder and think. Man being as he is, one of the things to think about is better weapons and strategy.

I am not up on all the wars but there was one between Chile and Columbia that Chile won. If you take the time to check out all wars, you may be amazed at how many times the country nearest the pole wins over the combatant nearest the equator.

Have you ever notice how the momentum of world events has moved around the globe from east to west? Go back a few millennia to the cradles of civilization originating around the main rivers in China, the Tigress and Euphrates, and the Nile in Egypt. Civilization then flourished in Greece before moving west to Rome.

From there it continued west to the western coast of Europe, like Holland, England, France, Spain and Portugal. It continued onward west to the New World and the settlements of the Eastern Coast of North America as well as Central and South America.

The western expansion continued across North America until it reached the West Coast. In the past century it has headed toward Japan and China and what is known as the Pacific Rim is hot developmentally. Soon this cutting edge of history will have returned to China and India where it began a few thousand years ago.

Item: Bremo High School is about to add a new wing of classrooms and a courtyard to the existing school, while also adding a TV production studio, a standalone physical education building, and expand the commons area. Concurrently, Mountain View Middle School will add an additional wing of classrooms for eighth grade students. Total cost for both is projected at $18.6 million and both are due to be completed in September of 2007.

Item: Annual Soap Box Derby held in downtown Bremo.

The visionaries who start companies are most often not the people who can best run that company once it has become established. Organized religion is no different. Moses is the visionary or prophet of the Jews; Jesus Christ the same for the Christians; and Muhammad likewise for Muslims. Muslins view the followers of all these three religions as people of the Book. They revere all of these prophets.

They also realize that the Old and New Testaments of the Bible were written by a great many authors, changed and modified endlessly…to the point that there are more discrepancies amongst the many manuscripts than there are words in the New Testament. Of the more than 5,000 surviving copies of the New Testament written in Greek, no two are alike!

The Old Testament is even worse with the oldest complete copy being from around 1000 A.D. Such finds as the Dead Sea Scrolls highlight the many changes and the hundreds of thousands of errors that exist amongst the various copies. Naturally, or predictably, the Vatican did all in its power to keep the Dead Sea Scrolls from seeing the light of day as long as it possible could. But then the Roman Church has a long and sordid history of being no friend of the truth. Like they say in Texas, "Never let the truth stand in the way of a good story."

The book, *The Dead Sea Scrolls Deception* presents nothing less than a new, highly significant perspective on Christianity. The oldest Biblical manuscripts in existence, the Dead Sea Scrolls were found in caves near Jerusalem in 1947, only to be kept a tightly held secret for nearly fifty more years, until the Huntington Library unleashed a storm of controversy in 1991 by releasing copies of the Scrolls.

In this gripping investigation authors Baigent and Leigh set out to discover how a small coterie of orthodox biblical scholars gained control over the Scrolls, allowing access to no outsiders and issued only a strict 'consensus' interpretation. The authors' questions begin in Israel, then lead them to the corridors of the Vatican, and on into the offices of the Inquisition. Can you believe that the Inquisition still exists? Maybe they should be charged with crimes against humanity.

With the help of independent scholars, historical research, and careful analysis of available texts, the authors reveal what was at stake for these orthodox guardians. The Scrolls present startling insights into early Christianity…insights that challenge the Church's version of the facts.

How could anyone in their right mind think that these self-contradictory ancient writings are the words of God rather than those of men? What an insult to God to attribute authorship to him, a book that sends many of its readers around the bend!

Would not a book that was truly created by God cause the reader to become a beautiful soul, a Mother Teresa or something like that...or at least enlightened? Anything but deranged!

Why would a book produced by God cause people to become narrow-minded, self-important, judgmental, mentally deaf, dumb and blind, cramped, self-righteous, insane, blood-thirsty, over-controlling, soul destroying, and just plain...well you get the picture; the opposite of the life and teachings of Jesus Christ.

The Muslims feel justified in putting their faith into the Quoran because of its means of origin. Muhammad was illiterate and those people were living at the time by oral tradition. He memorized and taught his words of God as they were given to him. He apparently was an epileptic who received these divine transmissions while he was either always, or most often having a seizure. I will simply leave that one alone.

After his death a committee was formed and those that had learned the Quoran directly from Muhammad came to agreement as to the correct wording to be written down. The Muslims realize how much rewriting, politics, and spin went into the Bible. The Quoran is quite different from the Bible in that it does not follow a chronological order but more or less goes from short passages to longer ones.

All of these religions went from the visions of their prophets to the bureaucratic types that produce and promote the growth and dominance of the organized religions. Like any organization, their goal becomes self-aggrandizement, enlargement, power concentration, control of their subjects, brain washing, and all the rest of it.

I may be wrong but I don't recall that Moses or Jesus or Mohamed ever got into erecting buildings. Jesus, as I recall was big on preaching to the multitudes in open-air forums.

Why is the Roman Catholic Church against birth control when human overpopulation is rapidly destroying our planet? Because they want to get even bigger than they are. It is just that simple and disgusting. The thrust of Christianity is the short-term exploitation of the Earth when what we need is a long-term ethical stewardship of our planet. We are all in the same boat, and it is floundering. We need to go back to the teachings of the original prophets and bring any out-of-control Earth-destroying organized religions to the curb.

If you want to read a most magnificently beautiful prophet, read *The Prophet* by Kahlil Gibran. Mr. Gibran, 1883-1931, a poet, philosopher, and artist, was born in Lebanon, a land that has produced many prophets. The millions of Arabic speaking peoples familiar with his writings in that language consider him the genius of his age. But he was a man whose fame and influence spread far beyond the Near East.

His poetry has been translated into more than twenty languages. His drawings and paintings have been exhibited in the great capitals of the world and compared by Rodin to the work of William Blake. In the United States, where he made his home during the last twenty years of his life, he began to write in English. *The Prophet* and his other books of poetry, illustrated with his mystical drawings, are known and loved by innumerable Americans who find in them an expression of the deepest impulses of man's heart and mind.

William Blake is quite an interesting read. Wordsworth's verdict after Blake's death reflected many opinions of that time: "There is no doubt that this poor man was mad, but there is something in the madness of this man which interests me more than the sanity of Lord Byron or Walter Scott." Here is one quote of William Blake, "Prisons are built with stones of Law, Brothels with bricks of Religion."

Item: Paul's Flowers a local landmark that opened its doors seventy years ago at 6th Street and Pacific Avenue is moving to allow for Bremo's downtown progress. The three businesses on that corner must make way for a mixed-use retail complex topped by offices, to be built by the Tim Ryan Construction Company.

Psychiatry describes two opposing forces, or the yin and yang of one force, as Eros and Thanatos. Eros is the force of life, life in all its exuberance...bursting forth. Children running and playing, teenagers making out in the back seats of cars, the joy of learning, singing, dancing, whistling while you work; these are all representations of Eros.

Thanatos is the death drive. Oppression, repression, over-controlling, stifling, cramping, torturing, and killing all stem from Thanatos. The obsession with establishing a National ID for every person is not a function of Eros. Recall the Nazi's policy of tattooing a number on each Jew that they took into custody. Time and again certain forces attempt to establish a National ID in the U.S. In the past these efforts have been beaten back by the Libertarians.

Bill Clinton attempted it under the guise of a National Health Care program. The Bush administration is using the post 9-11 anxiety to do the same thing using new, highly controlled Drivers Licenses. It is to be expected that governmental forces are naturally going to try repeatedly to gain more control over us. Balance between Eros and Thanatos is of course needed. But we should be very clear that we are dealing with Thanatos and just what the price to be paid for excessive control is. After all, it is the false desirability of central control that eventually brought down the Soviet Union.

The history of civilization clearly shows the trend of power. Power is moving from a total concentration at the top to a general diffusion toward the bottom. The Pharaohs had all the power. Kings had unlimited power until the Magna Carta in 1215. At that point a significant amount of the King's power devolved to the Aristocracy. This trend continued on down to powerful merchants and guilds.

Later the formation of labor unions brought power ever closer to the common man. Now with the advent of computers and instant communication, it is possible to enable people in the Information Age or the Age of Creativity to function with ever more personal power. I am writing this all alone in a cold truck, but with a laptop and a WIFI connection. With access to the Internet, and thanks to Google, I have available to me virtually all of the knowledge and research results existing on the planet. This is all mine on demand, and practically instantaneously. How fantastic is that?

What is America most famous for, most loved for? It is for our movies and our music, our culture i.e. our creativity. Creativity born of our freedom.

Sure, society is arranged to keep the workers subordinate to the elite, or as Balzac put it, "The rich will do anything for the poor, except get off their backs." But this is not the caste system that it once was. Upward mobility is more and more necessary every day if we are to remain a healthy, vibrant, innovative, and productive people.

For centuries, actually millennia, it didn't really matter what people thought. The time it took for news to travel from the event to the people was so great that by the time the folks learned about what had happened, it was old news with nothing much that could be done about it. That is hardly the case today with 24 hour TV and radio news broadcasts and both cable and satellite delivery.

Even the poorest countries today have TV and increasingly cell phones. All of these trends make it increasingly vital that the populations act with reason rather then blind faith in ancient often misguided and ill-informed concepts of truth and justice.

And yet we see today in this country, a massive effort to force nonsensical Creationism into our science classes...and this effort is endorsed if not led by our own United States President, George W. Bush! Since the word Creationism has so much negative baggage it has been re-christened Intelligent Design or Creationism Light by others.

This insanity takes us back to the famous Scopes trial in Tennessee over eighty years ago, and that takes us back to before the Age of Enlightenment. The battle is between Creationism and Evolution. As comedian Lewis Black says, "We have the fossils. We win." Not to mention carbon dating and all the rest of it.

The Creationists base everything on the Bible, on Genesis. But anyone who can read will easily see that Genesis I and Genesis II contradict each other over and over, and were obviously written by different people. The internal discrepancies in Genesis alone are enough to prove the patent falsity of that position. But beyond that, Creationism is one more insult to God and his very Creation. Evolution shows the true record of God's endless work over eons of time rather then the POOF of a piece of cake six-day miracle.

And this is followed by a day of rest. Folks, God doesn't rest, ever. God is what is. If God rested...that would be the end of it all. We are all a part of God's dream. It is man that rests every seventh day. It is worth noting that the Muslim Holy Day is Friday, the Jewish Holy Day is Saturday, and the Christian Holy Day is Sunday. If there were in fact a day that was holier than the others, don't you think that God would know which one it was? It is man who is confused and organized by self-serving forces of darkness or ignorance...not God.

What is startling to many is that in the seemingly enlightened United States of America, whose scientists are awarded about half of all Nobel Prizes, that more than one half of the people believe that Genesis is true and that Evolution is false! Such a dangerous collective delusion of religion is tantamount to a great illness of the human and national psyche.

The above is not true in England, France, Holland, or Canada. I suppose it must go back to the religious fringe, like the Puritans that were early to populate this country. We shouldn't forget that these religious folk in 1692 in Salem, Massachusetts managed to get another witch scare going and were quick to self-righteously set about the task of murdering innocent women and men. Fortunately calmer heads prevailed in the larger community and it was stopped at nineteen deaths.

The Court heard cases approximately once per month. There was no way to escape the stigma of being labeled a witch. Only those who pleaded guilty to witchcraft and supplied other names to the court were spared execution. Elizabeth Proctor and Abigail Faulkner were given respite 'for the belly' because they were pregnant. Though convicted, they would not be hanged until after they had given birth. A series of four mass executions over the summer saw nineteen people hanged, including a respected minister, a former constable who refused to arrest more accused witches, and at least three people of some wealth. Six of the nineteen were men; most of the rest were impoverished women beyond childbearing age.

Only one execution was not by hanging. Giles Corey, an 80-year-old farmer from the southeast end of Salem, refused to enter a plea. The law provided for the application of a form of torture called peine fort et dure, in which the victim was slowly crushed by piling stones on him; after two days of peine fort et dure, Corey died without entering a plea.

The possessions of convicted witches were confiscated, and possessions of persons accused but not convicted were often confiscated before a trial. Some historians hypothesize that Mr. Corey's personal character, a stubborn and lawsuit-prone old man who knew that no plea would stop the bloodlust, and knowing that he was going to be convicted regardless, led to his recalcitrance.

Does the above strike anyone as the work of God?

Despite the fact that our Founding Fathers were Renaissance men, followers and students of the Age of Reason and the Enlightenment, the first half of the nineteenth century saw the second 'Great Awakening' in the U.S. This became an Evangelistic Protestant guiding force in U.S. life.

Later in that century, Dwight L. Moody, the Billy Graham of his day was to preach against the four great temptations. These were namely, the theatre, ignoring the Sabbath, Sunday newspapers, and evolution/atheism.

Do you see how outdated this is after only a century and a half? Think how obsolete the stuff from millennia ago is! I image that even the most harebrained right wing fanatical Fundamentalist Christians of today think nothing of going to the theater or of reading a Sunday newspaper. Theocracy is just another name for repression and oppression, brainwashing and mind control. Make no mistake, these are morally evil liars, even if well meaning in a mentally disturbed way. As they say, 'The Road to Hell is Paved with Good Intentions.'

If you want a strictly mechanical understanding of evolutionary forces, read *The Blind Watchmaker* by Richard Dawkins.

Meanwhile the world is preparing for a possible pandemic, as health professionals are concerned that the continued spread of a highly pathogenic avian H5N1 virus across eastern Asia and other countries represents a significant threat to human health. The H5N1 virus has raised concerns about a potential human pandemic because:

- It is especially virulent
- It is being spread by migratory birds
- It can be transmitted from birds to mammals and in some limited circumstances to humans
- And like other influenza viruses, it continues to evolve.

Our President is okay with the foolishness that there is no such thing as Evolution and that the world was created six thousand years ago, but he doesn't hesitate to give the order to make preparation against this H5N1 virus should it evolve in our direction. But then this is yet another windfall of profits for Big Pharm.

I wonder how I could have traced my ancestry back seventy thousand years in a six thousand year old world? Just how big does the turd in the punchbowl have to get before people stop guzzling the Kool-Aid?

The whole concept of Holy Ground and Sacred Places is just more idolatry. Jerusalem is considered sacred by Jews, Christians, and Muslims. So how do they so often show their special love of this Holy spot? Why by killing each other there whenever possible! Hello?

All ground is sacred. All people are sacred. All of creation is sacred. Anyone following the Golden Rule would know that. When humans kill each other over a spot, they make that spot ugly. Jesus taught of beautiful ideas, principles, and concepts, not idols, relics, and extra special spots.

I like the city of Florence, Florencia, and in fact one of my all time favorite places to eat is there. It was once the home of such greats of the art world as Michelangelo, Leonardo Da Vinci, Rafael, Brunelleschi, Dante, Boccaccio, Giotto, Donatello, Botticelli, and Cellini to name but a few. But that was about five hundred years ago.

Today the city remains an art school center and overflows with art students. Why? Sure there is a well-developed art infrastructure there and it is probably a good place to study, but does anyone really think that Florencia is where any of those geniuses would be working now if they were alive today?

They were there at that time because it was easily deemed the most powerful, scientifically advanced, and artistically free place on the planet. The Italian City-States like Florencia and Venice, Venezia, were the greatest maritime traders and the richest towns in the Western World. There lived the wealthy and politically strong patrons of the arts. The reasons why these great men where there then, are no longer true about Florencia today.

If those greats were alive today where would they be? Who knows, perhaps New York, or Beijing, or Amsterdam, or well perhaps anywhere...but not Florencia. But followers follow and copycat, even if they are five centuries too late.

In making a point I have unfortunately and unintentionally dumped on lovely Florencia. Maybe it would help if I bagged on their old rival Venezia. This is actually justifiable as an illustration of just how horribly the average person can be mislead by following both political and religious leaders, especially when they are acting in concert.

Venezia is world class as far as charming cities go. It is a must see, to be sure. The winding walkways and shops, the famous bridges like the Rialto, the Grand Canal and the water-taxis, are all absolutely delightful. The Piazza St. Marco is the heart of Venice. Dueling orchestras lead you to dining establishments that have been operating continuously for many centuries and have been enjoyed by some of the greatest names in history. You may climb the Campanile, a 314 ft. tower and from the top you can look out over the city and the lagoon. It was built in the 9th century and often used by Galileo for his work.

This famous square is also bordered by the Doge's Palace and St. Mark's Basilica. People line up all day to see the treasures in the Basilica. The thing that is not mentioned is that virtually all of these treasures were not only stolen, but the Doge used the Fourth Crusade, 1201-04, to slaughter other Christians in order to obtain them! This treasure includes: the saint's relics whose theft was justified by a story that basically said, "An angel made me do it." And the Pala d'Oro, one of the richest and most precious altar screens in the world, covered with over three thousand precious stones and enamel icons inlaid in gold.

This Fourth Crusade was sanctioned by Pope Innocent III, who wanted to conquer Egypt, a center of Islamic power. They needed a port and ships, and that is why they turned to Venezia. The Doge agreed to help for a per head fee and also one half of all plunder. To make a very long and extremely sordid story short, the Doge deftly steered the expedition away from Egypt where Venezia had lucrative trade agreements, and actually diverted the Crusaders, by means of force and debt problems, to attack and loot, first the Christian City of Zara, and then the Holy Christian Orthodox Church City of Constantinople, the greatest Christian City at that time!

The crusaders knew it was wrong but had little choice. They owed the Doge money and saw the Zara loot as the means to pay their debt. The Doge also had a stranglehold on their supplies of food and water. Thus Christian crusaders began ransacking Christian churches and stealing everything of value! Despite these atrocities, the situation of the Crusaders had not improved as their half of the loot was not enough to repay the outstanding debt to Venezia having spent most of it buying food all winter in the captured city.

In 1203 the Crusaders arrived off Constantinople in 450 large ships and many smaller ones. Emperor Alexius III fled Constantinople on a ship after abandoning his city, his empire, his followers, his wife and his children. He took with him his favorite daughter Irene, some friends, and naturally he did not forget to bring 10,000 pieces of gold and many priceless jewels. There was much extortion and usurping of power. Eventually the city fell to the Crusaders. The sack of Constantinople, the richest city of all Europe was underway.

The troops were let loose. Thousands of civilians were slaughtered. Christian women and even nuns were raped. Churches, monasteries and convents were looted. The altars of churches were smashed and torn to pieces for their gold and marble by Crusaders who had sworn to fight for Christianity against Islam. The magnificent Santa Sophia was ransacked. Art works of incalculable value were destroyed for their material worth. The bronze statue of Hercules, created by the famous Lysippus, court sculptor to Alexander the Great was melted down for its bronze. The loss of art treasures in the sack of Constantinople is beyond measure.

The Venezians stole religious relics and works of art that are in St. Mark's Basilica to this very day...and they are collecting admission all day long from tourists who wish to see them.

Think of those thousands of men who walked clear across Europe in order to do what they were told was their Christian duty to take back Jerusalem from the infidels. They suffered untold hardships and what did their leaders end up having them do? They slaughtered fellow Christians, desecrated church alters, and raped nuns! All for the insatiable greed and power lust of wealthy old men!

If God was into suspending his own Universal laws, he sure missed a great opportunity with that Fourth Crusade! At the very least he could have turned the loot into lumps of coal or something. Funny how he is always meddling with school bus fatalities but missed both of the World Wars.

Of course Hitler was baptized as a Catholic. He was an alter boy, was confirmed, and had many ties to the Catholic Church. He made deals with them after he came to power and received much praise from high Church officials. When you come right down to it, Hitler's extermination of the Jews was right in keeping with many earlier attempts by Christians to slaughter Jews, ostensibly for religious reasons. Hitler and his pals were just far more systematic and efficient at it.

Did you ever stop to think and realize that every living thing around you is exactly the same age? Every tree and leaf, every bird and bug, every cat and dog, every virus and yourself, are exactly the same age? How can that possible be?

All life on earth viewed over time produces a tree of life. If you have children your branch will continue. If you do not it will end forever with you. You represent an unbroken line back to the very beginning of life on Earth. Your DNA and so forth came from your parents. The half-cell from your dad united with the half-cell from mom. It then went on doubling in a binary fashion, 2-4-8-16-32-64-128-256 until you were fully formed. You have added a lot of food and water to yourself, and gotten a lot bigger to be sure, but you are still composed of that original genetic material from your parents. Your parents got it from their parents all the way back through amphibians, fish, and so on. Right on back to the very beginning.

Or to start at the other end, at the beginning and move forward, we have single cells developing. After some time the single cells realize that by forming a ring their survivability is enhanced. The rings then join up to make tubes. The tubes or worms, our alimentary canal, then got fancy and added fins or legs and ever more complex organs and senses.

Your true age is not twenty or thirty years, your true age is the age of your DNA that goes back in an unbroken line to the first single cell critter. It has traveled down through the ages from parent to child. Any one who died prior to reproducing ended their line and is no longer represented. The same can be said for every single living thing around you.

The flowers on your desk also go back to that very same single celled beginning of life on Earth, the same with the tree outside your window, or the bird in the sky. We all share a common ancestry and our DNA while having traveled different routes and at different rates of Evolution, has all existed for exactly the same amount of time.

Erosion by water formed the first sedimentary rocks about 4 billion years ago. The discovery of fossil remains of life in ancient rocks from the Isua region of Greenland have been dated to 3.83 billion years ago. This makes them the oldest sedimentary rocks in the world. That would make every living thing you can ever see on Earth about 3.83 billion years old! Does not actual truth like that foster a greater reverence for all life? Does that not give greater understanding and meaning to an enlightened man who avoids stepping on an ant? That ant is his distant relative, they are both precisely the same age. He knows that.

Why spend so much time relating the above perspective? To illustrate how beautiful and fascinating reality itself really is. It is not necessary to immerse yourself in a detailed delusion about the world that you live in. We don't know where we came from or where we are going. What we do know is that we are here now in God's Creation. Let us appreciate and enjoy and study it for what it truly is, and not be distracted by those who would ask us for our money and sell us a bill of goods at best or too frequently, a load of hateful hogwash.

Deepak Chopra has written some very beautiful stuff and I highly recommend his, *The Seven Spiritual Laws of Success* as a book to live by. One of his riffs concerns the number of atoms that we breathe in out lifetime. The number is so astronomically high that it is almost certain that each one of us has breathed at least one atom that everyone else on the planet has previously had in his or her body. Not only that but it includes everyone living or dead. Thus we have probably all breathed into our lungs at least one atom that Moses, Jesus, and Muhammad had previously breathed into their bodies. 'All is One' is a lot more than just a catchy saying.

Item: 03-20-06 Monday—Government is Owed Billions in Unpaid Fines. A pipeline company was fined $3 million when an explosion killed three boys in Bellingham, WA. Nuclear labs were ordered to pay $2.5 million when they exposed workers to radiation and broke other safety rules. Coal mining firms were fines $1.3 million for violations that caused the deaths of miners from Alabama to West Virginia.

The above sounds good until you find out that the pipeline fine was reduced by 92%, the labs' fines were waived as soon as they were issued, and the mines penalties largely went unpaid. The amount of unpaid fines has increased sharply in the last decade. The uncollected amount is five times what it was ten years ago, namely thirty-five billion dollars.

Item: Since President Bush's election our national Debt has risen from 5.7 trillion dollars to an allowable 8.9 trillion with the recently raised debt ceiling. That works out to an increase of 56%.

Ronald Reagan left us a national debt of about $3.5 trillion. The national debt when Ronald Reagan took office was about $1 trillion. That included in it all the debt run up for the Revolutionary War, the War of 1812, the Spanish-American War, the Civil War, World War I, World War II, the Korean War, the Vietnam War and all the social wars of the 1930's and subsequent years. In other words it took the United States from 1776 until 1980 or more than 200 years to accumulate a national debt of $1 trillion. It took Reaganomics only eight years to increase the national debt from $1 trillion to about $3.5 trillion!

Despite the above, and the fact that Bill Clinton was running a large surplus, we are endlessly hammered with the message that Democrats are big spenders and that Republicans are fiscally conservative and against big government. Has truth become so totally meaningless and irrelevant?

Item: Muslims Are Worse Than The Nazis, says popular televangelist, the Reverend Pat Robertson. The accusation drew fire from a leading American-Islamic group that warned that the comments could spark violence.

The Council on American-Islamic Relations, CAIR, on Tuesday denounced Robertson's remarks as "lies, distortions and outright bigotry. It's a shame coming from someone who claims to be a man of the cloth," said Hodan Hassan, a spokeswoman for the group. "He is doing a lot more to increase tensions and maybe violence among different ethnicities and religions than sowing the seeds of peace," she said, maintaining that Robertson was using two passages from the Koran "deceitfully. It's outlandish and a total distortion," Hassan said, noting that the Koran contains numerous calls for inter-faith harmony and demands respect for other religions.
The Christian Broadcasting Network programming is broadcast in more than 180 countries around the world. Last month, Baptist minister Jerry Falwell called the Prophet Mohammed a terrorist, sparking international outrage and deadly riots in the Indian city of Bombay. Falwell later apologized. The wild-eyed Franklin Graham, son of the noted preacher Billy Graham, has also been accused of making outlandish and defamatory statements about Islam.

Item: Engineering Obesity—Yale's' Katz believes that junk food companies do just that, much the way tobacco companies were accused of tinkering with nicotine. Research shows that you are less likely to overeat plain baked potatoes than those drenched in butter, salt, sour cream and chives. Sugary cereals have more salt in them than many potato and corn chips. That is one way to make a cereal's flavor more complex and appealing, in order to get people to eat more of it.

I just ran a word count and this document is registering at one hundred and seven pages and over fifty thousand words. Now that is a lot of yammering! Sometimes the slant is to the left and at other times toward the right. It is my intention for it to zig and zag but to be overall fairly well down the middle and always realistic and pragmatic

Here are a couple of observations. While living in Mexico I was struck by the level of cooperation. I mentioned the schoolteachers who painted the school while on strike. Another time the shrimp season was postponed for two weeks and many of the local fishermen used the time to jointly contribute their labor to improve the public piers and docks from which they operated.

There were a great many examples. Then I learned of a simple test that was administered by psychologist to both Mexican and U.S. children, with startling results. A checkerboard was used with a child at either end. A token was put in the middle of the board. The rules were easy. The children alternated making one move on each turn. Whenever the token reached either child's side of the board, that child would get a treat.

For the Mexicans this was dirt simple. They each took turns moving the piece from one side to the other and each child obtained the maximum number of rewards. But not so with the children form the U.S., each time one child moved the marker one step towards their side, the other kid would move it back toward the center. Competition was the order of the day, even when it was totally self-defeating!

You may think from reading the above that I am opposed to competition and all in favor of cooperation. No, not necessarily. The GDP of all of Mexico at that time was less than that of Los Angeles County. Communism was in theory based on cooperation while capitalism is based on competition. We all know how that plays out. It used to be said that a young man who wasn't a communist at age eighteen didn't have a heart; and a man who was still a communist at age fifty didn't have a head.

James Michener's book about the Middle East is *The Source.* There is a remarkable analysis of two ancient towns and the early lesson they taught to man. One town had the brutal practice of demanding the blood sacrifice of the first-born male from each family. Or perhaps it was the second born male, it was many years ago that I read that book…same difference. Anyway, the god of this town was indeed a fierce and demanding one.

The second town could not have been more different. Here the gods were worshiped in temples that were well stocked with public prostitutes. The young women were selected for their beauty and raised to pleasure men. Naturally temple attendance was never a problem!

If a young man had been allowed to choose which of these two towns he preferred to be raised in, it would seem to be a no-brainer. But the fact of the matter was that the first town with the horrid habit produced a very strong society that always dominated and eventually defeated the second town with its love of pleasure. As stated, this was an early lesson and one that did not go unnoticed.

So there you have it, a cornerstone, if not the cornerstone of human civilization is human sacrifice. Now you can stop wondering why so many of our leaders freak out about sex but have no problem with violence. Those bone-breaking monsters crashing into each other at the Super Bowl were just dandy. Janet Jackson right booby was a national scandal requiring such an enormous backlash that poor old Howard Stern was knocked clean off the airways onto satellite radio. Oh my!

Speaking of James Michener, he wrote a book about Afghanistan that he called, *Caravans*. This was written long before the Soviet invasion. In this book Michener flatly predicted that sooner or later the Russians would have to invade. Not for economic gain or other low motive but because there was just no way that a society like the Soviets who based their culture on egalitarian principles and whose women worked in every type of job that there was, that such a society could not bear to tolerate the way that Afghan men treated their women. That the Soviet Union could no more tolerate such a situation existing right on its border any more than the U.S. could tolerate cannibalism existing in Baja, to make a dreadful and unfair to Baja, analogy.

Eventually the Soviets did just that, they invaded Afghanistan. And we as their sworn enemy aided the Afghans and provided them with Stinger missiles to shoot down Soviet aircraft. We also trained the Afghans in terrorist warfare and brought a fellow name Usama Bin Laden up to speed as well. We all know where this sordid business led and the whirlwind that we reaped and are still reaping.

Adrienne, ooops...sorry about that! I meant to inform you that I had stopped listing the surveillance ON/OFF times here, but I knew you would figure it out. It makes much more sense now to post that on DVR#3 with the surveillance data. It will also make this record easier for you to separate out and to deal with. I hate the amount of time I am spending spooking but I know of no other way to get this investigation where it needs to be. We have exactly 90 days tops to wrap up Phase I. Phase II must begin by May 02, 2006.

Item: I saw the most amazing documentary named Brainman. It investigated savants like Daniel Tammet and the man that the movie *Rainman* was written about, Kim Peek.

Most autistic savants appear quite strange due to a variety of disabilities but not so Mr. Tammet. The man can solve mathematical problems in his head with answers out to more places than calculators or normal computers can match. At one session he made good on his word to calculate the value of Pi, the fundamental constant that works for every circle, to 22,500 places! It took him about five hours of recitation with one break taken. His answer was exactly correct.

He does not knowingly make any calculations but merely records the odd shaped numbers floating in his mind. The correct answers to the most complex calculations simply appear to him.

Daniel Tammet stated that he knew perhaps nine languages and that he could learn any language in one week. To test him on this he was taken to Iceland where the language consists of some strange sounds used nowhere else. He was given a tutor who flatly said it would be absolutely impossible to learn that language in one week or anything like that short a span of time.

Unbeknownst to Daniel he was scheduled to be on a TV program in Iceland at the end of that week where he would be forced to demonstrate his ability to speak Icelandic in public. One week later Daniel Tammet did exactly that, brilliantly…with both good grammar and proper pronunciation!

He was also studied in San Diego and taken to Salt Lake City to meet Kim Peek. Kim peek is a living human Google. He knows virtually everything. He has a photographic memory with nearly perfect retention of everything that he has ever read. You can ask him the zip code, elevation, population, highway routes, or just about anything about anywhere in the country. He reads blazingly fast and reads one side of a book with one eye, while simultaneously reading the opposite page with his other eye.

NASA is now studying Kim, hoping to use MRI and CT scans to create a three dimensional model of Kim's unique brain structure with the purpose of better understanding him and his remarkable abilities. These new imaging studies are being carried out at Salinas Valley Memorial Hospital in Salinas, California in a joint project with NASA.

If you tell Kim your date of birth, he can tell you what day of the week you were born on. If you ask him what day that will fall on in one hundred years…he knows that also. His musical knowledge and abilities are equally amazing.

I bring these savants in here because if you really want to learn and understand this world, you must pay particular attention to the anomalies. These are the very things that are not taught in school. That reminds me of a popular book written many years ago. I believe that the title was, *Everything I Needed to Learn in School I Learned in Kindergarten.*

Actually it is amazing how little necessary and useful information that you actually do learn in school. There is no manual for marriage, or childrearing, dealing with your own possibly dysfunctional family, or so many other vital aspects of living. I had two years of algebra, plane and solid geometry, trigonometry, calculus both integral and differential, chemistry, physics, and other subjects that I have basically never used in my lifetime with the exception of perhaps some very simple algebra that I may have used a handful of times at most.

Item: My newspaper had a 3 x 5 purple sticker on it from the Holy Cross Lutheran Church. It states, "You don't get into Easter—Easter gets into you". There are a couple of crosses and three Easter eggs depicted. Here I am a detective and I have nary a clue as to what this could possibly mean. Easter like all Christian holidays was slapped on top of a pagan rite. Spring is the time to plant seeds and to fornicate…thus eggs are the perfect symbol. I am all for that, but really I would rather get into Easter, than have Easter get into me!

Did you ever watch a school of fish or a flock of birds and see them all turn at exactly the same moment? How can they do that? If people could do that on the freeway we wouldn't have the monster slow downs that we do. It is the cumulative effect of all the reaction times of the drivers that adds up to the long delays.

But the fish all turn in unison and the only way that can occur is if they are telepathically, mentally connected. Then there is the hive mentality, sometimes called a hive mind. Think of an insect colony like ants or bees, that individually behave seemingly independently, and almost unpredictably at random, but when observed of as a whole, they manage success far exceeding what any one of them could accomplish alone. Is the queen bee or queen ant directing the enterprise telepathically? Examples of human based hive minds include the scientific and mathematics communities, governments, and charitable organizations.

Bees were one of the first creatures ever to be domesticated by man and don't you see the similarity of the Pharaoh to the Queen bee? Or compare an ant colony to a Royal Court with its workers, nursemaids, soldiers, and princes.

When we lived in Mexico, we had three kinds of ants living within our compound. We were able to enforce our rules upon them with little difficulty. The tiniest ants were the only ones allowed on the patio. They cleaned up any crumbs and never bothered Tommy or I and our bare feet. But when we had visitors they would jump around and shout as they got regularly bitten by these ants.

The largest ants were out by our parking area. Twice a year there would be all kinds of commotion by their anthill opening and they would spend all day bring up and launching winged Queen ants...hundreds of them. Do you know that it is against Federal law to ship Queen ants in the United States?

The thing is, when periodically these ants would test the borders that we had set for them, we would put the hurt on them. They would then behave for about a year before a retest. Someone was getting the message and when that happened, they were all informed. You figure it out.

I don't doubt that humans all retain some telepathic abilities, though largely suppressed. If we could consciously pick up on the feelings of all other humans we would quickly go over the edge. Now the Internet is giving humanity a kind of hard-wired universal telepathic ability that we can turn off and on and control. This is and will continue to produce a sea change in human endeavor.

People with pronounced psychic abilities are able to use this telepathic realm in a useful fashion. Haven't you ever thought about someone and made a mental note to contact that person and then your phone rings and guess whom it is? Many are the tales of a person waking up at night in a cold sweat with the feeling that a relative has died and it later proves correct that the death did in fact happen and at that exact time. Identical twins are much more prone to this sort of thing because of their closeness and identical genetic structure.

C. G. Jung and Jungian Psychology saw the human psyche as made up of layers. First is the conscious mind. The ego is the term given to the organization of the conscious mind, being composed of conscious perceptions, memories, thoughts, and feelings. Those mental contents that the ego does not recognize fall into the Personal Unconscious. This is comprised of suppressed and forgotten memories, traumas, and all psychic contents that are either too weak to reach consciousness or that are actively suppressed by the ego because the latter is threatened by them.

Thus far Jung is in accord with his teacher Freud in supposing the existence of the Unconscious mind. This includes all that is not immediately accessible to everyday waking consciousness. Conscious and Unconscious are thus the two different parts of the psyche. Jung's great contribution however was to divide the Unconscious itself into two very unequal levels, the more superficial Personal Unconscious and the deeper Collective Unconscious.

Everyone has his or her own Personal Unconscious. The Collective Unconscious in contrast is universal. It cannot be built up like one's Personal Unconscious but rather it predates the individual. It is the repository of all the religious, spiritual, and mythological symbols and experiences of humanity.

The Collective Unconscious has as its primary structures, the deep structures of the psyche, what Jung called archetypes. This is a late-Hellenistic Platonic and Augustinian Christian term that refers to the spiritual forms that are the preexisting prototypes of the material world. Interpreting this idea psychologically, Jung stated that these archetypes were the conceptual patterns behind all of our religious and mythological concepts. In fact, behind our thinking processes in general.

Jung was led to the Collective Unconsciousness concept by a man who had accurate historical knowledge that he could only have come by from access to a Collective Unconsciousness, rather than through personal experience.

Could Gaia, the collective embodiment of all life on Earth…all life that is the same age and represents an unbroken lifeline back to the beginning, could Gaia be the source of our Collective Unconsciousness? Could she be the switchboard of our dreams and psychic abilities?

Did you ever think that you might be like a radio or TV receiver? The radio contains no news, or songs, or programs; but what it does have is the ability to pick such things out of the air and make them manifest. What if our minds are picking up the will of our Creator or even o Gaia from the energy field in which we live? We can exercise our self-will and go against this direction and suffer all the problems that flow from that, or we can do our best to follow this higher power and lead a charmed and marvelous life. To let go and to go with the flow, as they say.

Item: 03-22-06—The Today Show—Joe Nickell who has worked professionally as a stage magician, private investigator, journalist, and university instructor was on as an investigator of the paranormal. As a ghostbuster Joe has checked out all the major locations that are claimed to be haunted. Despite the fact that he would love to actually find a ghost, he has never found any legitimate evidence of one. He has naturally uncovered a whole lot of fraud however.

Nevertheless, fully 60% of the American population believes in ghosts. Probably the same impetus to believe religious myths, if ghost exist…there must be an afterlife. If there is an afterlife, I won't really die. I suppose most of these people also believe in Creationism.

Personally, I also like to believe in a spirit world. A dimension in which all who pass-on can go back or forward in time and observe anything or anyone that they choose. Knowing that everyone you ever knew or will ever know can at some future time watch your every move…something like that will tend to make you think twice before you sneak around doing things that you wouldn't want to be observed doing.

On the one hand we hear that 'Life is short.' and that 'You only come around once.' While on the other hand that 'The soul is immortal.' And 'The afterlife last for all eternity.' Many want to go to Heaven and live with God forever. Have you ever stopped to think what forever or eternity signifies? Sure you may want to live to be 100 if your health is good, but how about 500? Still in…okay how about a million years? Try on a billion…a trillion? Would anyone opt to withstand a trillion trillion years of existence?

What do people whose basic needs are being satisfied most complain about? That's right, being bored. The more we have, the more entertainment we want. That is why Las Vegas works and has been the fastest growing city in the United States for some time. That is why we have gone from one TV channel to hundreds. How boring would it be to live a trillion trillion trillion years? Be careful what you wish for.

The afterlife whether it exists or not is perhaps the biggest con of all times. The Spanish had a tri-part approach to colonization and exploitation. First in were the conquistadors to kill and subdue the indigenous population. These fellows were then followed by the Padres who pacified the locals and gave them the big snow job. Finally the business people came in to exploit them and operated the silver mines or whatever.

The poor natives that are now being worked to death in the mines for little or no compensation at all are constantly assured that their true reward will be waiting for them in Heaven! By and large this strategy worked almost everywhere.

There are only two possibilities here. If there is an afterlife, these folks are getting royally screwed in this life. If there is no afterlife, these folks are getting royally screwed in this life. In summary…these folks are getting royally screwed by the powers that be, by all three branches, the military, the religious folk, and the business class, all of whom are working together to make money on the backs of the original owners of that land.

Do you see here a motive to spread the truth or rather do you see it for what it is: oppression, repression, brainwashing, mind control, and economic exploitation. Always follow the money.

Religion has a long worldwide history of brutality. The Aztecs took it to new highs or lows when their priests would rip the still beating hearts out of the chests of their victims, and this was often done wholesale, by the thousands.

The Chief and the Medicine Man go back a long way. One had executive authority and the other spiritual authority. You could even attribute the Chief's hold to the left-brain and the Witch Doctor's sway over the right-brain. They might at times disagree but basically, just as with the Spanish system, they worked in concert. It is no different today.

Item: 03-23-06 Thursday—President Bush has been on the road all week propping up support for the Iraq War. This Iraq is an artificial country and quite a difficult stew indeed. The Shiites and Sunnis have five 'schools' of which four are Sunni and one is Shiite. The Shiites and Sunnis of Iraq are mostly Arabs. The Kurds are Sunni but non-Arab and they are the strongest separatists. A good book, that I have not yet read, on all of this is *Reaching for Power—The Shi'a in the Modern Arab World* by Yitzhak Nakash.

Item: A forty-one year old Afghan man is facing trial and the death penalty for converting from Islam to Christianity some sixteen years ago. His status as a Christian came out in some family legal squabble. The trial judge has already pre-judged him and stated publicly that it's a humiliation to Islam and that this man's head should be chopped off.

It seems that leaving Islam is a crime punishable by death according to Seria, i.e. Islamic Law. That means if your parents were Muslims than you have to one as well or be beheaded. In other words you cannot use your head to determine your philosophy or choice of religion. So in a way, why would you need a head if you can't use it anyway? Allahu Akbar!—God is Great! Yes God is great, but man can be such an abomination.

In fact Mr. Judge, it is not the man who converted that has humiliated Islam, it is you, sir. You have humiliated and disgraced Islam before the entire world. Is Islam so weak and unsure of itself that the only was to keep believers, nay subjects, is to retain them under threat of death by beheading? Does Islam not have sufficient value, worth, and truth to sustain membership? A reverse application of the Golden Rule to this benighted clod would mean chopping off this judge's head.

As a means of worshipping one's Creator such a law is totally absurd. As a way of building up your organization it makes perfect, if not misguided, sense. These religions are viruses and spread in the same way. As barbaric and harsh as the above appears to us, it is in fact less so than that practiced by Christianity during the Spanish Inquisition. There you not only could not leave Christianity but if you were Jewish you had to become a Christian or be burned alive. We are not different from these Muslims; we are just living in different centuries.

Do you think that the Spanish Inquisition is ancient history and should be forgotten? In 1632 Galileo was put under house arrest for agreeing with Copernicus that the Earth traveled around the Sun. His conviction was rescinded in 1992. Do you have three hundred and sixty years to wait around for a bureaucracy to be forced to spit out the truth?

In 1753 Sorbonne theologians forced Georges Buffon to refute his *Natural History* and state, "I declare that I had no intention to contradict the text of Scripture." In 1878 Alexander Winchell was fired from his position of professor of geology at Vanderbilt for teaching that there were men older than Adam. John Scopes was convicted by Tennessee for teaching Evolution in 1925.

It was in 1987 that the U.S. Supreme Court declared Louisiana's Creationism Act unconstitutional. In 2005 a U.S. District Court Judge had to rule that it was unconstitutional for Pennsylvania to teach Intelligent Design as an alternative to Evolution.

And to its everlasting credit, in 2006, the Vatican Newspaper rejected Intelligent Design stating, "...it does not belong in science."

We need to touch upon war now and again in different contexts. Regarding war and religion, both sides are often praying to the same God. All of our earlier wars were that way, the Revolutionary War, the War of 1812, the Spanish-American War, the Civil War, World War I, and World War II. A minister once said to Lincoln that it was good that God was on our side. Lincoln corrected him and said that what was important was that we were on God's side.

The Iraq War is a misnomer. The Great War aka WW I and WW II were wars. Korea was officially labeled a UN Police Action, but it was unquestionably a war. In a war, each side is relatively balanced and so the casualties are somewhat equal. Korea was definitely a war.

Viet Nam was a war although we had such superiority, particularly in the air that our casualties, though large, were a small fraction of those of our enemy. As soon as I saw those Buddhist monks begin to sit in the street, douse themselves with gasoline, and fire up...I knew we had lost that one.

The first Gulf War was a police action as we lost 148 in battle and 235 by other means, like drunken fights and vehicular accidents. Independent analysts generally agree that the Iraqi death toll was well below initial post-war estimates. In the immediate aftermath of the war, those estimates ranged as high as 100,000 Iraqi troops killed and 300,000 wounded.

According to Gulf War Air Power Survey by Thomas A. Keaney and Eliot A. Cohen, a report commissioned by the U.S. Air Force, there were an estimated 10-12,000 Iraqi combat deaths in the air campaign and as many as 10,000 casualties in the ground war. This analysis is based on enemy prisoner of war reports. The Iraqi government claimed that 2,300 civilians died during the air campaign, most of them during an F-117 Stealth Fighter strike on what was believed to be an Iraqi military communications center in Baghdad. It turned out to be an air raid shelter as well.

One infamous incident during the war highlighted the question of large-scale Iraqi combat deaths. This was the 'bulldozer assault' in which two brigades from the U.S. 1st Infantry Division used anti-mine plows mounted on tanks and combat earthmovers to bury Iraqi soldiers defending the fortified 'Saddam Line'.

While approximately 2,000 of the troops surrendered, escaping burial, one newspaper story reported that the U.S. commanders estimated thousands of Iraqi soldiers had been buried alive during the two-day assault. However, like all other troop estimates made during the war, the estimated 8,000 Iraqi defenders was probably greatly inflated. While one commander, Col. Anthony Moreno of the 2nd Brigade, thought the numbers might have been in the thousands, another reported his brigade buried between 80 and 250 Iraqis. After the war, the Iraqi government claimed to have found 44 such bodies.

When you lose a few hundred and the enemy loses tens of thousands, that is a Police Action. Let me elaborate. If you have two buildings full of an equal number of armed combatants, and they fight each other…that is a war. If a man runs into a building and it is surrounded by one hundred armed men who are after him, that is a police action.

By the above terms, the current Iraq War is really a police action. We took the country apart in a few weeks with limited casualties and have extraordinary superiority in almost all areas. But we are facing guerrilla warfare in a faraway land and that means an ever-mounting number of casualties.

The U.S. is very competent about war. We manage to have a war every ten years or so. That allows us to always have a sufficient number of war-experienced officers and men. We went from WW II to the Korean War, Vietnam, Iraq I and now Iraq II. By contrast the Soviets hadn't been in a war since WW II until Afghanistan and they were in no shape for it. Afghanistan was the beginning of the end for the Soviet Union. We took down the Taliban with the loss of only 221 of our men!

Warfare also allows you to test new weapons, systems, and procedures. Viet Nam was known for helicopter development, the M-16 assault rifle, night vision, defoliants, and many others. The Soviets tried that in Afghanistan. Iraq today is a testing lab for a wide assortment of remarkable devices. There is a glove that cools the wearer's entire body; a super radar that penetrates 12" of concrete to reveal people within a building, enemy fire locators, Wasp Micro Air Vehicles that are drones with 14" wingspans that can loiter for over an hour, 'Combat Zones That See', and a 'Command Post of the Future' a system that allows commanders and troops that are fielding intelligence and other info to share data real time across Iraq.

Did you ever consider the following? We are now struggling to maintain ourselves as the world's only superpower or hyper-power...the world's policeman. There are nuclear weapons all over and many countries without them could quickly produce them if so inclined. The weird and the wild, like North Korea and Iran either have nuclear weapons or are frantically working to produce them. Did it have to be so?

General George S. Patton was clear about what he thought the U.S. should do as Berlin fell and the European Theatre was coming to and end. The Soviets and communism were obviously our next major enemy, and they were on their knees. Europe and Asia were a wreck, but we were at the top of our game. Our country was untouched. Our weapons industries were running full tilt around the clock. We were the only ones who had atomic weapons. Our men were mobilized around the world.

Patton wanted us to take Russia on right then and there. Under those circumstances and especially with the atomic bomb it would have been no contest. Had we stepped up to dominate the planet at that time it would have been relatively easy to do, unlike now. Patton was extremely popular with the American people and the fear was that they would elect him President if he chose to run for that office. There are reasons to believe that General Patton was assassinated by U.S. Army Intelligence and the OSS, forerunner of the CIA.

I am not attempting to state that Patton was assassinated nor that we should have taken that historic opportunity to take formal world control. Certainly the way we did act was extremely honorable and far better than we could expect most other countries to have acted.

War and international competition spur development, so world domination by one country would probably have a tremendous stifling effect on all manner of progress. Still, one has to wonder what the world would be like today had Old Blood and Guts had his way.

The world's history is one of ever-larger groups fighting and combining. Tribes fought other tribes. Cities formed and fought other cities. Nations formed and fought other nations. Then we had two super-powers locked for decades in the Cold War. Obviously were the Earth to be threatened by beings from outer space, then all on Earth would quickly put aside their differences and unite to fight another world. We just seem to need an enemy of one sort or another to hate.

In WW II developed nations fought each other in a hot war. Since then we have sublimated that into cold or economic warfare. President John Kennedy made the race to the moon a warlike endeavor but did it as a peaceful pursuit. Could we not possibly achieve the transcendence to wage war on human overpopulation, ignorance, underdevelopment, starvation, pollution, and hatred as our common world-threatening enemy?

The first rule of politics is to divide and conquer. The sexes are needlessly divided, the races are divided, ethnic groups are divided; and all are pitted against one another. This makes it easy to foster fear and fear is the politician's friend. Fear allows populations to be guided, controlled, and taxed.

In Los Angeles for example, the Latinos are on the Eastside, the Blacks in South Central, and the Whites on the Westside. Each group fears and mistrusts the others. Do the politicians make any efforts to hold common events to bring these groups together? I never saw that in thirty years there.

What do I think about the Iraq War? At this point after I have gone after politicians, religious leaders, schoolteachers, and cops…you probably suspect that I am an anarchist or something like that. Not at all! Anarchists are left wing fanatics and as dangerous as those on the far right. Just imagine a world of more than six billion people with no governments! Fanatics are functionally if not legally incompetent, pure and simple.

It is usually a mistake to attempt to take responsibility where you have no authority, but where you do have authority, responsibility comes along with that authority. It is the misuse and abuse of authority that we seek to shed some light upon. Some of the misuse and abuse of authority is by individuals and some is institutionalized and systemic. Teachers don't get up in the morning and decide to miseducate their students. That is a result of a very old and outdated system that keeps on lumbering forth, propelled by its own massive inertia…and the very powerful teacher's unions don't help the situation.

So what do I think about the Iraq War? Like Bill Maher, I am intrigued by the grand design of fundamentally changing the Middle East in a positive way. If it works out it could be splendid. But it sure is rough going now.

Saddam Hussein was a brutal guy but you have to be brutal to some degree to rule that population. Americans are known for obeying signs, following instructions, and standing in line, but that is hardly the case in most parts of the world. But Saddam was at least a secularist. He couldn't stomach those Muslim fanatics. Saddam always wore a western suit; he fought against our enemy the Ayatollah of Iran, with our help. When we first had that anthrax scare it came out that the anthrax powder was identical to that of Saddam's but that story was quickly killed.

The anthrax in the letters came not from international terrorists, but from a U.S. bio-defense laboratory. Investigators determined the powder was a militarized anthrax strain developed at Fort Deitrick, in Maryland. Another irony is that Hussein got part of his anthrax starter kit from U.S. storehouses, which shipped cultures to Iraq on seven occasions between 1986 and 1988.

I hesitate to bring up the following thought, but will anyway. It in no way intends to trivialize or minimize at all the deaths or severe injuries of our loyal and brave troops over there. If a child of mine was lost there I do not know how I could go on. Nevertheless, when compared with one of the World Wars the number and percentage of casualties is a small fraction of those conflicts. The figures are so low in fact that I wonder how many of these young men, many in their teens, would have died in auto accidents on a weekend night after having too much beer, by racing or fighting or whatever.

Let me make this point as clearly as I can. While they are stationed in Iraq, they are under some heavy supervision by professional military personnel who have experience in dealing with young people in general and young men, at the height of their lifetime testosterone levels, in particular. Even under those conditions these boys manage to roll Humvees and whatnot.

The number of 18 to 25 year old males that kill and injure themselves and others on our highways and rural roads every week is staggering. My question is, what is the danger level comparison of being a young male civilian in the U.S. vs. being in the U.S. Army in Iraq? Is it possibly safer to be in Iraq? I would at least like to see these statistics.

Detractors talk about how many mistakes we made, like standing by and allowing the arms caches to fall into enemy hands and how Iraq has become a magnet that is attracting Jihadists and militant Arabs and fanatical Muslims from throughout the region.

Might that not have been deliberate and correct? Are we not there to fight these people over there rather than over here? Don't we want that small percent who are actually willing to take up arms against us to schlep over there at their own expense, identify themselves and present themselves to us for killing? Wasn't leaving the arms caches around, the bait that attracted them to travel over there at their own expense, identify themselves and present themselves to us for killing?

Do I think we had plans to invade Iraq again for some time? I do. Do I think that the highest levels of the U.S. Government had advanced warning of the 9-11 attacks? I do. Perhaps not in every specific detail but I do think we knew that it was eminent and probably that it would be commercial jets being flown into buildings, especially the Twin Towers. I am not saying that it was so; just that I personally believe that it was so.

In his vain attempt to obtain a FISA warrant, Minnesota FBI Agent Harry Samit testified that he had warned his bosses about Zacarias Moussaoui 70 times before the September 11 attacks, and raised fears that Moussaoui planned to hijack an airliner. He also admitted under cross-examination that he had accused his superiors of 'criminal negligence'.

Another example of many is that of Counter Terrorism Coordinator Richard Clarke who tried repeatedly to warn National Security Advisor Condoleezza Rice about al-Qaeda in early 2001 and was finally told in effect to shut up. I believe that the Administration knew full well what was about to happen and it wanted to maintain deniability.

I also believe that it is quite clear that FDR knew about Pearl Harbor and knew specifically of the looming attack. Further it is now also evident that he had deliberately adopted multifaceted policies, such as an oil embargo, that would virtually force the Japanese to attack us. I also agree completely with FDR's actions.

One thing I have learned never to do is underestimate our government. Remember when there was a general fear that the Japanese were going to buy up America and practically own the whole country? The last straw for many was when they bought Rockefeller Center; actually they bought the underlying mortgage not the title.

It was Calvin Coolidge that said, "The business of this country is business." It turned out that the Japanese had bought 'The Rock' at the top of the market and later sold it at a huge loss. They are just now coming out of a fifteen-year recession that has been Japan's worst ever.

Now it is China that is supposedly making fools of us because of the huge unbalance of trade in their favor. We are getting all their good and they are getting our money.

Look at it like this, the world consist of only two households, yours and your neighbor's. Your neighbor's family works all day, all year to make the most wonderful items and they are all sent to you, for your use and enjoyment. In return you give your neighbor pieces of paper. Whom do you think is getting the better deal?

If you go back to the U.S. prosperity of the 50's, to the good old days, you will find that while it was good for us, that was hardly universally true. Our consumption of the world's natural resources was many, many times our fair share based on our population. Even today with 6% of the world's population we are consuming 22% of all the oil produced. If we became richer and richer as much of the world became poorer and poorer, how long do you think it would be before a majority of countries would unite against us as their common enemy, and start gunning for us?

Let's picture a tribal village with fifty huts. Each hut represents a country. Although we are only one hut in fifty, we are taking in twenty-five percent of all the natural resources. How long would we last? It doesn't matter that we arrived at that position through strength and superior methods and techniques...the situation is untenable. The only lasting solution is for those in the other huts to become richer as we become, at least relatively poorer. Further, the more they are allowed to invest and take profit in our business, the better for all.

In the 50's most moms stayed home and took care of the house and kids. Dad earned enough to buy a home and occasionally a new car. That was then, this is now. Both mom and dad work, some with more than one job. Right there, even if we are somehow maintaining the same relative standard of living, we have become twice as poor if it takes double the work to keep our heads above water.

Our companies and our country are carrying massive debt loads now, rather than assets and cash like they did back then. The Japanese and the Chinese hold vast amounts of U.S. Government bonds and other securities.

A company that is rich in assets and cash with little debt becomes a takeover target. A raider will come in and buy it. Then it will be broken up and its parts sold. The raider takes his enormous profit and moves on. As the richest nation on Earth, we are much safer buried in debt.

Richard Nixon took us off the Gold Standard in 1971. The first OPEC oil embargo was in 1973. Do you think that these events are unrelated? That was when we got serious about equalizing the pressure with the rest of the world. You could think of that as a milestone in the march to globalization.

Item: An FDA advisory committee recommended Wednesday that the agency add information about a possible risk of hallucinations in children to the labels of attention deficit and hyperactivity disorder drugs. The committee also urged the FDA to develop a consumer-friendly medication guide explaining to parents that they should talk to their child's doctor about stopping the medication should hallucinations occur. This MedGuide also should note that ADHD drugs might increase the risk of aggressive behavior, although that can be a component of the disorder itself. And the guide should note that the drugs might increase the risk of heart attack, stroke or sudden death in patients who have undiagnosed heart problems.

Current labeling for the ADHD drugs, Adderall, Focalin, Concerta, Metadate, Methylin, Ritalin and Dexedrine, does not mention the possibility of hallucinations in patients with no history of them. "We read case upon case of these children who do experience these hallucinations, that is something that really struck all the reviewers. It is unlikely that the ADHD drugs are simply unmasking a previously undiagnosed psychiatric disorder that would explain the hallucinations."

Despite the above, the panel did not feel that the risk of hallucinations warranted a 'black box' warning, the strongest type of warning. In 2004, Nelson's panel did recommend a black box warning about suicidal behavior in children and adolescents who take SSRI, selective serotonin reuptake inhibitor, antidepressants. "In this case, you have overwhelming evidence of efficacy," Nelson said, adding that a black box might unnecessarily scare parents away from treatment.

The ADHD drug Strattera already has a black box warning about suicidal thoughts because of evidence from clinical trials, but no other ADHD drug label yet carries any information on suicidal thoughts.

Item: Death from Ritalin—Between the years of 1990-2000 over 569 children were hospitalized, 38 of them with life threatening hospitalizations, and 186 died. 12-year-old Adrian David Wade was born on November 09, 1991. 115 days after taking Strattera, with no signs, he committed suicide on October 23, 2004.

I singled out the above death because of what the father said afterward, "I even thought this drug was so wonderful I also put my youngest child on it. Two days later my 12 yr old son was dead. My son's suicide came out of the blue. He did not show any of the typical signs of depression, if any at all."

Launched in 2003, Strattera has been widely regarded as a safer alternative to the amphetamine-like medicines, such as Novartis's Ritalin and Shire Pharmaceuticals Group's Adderall, that have long been used to treat ADHD. That's largely because Strattera is the first nonstimulant prescription for ADHD, and hence doesn't pose the risk of substance abuse that the older drugs do.

Concern about Strattera's potential to induce extreme mood swings, which can lead to suicidal thinking, were noted in the Sept. 3, 2004, issue of the journal *Pediatrics*. The doctors, Theodore Henderson of Denver and Keith Hartman of Osceola, Wisconsin noted that a third of 153 children treated with Strattera at two clinics in their areas manifested extreme irritability, aggression or mania, a state of wild excitement typified by racing thoughts, insomnia, and inappropriate acts, soon after going on the drug.

Three had to be hospitalized, including one 11-year-old boy who stripped off his clothes, covered his body with markings using a felt-tipped pen, flew into a screaming rage and threatened family members with a sword belonging to his father. Three others were incarcerated in juvenile detention centers for violent behaviors.

There have been similar concerns about other ADHD drugs. Earlier this year the agency said that it planned to add cautionary language about psychiatric side effects, including aggression and suicidal thoughts, to the labels of several of the medicines, including Johnson & Johnson's Concerta, a time released form of Ritalin. Dr. Laughren says the agency also plans to ask Lilly to include a stronger caution on Strattera's label about its risk of inducing mania and similar mood destabilization, along with the new 'black box' warning out this week.

The message that patients using psychiatric drugs should be carefully monitored for possible mood destabilization, including suicidal thoughts is becoming a familiar one. Last year, the FDA warned that a class of antidepressants called SSRIs, such as Pfizer's Zoloft and GlaxoSmithKline's Paxil, have been shown in clinical trials to double the risk of suicidal thinking and behavior in children and adolescents compared with those given a placebo. About 4% of patients on the drugs experienced such symptoms, compared with 2% on dummy pills.

Indeed, the heightened concern about Strattera is part of a bigger, ongoing examination in medicine about the risks of widely prescribing psychotropic drugs to youngsters with relatively mild symptoms of depression, ADHD or other mental disorders. Says Dr. Henderson: "The bar has been raised for prescribing psychotropic medicines to kids."

Again the medium is the message. What could be a worse message to give to youngsters than that the answer to your problems is to be found in drugs? These kids and others not on them medically are already using ADHD drugs to 'party on'. What else could you reasonably expect to happen?

There is a Spanish saying that goes something like, "Dejar de luchar es comenzar a morir." Meaning that life is a struggle and when we stop struggling we begin to die. Drugs are certainly not the answer for our pampered kids without meaningful work to do.

13:30 ON
03-23-06 Thursday—Time for my 14:00 appointment at Affinity Massage with Greta. Oh what a relief it is! Stopped next door at the newly reopened MLK Library. What a nice Art Deco beautifully restored building it is. They have a Northwest Reference Room for in-house reading only. This is a veritable treasure trove of information, much of which I could surely use.
16:30 OFF

How far do you plan ahead for your family? Is it five years, ten years, maybe twenty years? How far ahead do you think the U.S. Government should plan ahead? Perhaps twenty-five years, fifty years, one hundred years, or more in some cases?

Our countries future, economy, and various other aspects are plotted on supercomputers. One can plug in different variables for the models and project out the most likely outcomes. Many complain that both parties, the Republican and the Democratic Parties have become more and more alike. Is that really surprising?

The shape of automobiles has become more and more alike as well. When you use a wind tunnel and computer analysis to determine the automobile shape with the least drag and therefore the best mileage potential, naturally everyone comes up with the same shape.

If the course of our country is plotted out at least a decade in advance, just how much influence can you expect that a four year Presidential Election cycle will have on current events? Did George W. or Dick Cheney single handedly take us into Iraq or were we destined to go into Iraq and that is what we needed the Texans for?

Item 03-24-06—Young preacher, Matthew Winkler was found shot to death. His wife and three small children have been found four hundred miles away. The wife has confessed to the crime.

Item: American Justice—The story told of John Emil List, a strictly raised devout Lutheran who had financial problems and was facing bankruptcy. Rather than have his family deal with the evils of poverty, and to insure their immediate entry into Heaven, John murdered his mother, wife, and three children. He was at large for seventeen years.

Item: A national panel of scientists reported Wednesday morning that the Feds are allowing too much fluoride in drinking water. This is putting children at risk of sever tooth enamel damage and adults prone to weakening of bones that could cause fractures. The EPA requested that the National Academies' National Research Council re-examine the current standard that allows up to four milligrams of fluoride per liter of water.

Adrienne, so you think this whole enchilada should be published in book form do you! I appreciate your enthusiasm but don't see how it could be done. Beyond the extreme difficulty of publishing any book these days, we would need our client's approval, and this is a work-product. Not to mention that I would probably reap sacks of hate mail for the rest of my life…or worse! If you want to peek into the pit of Hell…just poke a Bible thumper or a Jesus freak.

In addition I am working on behalf of Bremo and this town is full of churches. Of all the towns I have lived in, I love Bremo like no other, but I am not a product of this area. My notions would probably not sit all that well among many of the townspeople.

Now you have me wondering if I would write this differently, if I thought it would ever be published. Probably I would not. I am what is known as an automatic writer, or in this case an automatic recorder, and this stuff is just flowing and streaming, beyond that, ever since I worked for the government I automatically write with the potential of third-party review somewhere in the back of my mind.

What really keeps getting to me is how this endeavor seems to be acting as a magnet for material. No sooner due I raise a subject here but useful data starts flowing in by newspaper, mail, radio and TV, email, online and cable news, and person to person. I appreciate and look for synchronicity, but this is overwhelming. I can now in my own very small way, understand what Michelangelo's answer meant when he was asked how he had managed to make such an incredible number of statues during his lifetime. His reply was to the effect that he just got up each morning, wearily picked up his hammer and chisel and went to the marble. From that point on, some seemingly outside force took over and used his body to bang away on the stone all day.

You may wonder if I want to destroy all the church buildings. No, not at all. That is not about to happen. People need their religion. Religion has been called everything from a security blanket to the opiate of the masses. In 1927 Sigmund Freud published his *The Future of an Illusion,* in which he called for the shedding of the 'burdens of religious doctrines.' It hasn't happened yet. The communists did away with religion but that didn't work out either.

Church congregations can be wonderful social entities and serve many worthwhile purposes. Many have outreach programs that help disturbed children and the homeless. They have been historically a social center and place of refuge for immigrants. What I am railing against is the dogma and nonsense and the ruinous attempts to make more out of these millennia old writings than can reasonably be made. Once you pretend that the writings of man are the word of God you have opened Pandora's Box. In the misguided, at best, name of goodness you allow the darkest primeval reaches of the human psyche to justify every heinous crime imaginable against humanity.

Bear in mind that: The devil can cite Scripture for his purpose. — William Shakespeare.

If the so-called Holy Books were simply viewed and used for what they are, as ancient reference works, written by many authors, spinmeisters, committees, councils like those of Nicaea, and so forth; there would be no particular problem. But once you convince or imprint people with the lie that these books are the word of God, they are doomed. It is the mental struggle to reconcile all the irreconcilable contradictions that drives men bat-shit. How could anyone actually believe that the Creator of our Universe could have made such a total blunder out of just writing a book?

There is much good that can be learned from the Bible when seen for what it is, ancient writings. I have certainly not studied it personally but you can't help but pick up one thing and another. I understand that the Bible says something about, "...neither a borrower nor a lender be." I live by that, at least as it applies to friends and relatives, and have no doubt saved myself a lot of grief. If I can't break your legs...why would I loan you money? That last bit may not be Biblical...more likely Sammy the Shark.

I am getting off the track here, but did you ever notice that it is those people who distain money, if not downright shun it, who bad mouth those to whom money is important...that sooner or later, it is always those same people who hit on you for a loan? And then get all huffy when you turn them down! And of course if you are fool enough to make them the loan, they never pay you back.

Some of my best friends are flakes; in fact my best friend is a flake. I will do anything for my friends except loan them money. I might give them some money, but never a loan. Your friends and relatives are too important to destroy the relationship over money.

And I am not knocking flakes. If I were drowning near a road, would I want a couple on their way to church to come by or a flake? Give me a flake anytime. The church couple would be all dressed up and probably quickly look the other way as they proceeded to their front row pew. The flake would be most likely to stop and get all wet helping me out. He would then be a day late and a dollar short when he arrived at his original destination...as always.

Those brave clods that flew those commercial aircraft laden with innocent people into the World Trade Center's Twin Towers that were filled with innocent civilians from around the globe, those psychopaths thought that they were going strictly by a Holy Book. I really shouldn't pick on the Muslims here because the examples are endless and Christianity has more than its fair share.

A big problem with organizing spirituality into an organized religion is that the two are fundamentally incompatible. When you introduce hierarchy and money, spirituality gets the short end of the stick. Alcoholics Anonymous works better than any other program for good reason. If you are forced into a regular alcoholic treatment program you generally pay a huge amount of money and have a group leader with the authority to spring a UA, Urine Analysis, test on you, kick you out of the program, and perhaps even send you to the slammer.

With Alcoholics Anonymous there is neither financial burden nor an authority hierarchy. Each meeting attendee may put a dollar into the hat when it passes by, or not. The meetings are chaired and secretaried by members of the group and chosen by them for whatever period of time that the group wishes.

In this atmosphere spirituality and sincere goodwill abound. In fact I know of no other like situation, and have suspected that it is allowed to flourish only because these folks are so potentially dangerous as drunk drivers who can take anyone out at random; that the powers that be see no other choice but to allow this spirituality and deference to a Higher Power to flourish, without someone making money off of it. Yes I am surely a Doubting Thomas.

What I would like a reader of this to do is to stop sleepwalking through life and wake up. Just examine things and use the abilities that you received from your Creator. If you believe in an afterlife and Judgment Day, consider what that would mean. If you are just a follower who swallows everything hook, line and sinker, what would you have done in the days when young maidens were heaved into volcanoes in hopes of better weather from the rain god?

Well, you would have attended the service. You would have contributed your beloved daughter if asked. You would have gone along with the whole ignorant horror of it all. Then when it was your turn on Judgment Day, how do you think you would have fared?

You could offer the excuse that you didn't bother to use your brain, or follow your instincts concerning your daughter, because it was easier to just go along with the herd. Hey, everyone else was doing it! But what would be the point of Judgment Day if that old dodge would fly? All of Hitler's minions, and Stalin's and Pol Pot's and everyone else would be saying the exact same thing. Wake up, use it or lose it!

Item 03-24-06 Friday—Ominous Signs in Arctic Thaw—Thirty miles from the Arctic Circle, hunter Noah Metuq feels the Arctic changing. Fish and wildlife are following the retreating ice caps northward. Polar bears are losing the ice floes they need for hunting. NASA satellites have measured a meltdown of the ice sheets in Greenland and Antarctica in the past decade. Scientists in Colorado say the ice cap retreat in 2006 may be as large as that in 2005, probably the largest in the past century. The hardy Intuit are the "sentries for the rest of the world. They are the early warning. They see what is happening to the planet."

Do you remember as a child, putting one hand on an iron pole of some sort and spinning around until you got so dizzy that your mind was swirling and you could not walk a straight line or perhaps even stand up?

Our planet's circumference at the equator is about 24,900 miles or 40,000 kilometers. The Earth spins that much in one day of 24 hours. That means people on the Equator are traveling over 1,000 mph due to planetary rotation alone. Meanwhile someone standing at either pole would not be moving at all. Another good reason why it makes sense that all the favored nations have scientists stationed in Antarctica.

The folks who live somewhere between a pole and the Equator move at various speeds in between those mentioned above. Could this be another reason why the country nearest the pole usually wins a war with those closer to the Equator? Those guys near the Equator are just a bit dizzy?

Have you ever attempted to calculate just how fast you are moving by combining all of your known speeds? Our distance from the Sun is about 93 million miles, so times 2 pi gives us a circumference of 584 million miles. We travel that each year, so 365 days times 24 hours gives us 8,760 hours in one year. When you divide that into the 584 million miles, you get a speed of 66,666 mph. Thus if you live on the Equator you are traveling 1,000 mph plus another 66,666 mph.

But it does not end there does it? Our entire solar system is rotating around the center of our Milky Way Galaxy. The sun is about 26,000 light-years from the center of our galaxy, which is about 80,000 to 120,000 light-years across, and less than 7,000 light-years thick. We are located on one of its spiral arms, out towards the edge. It takes the sun, and our solar system, roughly 200-250 million years to orbit once around the Milky Way. In this orbit, we are traveling at a speed of about 558,000 mph.

But wait, there's more. The Milky Way Galaxy is just one galaxy in a group of galaxies called the Local Group. Within the Local Group, the Milky Way Galaxy is moving about 666,000 mph. Strange how this number 666 keeps coming up. We now have that fellow on the Equator traveling at 1,291,666 mph! And we are not done yet as the Universe is still exploding outward from the Big Bang!

Each day we wake up thinking we are in the same place, but at over 1.3 million mph, how far do we actually travel during our lifetime? An hour from now you will be well over a 1.3 million miles from where you are right now!

For those poor souls who are putting their faith into The Rapture, if you can ever get our speed up to that of light, the moment that we hit the speed of light, time would stop and we would all enter eternity spontaneously! But please don't hold your breath.

At this point you may well be asking yourself, "What is this lunatic off on now…I thought he was raving about religion?" Well that is what it was suppose to be, but to tell you the truth I must have gotten some bad oysters or something. If I am going to have vertigo…you are going to have vertigo.

Item: 03-24-06 Friday—Pope Benedict XVI has appointed 15 new cardinals. They were promoted from archbishop and are now considered to be Princes of the Church. Twelve of the fifteen are currently under age 80, making them potentially eligible to vote in a conclave to elect Pope Benedict's successor. There are now 193 cardinals in total, of whom 73 will be over 80 years of age. The total permitted to vote in a conclave to elect a new pontiff is 120, a limit established by Pope Paul VI in 1973.

The appointment of Hong Kong Archbishop Joseph Zen, an outspoken campaigner for religious freedom in China, signals that China is very important to Pope Benedict. The appointments are seen as a leading indicator of the Pope's intentions.

The Roman Catholic Church does its best work in the most primitive societies. Central and South American thinkers have long known that they must move from Catholicism to Protestantism if they are to continue to develop further. It is no surprise that the Catholic Church is growing at its fastest rate in Africa.

I would have no problem at all with the Roman Church doing its thing in Africa as a way for those folks to make a positive upward transition, if it weren't for their stand against birth control. That alone is so morally reprehensible as to in my mind be one of the worst crimes against humanity imaginable. And the only reason, the real reason, is just to swell their numbers…like a newspaper increasing its circulation.

Beyond that, the AIDS epidemic is devastating Africa and the Catholic Church's opposition to the use of condoms is like throwing gasoline on a fire. Shame on you! Would we allow any non-religious group to get away with that without comment? But since it falls under the shield of a religious organization it gets by with it. We may think, yes it is horrid but that is how those people are.

Well, if it is wrong and harmful, stop them, whoever they are. People have been speculating on the arrival of the Antichrist for centuries. What if he has already been here for centuries and is here now? Doesn't it look like it? Could we have possibly slaughtered more people in the twentieth century than the tens of millions that we did? Wake up and smell the cordite and the napalm.

Looking for the Antichrist is like looking for the Lost Tribes of Israel. If you take the number of people in the lost tribes and extrapolate the population up to today, you are looking for maybe 500 million people. This is just one more case of not being able to see the forest for the trees.

I have been beating up on the Popes for good reason but a man like John Paul II is richly deserving of praise for his courage in standing up to the Communists when he was a young man in Poland and afterward as Pope. He certainly seemed sincere, well-meaning, holy, and all of that. Nothing however can excuse the Church's stance favoring increased human population; not with tens of thousands now starving daily and the entire planet under increasing stress.

The so-called Pro-Life people, you know…the ones who love the death penalty, are forever yammering that abortion is murder, even the morning-after pill. Well then, what do you call promoting overpopulation on a planet already so dangerously overrun with human beings that the ecosystems are dying along with tens of thousands of actual people, not zygotes, but living people are dying by starvation on a daily basis? I could justifiably call that the mass murder by criminal policy of over ten million people per year.

When human overpopulation is the root cause of almost every ill on this Earth, why are our best minds not making the needed recommendations as opposed to the matter being largely left in the hands of mostly well-meaning but desperately ignorant people who are guiding their lives and our planetary destruction based on the musings and mutterings of ancient illiterate mystics? How can this possibly be?

We have truth in lending laws and truth in advertising laws and the like, but as soon as something falls under the heading of religion, all bets are off, and anything goes. If a teacher began telling her students that two plus two equaled five, it would be quickly stopped and corrected, but a religious leader, and anybody and everybody can become one overnight, can fill the heads of people with the most preposterous and dangerous misinformation known to man without any repercussion.

Let's get real and face life squarely. Life is beautiful. Life is magnificent. But the Earth is not Disneyland, it is an abattoir, a slaughterhouse if you will. Every fraction of every second, trillions of trillions upon trillions of life forms are killed and consumed by other life forms. Life feeds on life. That is how it is. That is how God made it. God made man and man made Disneyland. At the moment of our birth, our death certificate is signed. No one gets out of here alive. We shouldn't want it any other way.

Being at the top of the food chain makes it easier to ignore this reality, at least on the surface. Even so, the food chain like everything else is not a straight line but a cycle, a circle. We are born with the worm eggs inside us that will one day consume us. We are on the menu of rats.

Rats mirror the human population at about seventy-five percent. A town of ten thousand people will have about 7,500 rats. A city of ten million will have over seven million rats. When you see a picture or cartoon of a graveyard, what do you often see depicted there? Rats! Now if you were a rat that ate old dead people, what would your dream be? Probably it would be eating a fresh new baby. Does that not happen in the worst slums? Or what about drunks passed out in alleys that awake to find parts of their face, fingers and ears nibbled off?

Rats are a lot like us, which is why they are so valuable as research animals. Recall the 1960 movie, The Time Machine by H.G. Wells. It tells of a future where there are two races, the above ground Eloi, a mild gentle race, and a cannibalistic underground race, the Morlachs.

At the time of the dinosaurs our ancestors were tiny shrew-like critters. Obviously at some point, we and rats had a common ancestor. I wonder when we decided to stay above ground and they went underground? It is only because we and rats are so much alike that they are used all day long in medical experiments, both physically and psychologically. We don't call it a rat race for nothing. People and rats react to stress often in similar ways, even to becoming homosexual when packed to closely and overstressed, like in our prisons.

My Saturday newspaper has a large article with pictures titled Rat Fancy. It begins by telling about the Pacific NW Rat Fancier Club's fifth annual show where rats are judged for Best of Show. The North American Rat Registry has been working on a national database of pedigrees. So far they have 8,600 registered. Rats learn their names and do tricks. "Once you go rat, you never go back."

Item 03-25-06 Saturday—NPR's Car Talk [www.cartalk.com/]—A reasonably sized beer belly acts as an internal airbag that enhances survivability of men in auto accidents. Finally some really good news!

Item: Mary Winkler, 32, was arrested on murder charges and confessed to the slaying of her husband of ten years, Matthew Winkler, a popular charismatic Fundamentalist Christian Church pastor. Mary had fled from Tennessee to Alabama with her three daughters who were present at the murder. The poor Golden Rule.

Item: A tortoise has died in a zoo at the venerable age of 255. The giant Aldabra tortoise was brought by British seamen from the Seychelles Islands as a gift to Robert Clive of the British East India Company. Clive died in 1774. For many years the tortoise had been living in a zoo in the East Indian city of Kolkata, formerly known as Calcutta, where it was one of the star attractions.

Adwaitya, The Only One, spent his early days in Robert Clive's garden. He was later transferred to the Alipore zoo after it opened in 1875 and delighted the zoo visitors for 131 years. Records show the tortoise was born in 1750, but some have claimed he was born in 1705. The zoo will use carbon dating to determine his true age. I guess there is something to be said for life in the slow lane!

Item: Barbara Bush's donation to the Bush-Clinton Houston Hurricane Katrina Relief Fund required that some of her gift be spent on software from her son Neil Bush's Texas firm. "Donors who direct that their money be used to buy products from a family business set a bad precedent. If everybody started doing that, it would ruin our whole system for tax-exempt organizations, because people would be using them to benefit their business rather than for the public benefit.

That's not why our government gives tax deductions for donations. I hope other donors across the country don't start dictating that their contributions go to their family business. That would be a rip-off of our tax system," said Daniel Borochoff, President of the American Institute of Philanthropy, a charity watchdog group.

The software firm in question is Austin-based Ignite Learning. It has investors in the United Arab Emirates. I have deliberately avoided the whole political firestorm over Dubai Ports World and the attempt to have this UAE outfit help run six U.S. ports. The matter is complex and just too easy and perhaps tempting to demagogue.

Item: We are building four huge bases in Iraq with franchises like Burger King, Pizza Hut and even a car dealership. It doesn't look like we are about to pull out anytime soon.

Item: According to this Pew poll, Americans favor torturing detainees in some circumstances by a wide margin. Most disturbing are the high numbers of self-described Christians favoring torture: only 26 percent of Catholics oppose it in all circumstances, while only 31 percent of white Protestants rule it out entirely. If you combine those Christians who think torture is either never or only rarely acceptable, you have 42 percent of Catholics and 49 percent of white Protestants.

The comparable statistic of those who are described as secular, which I presume means agnostic or atheist, is 57 percent opposition. In other words, if you are an American Christian, you are far more likely to support torture than if you are an atheist or an agnostic. Christians for torture…it's a new constituency!

Item: One man in the cross hairs is Dr James Hansen, director of NASA's Goddard Institute for Space Studies, GISS. You may remember him from his announcement that 2005 was the hottest year in a century. According to an article in the New York Times, the White House has been attempting to gag Dr Hansen following a speech he gave calling for reduced CO_2 emissions in order to curb climatic change.

The scientist, James E. Hansen, longtime director of the agency's Goddard Institute for Space Studies said in an interview that officials at NASA headquarters had ordered the public affairs staff to review his coming lectures, papers, postings on the Goddard Web site, and requests for interviews from journalists. Dr. Hansen said he would ignore the restrictions. "They feel their job is to be the censor of information going out to the public," he said.

This news comes at the same time that the UK government, who along with most of the rest of the world can accept reality for what it is, have issued a report concerning the likelihood that the Greenland ice cap will melt, raising sea levels by seven meters, over twenty one feet. Environment Secretary Margaret Beckett said the report's conclusions would be a shock to many people. "The thing that is perhaps not so familiar to members of the public... is this notion that we could come to a tipping point where global change could be irreversible," she told the BBC. Meanwhile transplanted oil lobbyists are in the White House acting under the ostensible guise of environmental protectors.

Sadly, it is yet another in a series of scientific papers, official reports and assessments that have become increasingly pessimistic over the past few years. Whereas interviews with scientists always used to stress the possibility that a concerted global effort might alleviate the problem of global warming, these days it seems everyone is starting to resign themselves to our eventual fate. Meanwhile we have these dying old rich men killing our Mother Earth for cash...men who already have far, far more than they will ever need.

If you want to scare yourself out of your socks, read *The Weather Makers* by Australian biologist Tim Flannery [www.theweathermakers.com/] and *Field Notes From a Catastrophe* by journalist Elizabeth Kolbert.

People are motivated largely by the two opposite emotions of greed and fear. Stocks move up climbing a wall of greed, people hoping it will go ever higher, far past the true value; and then they come crashing down, with panic selling driven by fear of ever lower prices, way below a reasonable value.

Item: 03-26-06 Sunday—Nationally recognized Bremo's Gold Mountain Golf Complex to host the July 10-15 U.S. Amateur Public Links event. Admission to the Public Links is free.

Item: 03-27-06 Monday—Kitsap County Seeks a Vision for the Future—Kitsap needs to find room for 100,000 new residents over the next twenty years.

According to a Harvard and Princeton poverty experts, and counting Black inmates normally left out of Federal jobless studies, the real jobless rate for Black male high school dropouts in their twenties, soared to 65% in 2000! So if you drop out of school, speak Black English, and can't get drafted by pro-sports and make it as a rapper; it look pretty bleak. Wake up Black Community!

Item: 03-28-06 Tuesday—What a total bummer, circumstances forced me to blow off the Tuesday YMCA Dedication! Not that the $10 Gs wasn't for a good cause and with effort I can compensate for civic heavyweight contacts but I was looking forward to meeting Mayor Bozeman and talking to those little rascals. I must remember that the Universe is unfolding exactly as it should be.

What a great organization, the YMCA is. One that actually does live up to what are supposed to be Christian principles. That is Christian as in Jesus Christ, not mega-business. I had never really thought much about the YMCA before, nor did I ever plan a lifelong affiliation. In the early 50's the boy next door and I would take an intercity bus each day and go to the YMCA in Pawtucket, RI. Those were always good times. It was ten years later when I pulled into LA from my cross-country bike run in 1964 that I stayed at the YMCA in downtown Los Angeles on

Hope Street. That area is all gone now and replaced by the Bunker Hill Redevelopment Project.

It was perhaps another fourteen years later when I began running marathons. I ran the first one over the Coronado Island Bridge in San Diego and ended up in Charger Stadium. Less than thirty days later I ran my second one in San Francisco. It started at the YMCA I think on the Embarcadero, went over the Golden Gate Bridge, up around to Sausalito and was just beautiful. It ended on some Heartbreak Hill and a hydrofoil returned us to San Francisco. That YMCA had a really great location. It was then perhaps twenty-five years later when Xiao-Ping and I noticed a local dance with 50's music and it was at this Bremo YMCA.

Gifts are both horizontal and vertical. When you exchange birthday or Christmas gifts with someone, that is a horizontal gift. Examples of vertical giving are when a mentor helps you in life. You don't pay that person back. That person is making good on help they received long ago from someone who mentored them. Your turn to pay that debt will come years in the future when you mentor a younger person yourself. And so it was with my donation here. I am indebted to this YMCA for giving me such a splendid opportunity to discharge, at least partially, some very old debts.

Vertical or intergenerational giving is as old as humanity. It is one of those wondrous things that bind us together and advance our evolution as a species. This is just one more vital aspect of life that is not taught in school. Has anyone bothered to sit down and enumerate what the learning goals should be for our children, to justify the sacrificing of most of the best years of their life, in order to attend these mandatory classes?

An interesting side-note, when I was talking earlier with Glen Godfrey the Executive Director for this YMCA facility, I had described that old four story brick YMCA building in Pawtucket, RI. It had a swimming pool in the basement and a basketball court with a tall ceiling and a running track that ran along a mezzanine over the court. Glen had gone to a YMCA as a boy somewhere in the Midwest or certainly very far from RI and his YMCA was identical to mine. This was like an early McDonald's franchise that had erected identical buildings all over the country.

Item: 03-29-06 Wednesday—A charity foundation's former accountant pleaded guilty to embezzling $237,000 from a heart disease research fund to pay a dominatrix to beat him. Well, he did get that part right about his needing a good beating.

I have just pulled a double all-nighter. Sometime around four or five this morning I began watching a cable movie *The Village* with an interesting cast of Joaquin Phoenix, William Hurt, Sigourney Weaver, Adrien Brody, and Bryce Howard. I thought that Brody was Brazilian as he is all the rage down there, but in fact he was born in NYC. His mother is the Hungarian-born photojournalist Sylvia Plachy, and he attended the American Academy of Dramatic Arts and High School for the Performing Arts. Adrien grew up an only child in Woodhaven, Queens, where he often accompanied his mother on assignments for the Village Voice.

Anyway this weird movie had a religious sect living a 19th century life out in the woods. The well-meaning church Elders had told the group a pack of silly lies to keep them from leaving. Basically they had invented a really scary creature that roamed around and they had even constructed one. After a murder was committed and a blind girl had successfully gone to town and back, the Elders took a vote on whether or not they thought it would be a good idea to continue foisting this pack of lies on their congregation, or to tell them the truth. They quite proudly, happily, and unanimously voted to continue teaching the lies!

Maybe it makes sense when dealing with primitive people who are still talking to tree spirits, to make up some wild stories that they are inclined to believe. But why on Earth would we in the United States today think that it is a good idea to fill children's heads with ridiculous stories, absurd tales and just plain lies and bogus information? When you put garbage in…you don't get rational thought out.

Teach them ethics and sound philosophy instead. I was really struck when watching TV in China, how different the programming was from what you get here. The shows, other than the soap operas, both modern and Imperial times, strove to be high-minded, educational, and positively motivational. They had all the Discovery, History Channel, Biography, and learning shows. What they did not have was all the senseless and gratuitous violence, the car chases going the wrong way on the freeways, the ever more exploding automobiles, drive-by shootings and all that soul destroying crap.

Not that the Chinese are angels by any means but they make an effort not to poison their airways and the children's minds. We used to do that here. I mentioned Popeye, how about Howdy Doody? It does seem kind of dumb now but the theme was to condition youngsters to be friendly and say howdy to people. Or Mr. Rodger's Neighborhood…that is a far cry from very young children getting wasted in botched drive-by shootings.

Item: 03-30-06 Thursday—The 2005-06 flu vaccines were for type A influenza, but the type of flu that folks are getting is type B from Hong Kong. That pesky bug doesn't seem to realize that Evolution doesn't exist.

Item: Puget Sound Steelhead are being proposed by the Feds for listings as a Threatened species.

Item: That Afghan man threatened with death for conversion to Christianity received asylum in Italy, over the objections of some Afghan lawmakers who didn't want him to leave with his head on his shoulders. There was so much clout from the U.S. and the Pope that he was declared non compos mentis, balmy, and spirited out of the country.

Item: I couldn't make this stuff up! In early January twelve of West Virginia's thirteen miners were pulled out of the mine deceased, and the sole surviving miner, Randall L. McCloy Jr. survived. Yesterday it was on TV that the street that Randall lives on has been renamed Miracle Road. Medics estimate that had he been trapped another four minutes he would have died. No laws of physics were violated, no Divine intervention, just a near miss. It is just so important to our Elders that we remain buried in a swamp of lies and misinformation that they will even re-name streets.

These snow jobs are everywhere. The busier and more overworked we become, the easier it is to perpetrate them upon us. I mentioned that I had made a bundle in the stock market. Almost daily I get mailers promising to make me rich. From my experience the advice contained in these mailers will affect you financially all right…they will make you broke. Why would these people who profess to know how to make people rich spend their time trying to make you wealthy, rather then themselves?

Around 1997 I received a newsletter from the famous Louis Rukeyser. In it, all or most of the stock analysts, strongly advised buying Chesapeake Energy, CHK at somewhere between $20-30 per share. I bought one hundred shares at a coast of over two thousand dollars. I didn't pay any attention to it. In 1998 when I was in Maine I finally checked on it and it was trading for under a dollar making my holding worth maybe $65!

My first thought was horror and I planned to dump it immediately but then I reasoned that the gas and oil were still in the ground and the long-term charts showed that the prices were very cyclical. The more I studied it the more I believed that CHK would someday again hit $30. Then the oilmen, the Bush Administration, captured the White House. Now it was to me a no-brainer. I figured that if I had 33,333 shares and it hit $30 I would have a million dollars.

I eventually accumulated 35,000 shares at a couple or so dollars per share. Six months ago CHK broke $40, making 35,000 shares worth 1.4 million dollars. Here is the interesting part, when CHK was going for $1, $2, $4, and so on, nobody was telling me to buy it. But when it eventually again reached over $20 and $30 all kinds of creatures crawled out from under their rocks and urged the purchase of CHK. The more you listen to this sort of advice the more certainly are you doomed.

What is going on here is that the people in the know are buying stocks at the bottom of their cycles when they are low and then when they reach near the top of the cycles they tell you to buy it. That way they can bail out at the highest possible level and leave you holding the bag. Now doesn't that make a lot more sense then that these money-loving guys are getting up early every morning trying to make you rich?

The above is a vast over-simplification. There are numerous dodges and outright scams like those run using worthless stocks by the pump and dump artists who send unsolicited stock advice where they give you the name of the miracle stock for free. This is a mob favorite. But so much of the data streams that we are increasingly inundated with make no attempt to tell us or our kids the truth or inform us of something that might be good for us. Instead they tell us what we want to hear and then rip us off or make us sick, over and over again.

Like attracts like, nutcases often work in the psychiatric field, sadist often work in prisons, pedophiles are found in and around schools and Boy Scout troops, and people who love money gravitate toward money sectors like the stock market, or banks, or whatever. Their motive is not to make money for you, what they want is to take your money or at least make as much money as possible off of you.

Item: 03-31-06 Friday—Nine Year Study Shows Prayer had No Beneficial Effect. In the largest scientific test of its kind, heart surgery patients showed no benefit whatever when strangers prayed for their recovery. And patients who knew that they were being prayed for had a higher rate of complications!

Forgive me but this reminds me of an old story. Sam from Boston was visiting Jerusalem. Each day his walk would take him past the Wailing Wall. Standing and praying at the wall each time he passed was an old Jewish man.

It didn't matter if Sam walked by at 7AM, Noon, 4PM or even later, he would always see this same man praying. Finally Sam approached him and asked how long he had been coming to the wall and what he was praying for.

The old man replied that he had been praying at the wall for almost thirty years. He stated that in the morning he prayed for peace and brotherhood among all of God's children and in the afternoon he prayed for an end to disease and hunger.

"Wow," said Sam. "That is really remarkable! What does doing all that for so long make you feel like?"

The old man replied, "I feel like I have been talking to a stone wall!"

I am not speaking against prayer, just being realistic. Praying for others may be a complete waste of time but that doesn't mean that it can't have a beneficial affect on the one doing the praying. It has been said that prayer is asking God the question, and that meditation is calming your mind so that you may receive the answer. We ought never to underestimate the transforming power of imagination. Many breakthroughs can come to us when we are meditating or are asleep.

Living a life of good karmic deeds and following true spiritual laws, in my experience, are immensely fruitful. Pretending that there is an invisible fellow in the sky whom you can treat like Santa Claus and submit detailed requests to is not only a dreadful waste of effort but the lack of positive response to your devotion and the following of nonsensical rules can lead to mental problems and depression. The thing to bear in mind is that: God helps those who help themselves.

We not only treat our zoo animals much better than humans, at least as far as diet is concerned; but we will treat our robots far better than our fellow humans. NOVA last night had the Desert Robot Race. Major outfits and Universities like Carnegie-Mellon compete each year to create robot vehicles that can avoid obstacles and win the race.

It is very difficult and last year they all failed rather miserably. DARPA [Defense Advanced Research Projects Agency] those tricky guys who created the Internet, are behind it. Can you imagine anyone deliberately programming these costly robots with nonsense, lies, and garbage?

Lies may seem comforting but there is always a heavy price to pay. People who pray and go to church and believe that this will insure that God will be kind to them are being set up for double tragedy and magical thinking. Additionally, note the insightful epigraph at the end of the movie Capote that reads, "More tears are shed over answered prayers than unanswered ones."

When bad things inevitably happen to them and their loved ones they are naturally confused by this worldview breakdown. If you are in the wrong place at the wrong time you will have a problem irrespective of the amount of time previously invested praying or squeezing beads, lighting candles, or worshipping idols. The only exception is Paula Abdul on American Idol. She can squeeze my beads any time.

The people in the path of the Christmas Tsunami or a great Peruvian earthquake, or other natural disaster were not evil, merely unfortunate. There is an old saying about God seeing every sparrow fall. That only heightens the lie. It indicates that God is this invisible fellow in the sky who is a bird watcher. God is the sparrow and the sky, or rather the sparrow and sky are made up of the energy field of existence that we would call God; not separate and detached. Life and death are endless and just names for different parts of the same cycle.

April 2006

04-01-06 Saturday — I pick up my mail and find that I have been sent, *Your Commemorative Papal Rosary and New Guide to Praying the Rosary*. This is from Food For The Poor, Inc. It is from FL and anything I get from Florida or Utah I assume is a scam until proven otherwise. Worry beads sent to me...do you think I am irritated? The snow job technique is fully employed with a listing of twenty mysteries broken down into four different categories. The snow job has you so bogged down in details that you lose sight of the fact that you are swimming in a sea of made-up bullshit.

They ask me to pray for these poor people, a complete waste of my time, but fortunately they don't forget to also ask me to send them money. After hurling this thing into the circular file I run them online and find out that in fact they are very legitimate, have a low administrative overhead, and do great work in Latin America. I know if I send them money they will never get off me and I prefer to give larger amounts to a select few charities rather than be plagued endlessly by hundreds of them. But I don't want them to be out the cost of this mailing so I decide to anonymously send them some cash.

Item: Fidgeting in School May be a Plus—Rochester, Minnesota—The fidgety students in Phil Rynearson's class-room get up and move around whenever they want. Stretching, swaying, balancing on exercise balls are the point of this experimental classroom to see if moving a little will combat childhood obesity. It appears that these students are more focused on the curriculum than the control group. Gee what a revelation, moving is better than being drugged! What ever happened to common sense?

I never set out to rant endlessly about overpopulation, religion, schools, and the rest of it. My first reaction as this began to unfold was surprise. But now I am thinking that since I was born 64 years ago and have lived long enough to see my planet being not only destroyed by the net addition of four billion people, a tripling of the population; and beyond that, both the religious leaders and political leaders often aiding and abetting that situation…I have not only a right to be royally pissed off but have a duty to say something about it. We should all be mad as hell and unwilling to take it anymore.

These people who trumpet their great belief in Jesus Christ rather than following his morality have been around for a long time. Thomas Jefferson referred to them as pseudo-Christians.

Thomas Jefferson once went thru the Gospels with a razor cutting out the parts that he found implausible. He also stated, "The God who gave us life, gave us liberty...including the liberty to believe or not to believe." The Founding Fathers were not conservative Christians but rather rational men and products of the Age of Enlightenment.

You have to realize that people of either the far right or far left are mentally unbalanced. They are using only half of their brain, see only one side of things, and are totally convinced that they are absolutely correct and that the vast majority is wrong. Fanatics, in other words, and they are potentially if not actually dangerous.

It is like listening to one person in a divorce proceeding. One side has you totally convinced that they are a saint and that their former partner is a monster who is lucky to remain alive. Then you hear the other side and everything shifts 180 degrees. The people of this country are generally centrist who drive on down the road but on occasion we have been known to drive off onto the right or the left shoulder.

I realize that I have not slammed the Jews much, if at all. I know little of that religion but think that there is no authoritative hierarchy, and that the rabbi is a regular member of the group that is elected by the group. If that is so, it sounds really good to me in comparison to Christianity and Islam. We in the West tend to think that newer is better, but here it looks like the Jews had the better idea, then came the Christians who got really ugly with religion, and finally along came Islam and they are…what are they doing with it? Why are they beheading people and chopping off hands?

Getting back to the rabbi approach, isn't there something in the Bible about, "whenever three or more are gathered together in my name…" Now that is all about the Holy Spirit. That does exist as a sort of local telepathic state. If forced to go to a church service I would choose a Black church where they do a lot of get-down singing. Now that is spiritually fulfilling and uplifting. That is what it is all about. Dancing only makes it better. That same spiritual bond can happen with a team, a crew, a jury, or between an audience and an entertainer.

But those Orthodox Jews, the ones with the funny hats and weird rules like you can't shake hands with their wife or be alone in the same room with them, and a host of others. I have a few problems with some of these folk. No doubt the majority are good people, unfortunately the few that I have known have tended to be quite arrogant and seemingly view anyone who is not an Orthodox Jew as practically sub-human. This allows some of them to sleep well at night while perpetrating frauds, smuggling Ecstasy from Holland into NYC for sale to goyim, and other antisocial deeds. Others were just ludicrous, wacky, and fanatical nut cases. Now whom have I missed?

Item: A Dog-Eat-Dog Show—Competition is ruff at the Peninsula Dog Fanciers Club show. I look at some of these inbred dogs and want to barf. Dogs are tame wolves. An interesting side note is that if a female dog bears the pup from a wolf…the other dogs will kill it. But if a female wolf bears the pup from a dog…the wolves will rear it.

Anyway, the more a dog looks like a wolf, like a German Shepherd or an Alaskan Husky, the healthier and more complete the animal is genetically. These show dogs have been inbred into grotesque shapes and have all manner of deformity problems like bad hips, jaws, and so forth. A certain amount of breeding for specific traits is understandable. Horses are bred and cows are bred, but not to such extremes that they look like goats, or gargoyles.

Every year we put to death about as many stray dogs as are bred. Thus if dogs were not bred, we wouldn't have to put any to death. The more you inbreed any animal the more you harm it. Mongrels have always been known as smart dogs. My cat Gravity and dog Teddy both came from the Kitsap Humane Society and both are magnificent animals. German Shepherds make good seeing-eye dogs because they are genetically complete.

Gold fish have been genetically bred into weird shapes for a millennium by the Chinese. If you take those telescoped-eyed and other weird goldfish and interbreed them, you get back to the complete goldfish. I have raised goldfish for over forty years. They are an extremely strong and hardy fish. I have some now that hibernated this past winter in Dragon Pond in the bird sanctuary in the back yard.

If they are so strong, why do they die in the little bowl that they come in? Because every inch of fish requires a gallon of water and that bowl holds only a fraction of that. This is done deliberately so that you can be sold more goldfish. That is why you see them on the surface attempting to breath air. How is that for cruelty? That they manage to live as long as they do without sufficient oxygen is a testament to their hardiness.

People are no different. I think it is Brazil that is that rare country that has a national policy in favor of racial interbreeding. The more interbreeding the more complete the genetic pool. Many of the most beautiful people on Earth are Eurasian, or other widely mixed groups. A mixing of all people on Earth would be what produces a master race; not inbreeding that produces sickness and imbeciles. Not convinced yet? Salma Hayek, Tiger Woods, Issa Bayaua…case closed.

The Pennsylvania Amish are a good example of the bad that inbreeding brings. The Amish are Anabaptist whose ancestors were invited to Pennsylvania by William Penn personally. Of the 200,000 in the U.S. today, about 25,00 live in Lancaster County. The Amish and their spiritual cousins the Mennonites have an inordinately high incidence of genetic based diseases that affect very young children. Many of these afflictions are disabling or fatal but some could survive with proper medical care. A typical Amish response to this situation is to say, "Disabled children are sent here by God to teach us how to love."

The above are the folks who our President told that he hears God talking to him. Enough said.

Item: Brazil is expected to reach energy independence next year. That goal was set back in the 70's. At this time last year I went to Galeão Antonio Carlos Jobim International Airport in Rio to meet my youngest son Tommy arriving from Los Angeles. It was April 5, his 23rd birthday.

Our guide, Ricardo Barbosa drove a car that like many others and virtually all taxis was running on propane. It had a large propane tank in the trunk. They will also run on gasoline. The savings is 60% with a reduced yearly registration fee. The gas stations in town had propane and all had ethanol from vegetation. I was totally impressed by what they were doing in this regard.

Another interesting thing in Brazil was that all the large trucks and busses had tubes running into the tires from the axle hubs. We learned that they could run air continuously into the tires from compressors. This not only maintained the tires at the optimal pressure for mileage, wear and safety, but in the event of a puncture…the incoming air would keep the tire inflated until it could be fixed or replaced!

Item: Wrestlers Pin Down Spirituality—Ministry combines wrestling with sermons to attract an alternative crowd. I'll spare you the details. Is there anything that they won't do with a straight face?

Why would we spend many times more to incarcerate minorities, in crime academies, rather than invest in the schools and infrastructure of their communities? Why have prisons become such a big business?

- The U.S. has nearly two million people incarcerated.
- One out of 150 Americans, are behind bars. This doubled in the past twelve years.
- Daily 1.96 million U.S. children have a parent or close relative incarcerated.
- One out of three young African-American males is under criminal justice supervision.
- For every black male enrolled in a California college, five are behind bars.
- For every Latino in a four-year college, three are incarcerated.
- The number of women inmates has tripled since 1985.
- 78% of the women in state prisons are mothers.

The increase in incarcerations has dramatically increased jail costs. The average annual cost of keeping an adult prisoner ranges from $30,000 to $75,000 and the costs of building and maintaining prisons jumped from $7 billion to $38 billion between 1980 and 1996.

Statistics like the above have caused a radical change in the thinking of such conservatives as William F. Buckley. In a 1995 statement to the New York Bar Association, he reasoned, "… one dollar spent on the treatment of an addict reduces the probability of continued addiction seven times more than one dollar spent on incarceration. Looked at another way: Treatment is not now available for almost half of those who would benefit from it. Yet we are willing to build more and more jails in which to isolate drug users even though at one-seventh the cost of building and maintaining jail space and pursuing, detaining, and prosecuting the drug user, we could subsidize commensurately effective medical care and psychological treatment."

Princeton University professor John J. DiIulio Jr., a leading conservative criminologist writing in The Wall Street Journal declared, "The nation has maxed-out on the public-safety value of incarceration. Until recently, increased incarceration has improved public safety. But as America's incarcerated population approaches two million, the value of imprisonment is a portrait in the law of rapidly diminishing returns. The justice system is becoming less capable of distributing sanctions and supervisions rationally, especially where drug offenders are concerned. It's time for policy makers to change focus, aiming for zero prison growth."

DiIulio and Buckley join a growing chorus of academics, law enforcers and intellectuals from across the political spectrum critical of a criminal justice system that distinguishes the United States, along with Russia, as having the highest incarceration rate in the industrialized world. Where the number of Black men in prison is four times higher than that of South Africa during apartheid. Where people who kill White persons are far more likely to be executed that those who kill minorities. Where as other countries abolish the death penalty, capital punishment is on the increase. Where in 24 states people can be put to death for crimes they committed as children. All of this is carried out at staggering costs.

The United States currently arrests more than 700,000 people a year for cannabis, i.e. forbidden plant smoking. The U.S. rate of incarceration is generally 5-8 times that of comparable industrialized nations such as Canada and the countries of western Europe, where it currently stands in the U.S. at 699 per 100,000 population, the nearest nation Russia, is at 644.

Marijuana offenses at the Federal level = $500 Million Annually for Incarceration Costs
Marijuana Offenses at the State level = $1.3 Billion in Annual for Incarceration Costs
Marijuana Offenses at the Juvenile level = $200 Million in Annual Costs of
Marijuana Offenses Pre Sentence Incarceration = About $83 Million Per Year
Marijuana Probation Across the United States = $60 Million in Costs Annually
Marijuana Offenders Lost Wages Due to Incarceration = $4.2 Billion Lost For 2002
Marijuana Arrests = $779 Million Each Year

When you consider that the drug czar's office has claimed that 77% of illegal drug users are employed, one has to wonder what is accomplished by the double cost to society incurred by jailing them. Not only is it costing a fortune to keep them warehoused, but society is also losing the monies they otherwise would earn and contribute to society.

We bear some three quarters of a million arrests for marijuana each year in the United States and about 135,000 persons are currently in prison after being convicted of either a state felony or federal marijuana offense. This costs more than $7 billion per year. At the time when the above was compiled the U.S. States were reporting a combined $40 billion shortfall. States face the direst fiscal situation since World War II according to the National Governors Association.

A Rand Corporation report shows beyond reasonable doubt that the already discredited 'gateway theory' of marijuana use leading to heroin or cocaine use is simply not likely.
"Marijuana use among adolescents does not appear to act as a 'gateway' leading to the use of harder drugs such as cocaine and heroin." It's clear that at such an enormous cost, there is some value to be gained by considering the wisdom of jailing tens of thousands of Americans for no other reason than possession of a plant that is currently considered politically incorrect.

Britain's Home Office said, "The analysis, based on recent survey data on nearly 4,000 children and young adults, finds: No significant impact of soft drug use on the risk of later involvement with crack and heroin. Very little impact of soft drug use on the risk of later involvement in crime."

Dutch marijuana shops quite successfully and happily passed their thirtieth anniversary. The Ottawa Citizen in a story on December 19th reported, "Quebec court Judge Gilles Cadieux, who had postponed making a decision on the case about ten times, said that the absence of a legal source of marijuana takes away the right to life and liberty for those who need it."

The issue has been brought to a boil in Santa Cruz, California where federal authorities reportedly handcuffed a paraplegic to a bed in a medical marijuana case that sparked nationwide outrage.

From the WAMM Website: "A hearing has been set for the Motion to Return Property filed shortly after the DEA raid on Women's and Men's Alliance for Marijuana, WAMM, a Santa Cruz based medical marijuana cooperative. The motion requests the return of all personal property including 137 medical marijuana plants taken in a DEA raid in early September from the 238 patient's collective garden.

I don't personally advocate marijuana use, but if all the alcohol drinkers in the country switched to smoking grass we would live in a much more peaceful environment with less crime, less fighting, and far fewer automobile accidents. The population would save the $90 billion each year that is now being spent on alcohol.

They don't call pot weed without reason. It grows like a weed and everyone could easily supply his or her own needs. The only reason why marijuana is expensive and generates enormous and socially corruptive profits is because it is illegal. Marijuana is obviously wrongly classified as a Schedule I substance under the Controlled Substances Act. Schedule I drugs have the highest abuse potential and include heroin and cocaine.

Would our government really do this much harm to society just to protect the loss of these billions to the alcohol industry? What was the first major test of Federal Power in the United States? Wasn't it the putting down of the Whiskey Insurrection or Rebellion by George Washington in 1794?

The DEA budget goes up and up and up. Do drug induced deaths by number or rate come down? No they do not. In 2000 New Mexican Governor Gary Johnson said that last year there were about 450,000 tobacco-related deaths, 150,000 alcohol-related deaths and 100,000 prescription drug-related deaths reported nationally. He compared those statistics, which were all the result of using legal, controlled substances, with the 5,000 cocaine and heroin related deaths nationwide last year.

Johnson said that people want to put drug pushers in jail but they don't truly understand who the pushers are. He said the profile of the average pusher is a single mother of three children, who is selling cocaine to get extra money to support her own habit. He said when the mother is caught after the second or third offense, she is sentenced to 15 to 20 years in jail under federal law and the children are placed in state care.

He said that fully 60% of the people in Holland use recreational drugs, and that country has one-fourth the violent crime rate, one-fourth the homicide rate and one-tenth the incarceration rate as that of the United States.

Item: 04-02-06 Sunday—Now that South Dakota has banned abortions, even in cases of rape, incest, or both, Native Americans are considering opening an abortion clinic on one of their reservations in order to provide service to South Dakotan women.

This document, whatever it is, has reached 145 pages and is gaining steam. Almost all of the material pertinent to this case-file is now being reported under our Surveillance File. I have come to accept that this is meant for readers currently unknown to me. A shift in approach and a little background is in order.

I was born in Providence Rhode Island. After arriving in Los Angeles on my bike in 1964, I worked as a repo-man and bill collector, a Fuller Brush man, and later a government investigator. I climbed rapidly through the collection and investigative ranks of I, II, III, IV, V/Head/Division Chief, and VI/Division Head.

Somewhere in there I took a college equivalency test and entered law school at night. I took criminal law, torts, contracts, and domestic relations. My criminal law teacher was Vince Bugliosi, the brilliant prosecutor of Charlie Manson, author of the book Helter Skelter and many others. He was perhaps the most interesting and enjoyable teacher that I was ever lucky enough to encounter.

I also got into real estate and computer hardware. I was the head painter, plumber, and repairman of my homes and rental properties. I attained financially independent in my late thirties. I have held a Private Investigator's License for many years under the name Beagle Detective. I raised my youngest son in Los Angeles, Baja California for five years, and finally on Whidbey Island in Washington State. I play the markets for capital gains.

What do I want to do about all these pesky churches? The Institute for Social Research at the University of Michigan periodically conducts the World Values Survey. It polls a statistically valid sample of adults from a total of 60 nations. Some of the findings from their 1995-1997 survey follow:

The United States has a higher level of church attendance than any other country that is "at a comparable level of development."

53% of Americans consider religion to be very important in their lives. This compares with 16% in Britain, 14% in France and 13% in Germany. The importance of religion has been declining in developed countries. In those countries which are "experiencing economic stagnation and political uncertainty," the importance of religion is higher.

Political scientist Ronald Inglehart, one of the authors of the Institute's 1998 survey commented: "Although church attendance is declining in nearly all advanced industrial societies, spiritual concerns more broadly defined are not. In fact, in most industrial societies, a growing share of the population is spending more time thinking about the meaning and purpose of life."

These numbers are somewhat suspect. Church attendance data in the U.S. has been checked against actual values using two different techniques. The true figures show that only about 20% of Americans and 10% of Canadians actually go to church one or more times a week. Many Americans and Canadians tell pollsters that they have gone to church even though they have not. Whether this happens in other countries, with different cultures, is difficult to know.

The Institute's 1998 study involved almost 166,000 people. They found that church attendance was in decline in 15 of 19 industrialized democracies. Only two showed small increases: Northern Ireland and Great Britain. Attendance in East Germany continues to decline, having dropped from 20% in 1991 to 9% in 1998. Five of eight ex-communist societies show an increase in church attendance.

Item: Anthony's Home Port will open its latest restaurant next Saturday in downtown Bremo. This is another big plus for the redevelopment!

The main thrust of this report is not about religion, but about how human over-population is destroying our planet, at least for human habitation. This is clearly irrational in this day and age. If we were all on a ship, would we tolerate people drilling holes in the hull? If we did we would deserve to go down with that ship. Many religious and political leaders for the most venial gains are doing just that, drilling holes in the ship that is providing us with life. They can only do that by the means of mass delusions that only organized religion can get away with.

Do you think that there can never be a Theocracy in the United States of America? Guess again…there already is one in Utah and it is growing at an alarming rate worldwide. I was in Salt Lake City some years ago with my family and we planned to spend the night there. Ground zero where the temple is was beautiful but as soon as you got away from that it was the bleakest, most depressing large city that I have ever had the misfortune to be in. Even the radio was exploitive, repressive, and controlling. Thanatos so permeated the atmosphere that we had to drive on to sleep in a less oppressive atmosphere.

The temple is literally at ground zero. The streets are numbered beginning with zero at the temple and go up from there in all directions, north, east, south, and west. The freeway exits have no street names, just a number that indicates how far away you are from this temple!

One of their most bizarre mass hallucinations is that you have to research your ancestry and give them each a pass into heaven or they will rot in hell forever! Their founder, Joseph Smith had a history as a petty thief and con man. He sold magic rocks or something. Then he claimed that God gave him these golden tablets of some kind by way of an angel named Macaroni or some such thing.

The really far out fact is that no one else ever saw these golden tablets, no one…ever. But of course since we are dealing with religion, that didn't matter. Joseph Smith taught that a man who took ten wives with him to heaven had ten times as much chance of becoming a God of his very own planet, than did a man who took only one wife!

I know that it takes all kinds to fill the freeways but why is it that the wackier the ideas, the more the holder feels compelled to force his or her cockamamie notions, or I should say false beliefs onto others? I suppose the more people you can get to subscribe to your particular brand of insanity, the more favorably you are able to value yourself. Misery loves company and delusion loves reinforcement.

Many religions demand that you have faith. Now faith is fine. I have faith that the sun will be around mañana, in mankind, in my family, in my neighbors, and many other things…yet I can still remain rational. But if someone tells you that you must have faith in something irrational like that 2+2=7; then that is not faith. That is a demagogue, conman, or a scammer trying to sell you the Brooklyn Bridge. Or as Mark Twain put it, "It was the school boy who said, 'Faith is believing what you know ain't so.'"

An interesting read on the subject of religion can be found in the little known work, *Letters From The Earth* by Mark Twain. It can be found on the Net.

Here is an even wilder example that illustrates just how much desire there is in people to believe in something beyond themselves, and how little it takes to set them off. The February issue of the Smithsonian has a lengthy article on page 70 titled, *In John They Trust*. It seems that some South Pacific villagers worship an American known as John Frum and believe that he will return and bring them great wealth. They dance in his honor every February 15th, on John Frum Day. According to legend John Frum first appeared to the Elders in the late '30s and this Yank Messiah reappeared during WW II dressed in white...U.S. Navy whites.

They have all kinds of details and each man marches with a length of bamboo as though it was a rifle. They have USA painted in red on their chests and back. They believe that John Frum is living in their volcano and of course the headmen talk to him on a regular basis. When some scoff and ask them how they can keep waiting for the return of John Frum, they reply, "You have been waiting two thousand years for Jesus to come back...how long are you going to wait?" There is no doubt in their minds that John Frum is far more powerful than Jesus Christ.

Lets go back to the prophets Moses, Jesus, and Mohammed. Moses gave his people concepts, the Ten Commandments, Jesus gave his followers concepts, parables, and Mohammed also gave his followers concepts.

Moses found his people worshipping a golden cow and freaked out at the organized idolatry. Jesus, who conducted his preaching outdoors, went into the temple and raised hell in there. Mohammed rebelled against the organized idol worship of his time and started his own teaching.

Can you see Moses running a movie studio churning out mind poison for children? Can you see Jesus burning people alive, molesting children, and condemning people to hellfire en mass for failure to go to church? Can you see Mohammed cutting off the heads of those who choose not to follow him?

The point is that many great prophets have given us many wonderful ethical concepts to follow. Organized religions are something else. Most act the same way that any large and powerful organization or corporation acts. These are bureaucracies that want to grow and become ever richer and more powerful. They are just like newspapers; they want to increase their circulation, authority, and revenues. They are the works of men. That is the exact opposite of what the original prophets expressed and espoused.

Why do many Sunnis and Shiites hate each other? It goes back 1400 years to a disagreement over who would succeed Mohammed. It was not a religious issue at all but it has now become a religious division. What would Mohammed think about that?

Back in ancient times the Pharaohs claimed that they were a direct link to God. Later Kings pulled the same scam. More recently the Emperor of Japan was still getting away with that. And today the Pope is still at it. And so is the head of the Mormon Church! Not only that but they make a claim of selected infallibility, despite the fact they have made thousands upon thousands of errors.

Funny how God talks to the Pope, talks to the Head Mormon, and even talks to George W. but God tells them all something different. What are we to conclude from that? Are they all hallucinating? Does God speak with a forked tongue? Is somebody putting us on? Or are they all pulling our leg?

The historical trend is toward ever more decentralization of power. Today, computers and instant communications make that possible for almost every human on our planet. And it is our planet; it does not belong to governments, corporations, or to these demagogues, conmen, and charlatans.

There is no way at this time to do away with these organized religions but a revolution is certainly called for and way overdue. When the ship's masters are sinking the ship, the crew has no choice but to take matters into their own hands. If Moses, or Jesus, or Mohammed were alive today, let me assure you that they would be leading the charge. They were concerned with the welfare of their people, not in self-aggrandizement.

Temples, churches, and mosques are good places for subscribers to socialize and do good works. But such scams as pretending that their books were written by God, that you must substitute false-faith for reason, that God will reward you for heinous acts, that they are authorized by God to issue or carryout death sentences, that they are a direct link with God, and really anything else that they can not prove is a fraud and like every other organization, they should be held accountable for false advertisement and outright fraud.

Are we saying there should be no sermons? No. There are so many worthwhile topics other than hellfire, damnation, and someone living in the belly of a whale. How about waste as a topic? With people starving to death at an alarming rate as we sicken and die from obesity, with the Earth ever more stressed from over development, wouldn't waste make a good topic to be gone over and over again? The list of both worthwhile and rational subjects must be nearly endless.

For example, the 1973 oil embargo scared us for a while. Cars got smaller and showed the tested mileage, appliances became much more energy efficient and bore new energy use labels, houses got insulated and sealed, we were told to dial down to 65 degrees in the home and highway speeds were lowered to 55 mph.

So how did we end up with an SUV craze in the 90's? Well, for one thing SUVs just happen to be exempt from the automobile fuel consumption restrictions. People are becoming ever more afraid and think than an SUV offers better protection. Aside from the fact that the SUVs have a tendency to rollover, there are two ways to be safer in a vehicle. One way is to have them all bigger like an SUV and the other way is to have them all smaller.

Of the two ways, it is far superior to have them all smaller. It is no different then with prizefighters. The heavyweights can easily knock each other out as they have the mass to break heads and jaws. The flyweights are faster but rarely can cause a knockout, as they don't have that skull-crushing power. As size increases, strength goes up by the square but weight goes up by the cube. That is why ants are skinny and can lift many, many times their own weight. Elephants have huge legs and cannot lift even half their own weight.

Two SUVs crashing into each other will cause much more damage than two small cars. The small cars could have just as strong a steel protective shell and would get far superior mileage. Our leadership is failing us dramatically at every twist and turn.

Much too often religion is a legal bastion for the wolves in sheep's clothing that prey upon rather than pray with their flocks. And they are the only ones with a tax-free status to do this! If a priest can be prosecuted for molesting his members, the separation of church and state does not confer blanket immunity from prosecution.

Whoa, you say! We don't want the government controlling our religion, that's what the commies did. True we don't want our religions controlled by the government. People must be free to gather and pray and worship God as they see fit.

But when they act as schools and fill the children's heads with absurd falsehoods that is quite a different matter. When is enough going to be enough…when they start teaching that the Earth is flat? At the very least they should lose their tax-exempt status for doing that. Why should the taxpayers subsidize the fouling of our young citizens' minds?

Right now these tax-exempt organized religions are pushing to jam this nonsense of Creationism into our public schools. What should be happening is our government should be demanding that reality based Evolution be taught as science in religious schools and during home-schooling. That is where the battle line should be drawn.

I understand that the rise of the Fundamentalists in recent times is a backlash. It is a backlash against the speed of social evolution, to the ubiquitousness of porn on the Internet, to the universal bombardment of sexual images in advertising and the media, to the freedom of verbal expression that offends many from the old school, and much else.

But this religious-based backlash has gone so far that when they attempt to push the rest of us back beyond the Renaissance, that itself produces its own a counter-backlash by religious moderates and secularists.

What exactly does the First Amendment to our Constitution say?

Bill of Rights — Amendment I

"Congress shall make no law respecting an establishment of religion, or prohibiting the free exercise thereof; or abridging the freedom of speech, or of the press; or the right of the people peaceably to assemble, and to petition the government for a redress of grievances."

Congress shall make no law respecting an establishment of religion — That protects us from a state religion and from a Theocracy.

Or prohibiting the free exercise thereof — That protects people who want to exercise their religious freedom from being stopped by the government.

But what if a group says that their religion calls for shooting up with heroin every Sunday morning, or eating their deceased relatives, or making human sacrifices of their children, or committing genocide against a rival church membership, or anything else that would be unacceptable if it were done without invoking the name of religion or of God?

Freedom of religion means freedom to worship God as you see fit, not to harm other people or society or commit crimes or atrocities in the name of God. God doesn't need you to act in his name.

Theocracies are a universal disaster. You can work for God or man but not always both. How many times does history have to teach us that? Theocracies are worse than garden-variety dictatorships. Religious hierarchies are a disaster. The congregation should at least have veto power over their spiritual leaders. They should be able to pick their preacher and not just have one transferred in from Lithuania by the Vatican or whomever. I was wondering how I could possibly knock those good Lithuanians!

The Roman Catholic Church is the perfect example of a top-down organization. Edicts, fiats, decrees, and ukases roll on down from on high. They are purported to be from God, infallibly related by the Pope. But try to effect change from the bottom up and you may as well just ram your head into a stonewall. It is the equivalent of attempting to chat with Pharaoh.

I once sent the Pope a multiage letter in both English and Italian in which I respectfully requested a certificate of excommunication. I offered to pay whatever fee was necessary for the best calligraphy. They had issued such certificates previously to me for such things as baptism and their other rites and I wanted a complete set. It may not surprise you to learn that they did not even give me the courtesy of a response, not even a, Go to Hell!

But just as communism was a necessary transition for the Russians and the Chinese, I suppose theocracies may at times be necessary transitions as primitive peoples evolve and develop. But there is no excuse for them in advanced democracies.

Having said all that against organized religions, I am reminded that the YMCA is able to walk the walk and forgo the talk. They accept all without any regard to the member's religion and spout no religious bullshit, or dogma as they call it...but BS is BS no matter what you call it, and they do their best to help all people in a most positive way. That would be my model as to what an evolved and revolutionized religious organization would be like in the modern world.

They also have a hierarchy but it doesn't dress up in silly clothes, carry silly miters, burn incense, hate sex, pretend to do magic like turning bread into God, or spout mumbo jumbo. That stuff may be necessary for early development but it has no place in an educated society.

Item: I never watch Dateline but just happened to catch it last night. The subject was *The Jesus Papers*, a new book by Michael Baigent, one of the authors of *Holy Blood Holy Grail*. The latter preceded Dan Brown's widely read *The Da Vinci Code* that claimed to prove that Jesus was married and has living descendents today. In fact, Dan Brown has been sued by Michael Baigent. The case is made in *The Jesus Papers* that Jesus survived the crucifixion and never claimed to be anything more than a mortal man.

I have no idea if any of the above is true but it is good that people are questing the so-called authorities that have a track record of having been withholding truth and promulgating falsehoods for centuries. If there is proof of any of this it no doubt lies deep and securely hidden within the Vatican.

What do I think of *The Da Vinci Code* or *The Jesus Papers*? What I think is that it is interesting but it doesn't matter at all one whit. Whether Jesus was married, or had a child, or if his bloodline continues or not, if he did or did not die on the cross…none of that really matters. That is all more idolatry. What matters are the concepts that he put forth. That was what he was attempting to do, promulgate good positive concepts for the benefit of mankind.

I really want to get off this topic of religion. Obviously there are many wonderful people who do great work in this area and serve their fellow man admirably. But there are also severe and fundamental problems, and endless cover-ups of them.

Even today with the case noted above with Mary Winkler confessing to murdering her husband Matthew Winkler, a popular charismatic Fundamentalist Christian preacher. They were seen as the perfect couple with three perfect kids. She was the perfect wife and mother, and he the perfect father and husband. After ten years of all this perfection, Mary puts two caps in his back, in front of their children. Huh?

I have never heard of a murder like this where the motives were not immediately leaked and all over the news. But not here...not a peep! The reason given is that they don't want to harm the children. Really, like all the other murderers haven't had children? The child excuse is a lie to cover up a cover up...as if God is so feeble that he needs us to lie for him.

Item: 04-03-06 Monday — USS Honolulu set for One Last Voyage to PSNS in Bremo. The 360-foot nuclear attack sub will leave Pearl Harbor on April 15 after a farewell ceremony. She has been in service since 1985

This document began as a really great way to pass surveillance time, and that is some of the most boring time imaginable. And it works like a charm. So well in fact that I did lose a couple of targets due to being so wrapped up in this venting and online research that the time got away from me altogether. What is going on here, or what I finally realize is going on here, is the ranting and raving of a man born in 1942, reacting to the daily news while trying to make sense of a world that seems not to compute.

I was very young during the latter years of WW II, but I remember the blackout curtains, the food and gas rationing, and more. The family next door to us somehow brought in a little girl from Germany. Whenever planes flew overhead, and that was common, this child would absolutely freak out.

It is not a typical intergenerational thing of thinking that the world is going to hell in a shopping cart in the hands of a younger generation. It is the dreadful sinking feeling at some gut level that his generation has not done enough to preserve our planet for the future generations to come. If we lose the whole enchilada, it could well be during my lifetime, on my generation's watch as it were.

I was born on a planet that had clean air, plenty of fish, ample drinking water, unspoiled rainforest, large old growth forests, healthy reefs, safe National Parks, and all the rest of it. We owe it to our descendents to see that they inherit the world in the same or better condition. But that is not the way things are going. Not by a long shot.

Our value systems seem to make little sense and our priorities are horribly out of order, and on a grand scale. What is more frightening is that when you project current trends they almost all point to an ever more dire situation. We even appear to be approaching possibly irreversible trigger points or thresholds in the very near future. Yet our leaders insist on doing things ass backwards.

If you keep adding fish to an aquarium, what happens is this. As it gets more and more overloaded, the ammonium level starts to climb from the urine. But nothing happens until all of a sudden it passes a certain threshold level and then a quick and major die-off occurs. A few will survive and the ammonium level quickly drops. Mother Nature has a vast array of such checks and balances.

No I don't think man can destroy the planet but he can certainly destroy civilization as we know it. God, Mother Nature, the Higher Power, or the Energy Field of Pure Potentiality, whatever you want to call it, is the great recycler. Creation is the great recycler. The Earth recycles continents, mountains, oceans, life forms, you name it. No matter what we do, eventually balance will be restored.

A grove of bamboo at Hiroshima in 1945 at ground zero survived the atomic blast and, within days, sent up new shoots. One species of bamboo has been known to grow over four feet in 24 hours. New shoots emerge from the ground with the diameter they will have at their mature height, which will be attained within 60 days. While traveling in China I was amazed at the lashed together bamboo scaffolding that is used when erecting buildings of a dozen or more stories. Bamboo is a grass, not a tree.

But we have gone a long way toward depleting the fossil fuels like oil. If we can continue without a major setback, we will be able to transition to other fuel sources. But if we blow the whole game, how would future generations coming along after centuries or millennia be able to replicate what we have done? The oil that we did it on will be long gone. This could be a one-shot deal. It will take many millions of years for the planet to renew that oil.

Global warming has a lot to do with our burning of fossil fuels. To be fair and balanced, things as far-out as termite farts are a major contributor to global warming as well. This whole situation is a shame when you stop to realize that we are awash in free clean energy. Sunshine is the natural energy that our planet lives and thrives on. Then you have tidal movement, wind, geothermal, nuclear fission, nuclear fusion, and more. We are so close but we just don't yet quite know exactly how to capture it all economically. What a tragedy it would be to come this close and then to blow it. The gods would have to really crack up laughing at us over that.

According to no less an authority than HBO's Tony Soprano, "If you make a model the size of the Empire State Building, and flat on the top of the spire you put a postage stamp, the model would represent how long the Earth has been here, the spire would represent how long life has been here, the thickness of the stamp would represent how long human beings have been here, and the thickness of the ink on the stamp would represent how long we have been sentient."

The big political football lately is immigration. That is a buzzword for Mexicans and other Latinos crossing our southern border illegally. I have seen and been involved one way or another in this area for decades.

In the early sixties, I was escorted through a Los Angeles detention center by an INS agent. It was the day before Christmas and the detainees were jammed into a large glass cell. They pleaded to me for help. The agent related stories about how such people were so often abused. One trick of a huge outfit by the name of MissionPak, that was known for their Christmas Fruit Packs, was to use the workers labor until all the work was done and then blow the whistle on them to INS just before payday in order to cheat them out of their hard won earnings. He was proud that the INS had recently changed its policy and made the employers payoff the workers before the INS hauled them away.

At one time I oversaw the collection of the Los Angels County USC Medical Center's hospital bills. This was the primary place for medical treatment, including Unit II or Women's Hospital that provided OB/GYN services for much of Los Angeles County's Mexican Community.

I have met with the U.S. Consul in Tijuana to establish immigration policy in the above regard. When President Reagan first called for a general amnesty program, I had the task to see that a private business in Los Angeles was wired up with fifty terminals to process these undocumented workers. This was done but the program was delayed for a long time.

The notion that these people take more than they give is just a huge political lie. More of the divide and conquer strategy. They unquestionably give so much more than they could ever possibly take.

Around the year 2000 I had occasion to spend some time in and around Soledad, located in the Central Salinas Valley of Monterey County in California. That last sentence about says it all: the city, valley, county, and state names...are all in Spanish.

I was just amazed at Soledad, King City, Greenfield, and other towns thereabouts. To all appearances they were populated, owned, and run by people ethnically Mexican. They were small towns and that makes it easier, but they were the cleanest, nicest, friendliest, and most model little towns that I have ever been in. If you just looked like you were even thinking about crossing the street, the pickup trucks and cars would stop and offer you the right of way with a smile.

I had occasion to visit a library as I had to get online to trade some gold stocks. The library had a good size group of young children there being read to by a librarian. I felt like I had stumbled into the twilight zone and had gone back in time a half century. It was so charming and beautiful.

Now with all that said, I realize that there are some really bad-news dudes out there. Prominent gangs like: the Mexican Mafia, Nuestra Familia, Florencia, Syndicato Tejano, Maravilla, Calle

Diesiocho, and perhaps the worst Mara Salvatrucha or MS-13; are not the kind of residents that we want, but they are a very small fraction of the Latino Community.

Mexicans as a rule are excellent workers, in fact a job, a trabajo, means everything to them. Their family values are real, strong, and true as opposed to this bullshit rightwing political rhetoric that is so abysmally used and abused.

I don't see the Mexican Government ever changing in its dealings with the U.S., nor do I blame them. But you have to be realistic. What they do is to agree for a quid pro quo, to whatever we demand. Then they go ahead and do what they always did. This happens over and over and over.

If a person invests in land by the shoreline in Mexico, once they have your money, funny things happen sooner or later. The recorded papers disappear, the survey marks get up and walk off, or the papers are found to have one legal flaw or another. The rule of Gringos who know the ropes down there is to never invest more than you are prepared to walk away from. Don't get me wrong, it is so beautiful and the life style is so wonderful that it is worth it. But if you want to heed the best advice you will ever get in this regard: Rent, don't buy.

How can I accept the above? As previously stated, the last time I checked, around 1988, the GDP of Los Angeles County was greater than that of all of Mexico. They know full well that if they play fair, they will be overrun and all the best property gobbled up by the Gringos. They see it as having no other choice.

I don't want to get into Immigration Reform but obviously we need the workers and a border crackdown is essential but it must be offset with a legal way for the workers to enter the U.S. These workers also need some way of gaining legal status and eventually citizenship. Hopeless Guest Worker Only programs like they attempt in Europe do not work and have terrible repercussions in the long term. By the same token, when an undocumented individual is convicted of a serious crime, they need to be deported.

What happens now is that most of those rounded up that are here illegally are simple dumped back over the border. There are cases where some have managed to get back to Los Angeles before the agents who had bussed them back to Tijuana. This is rare but it has happened.

The other option is a formal deportation. When that is done they are in trouble if they are caught back in the United States. When they are bussed and dumped, they are free to sneak right back in. Legally free that is, they still have to pay another 'coyote' to lead them. The deportation method is rarely used because it is costly and time consuming. But that is no good excuse. Congress could simply change the laws in this area and streamline the process. If you commit a serious crime and are here illegally, you should serve your time, be deported, and never come back…or else.

A downside is that the Mexican fertility rate is very high and adding to the overpopulation nightmare. Thanks again to the Catholic Church. At the rate that they are going they will regain the Southwestern United States that they lost in the Mexican American War of 1846-1848

By the time President Polk came to office in 1845, an idea called 'Manifest Destiny' had taken root among the American people, and the new occupant of the White House was a firm believer in expansion. The belief that the U.S. had a God-given right to occupy and 'civilize' the whole continent gained favor as more and more Americans settled the western lands.

The fact that most of those areas already had people living upon them was usually ignored, with the attitude that democratic English-speaking America, with its high ideals and Protestant Christian ethics, would do a better job of running things than the Native Americans or Spanish-speaking Catholic Mexicans.

Manifest Destiny did not necessarily call for violent expansion. In both 1835 and 1845, the United States offered to purchase California from Mexico, for $5 million and $25 million, respectively. Not surprisingly, the Mexican government refused the opportunity to sell half of its country to Mexico's most dangerous neighbor. So instead…we took it.

Item: 04-04-06 Tuesday—Bremo's Economic Roundtable has invited the Bremer Trust Board to discuss development on the strategically located downtown JCPenney Building. This building takes up an entire key city block and is currently used as a parking structure. There is talk about a downtown grocery store, multiplex movie theatre, and who knows what else. The Bremer Trust owns ten downtown properties and this one is the biggest moneymaker.

Item: Miracle Crash in Dover, DE. Wow…another miracle in my lifetime! The laws of physics have apparently once again been Divinely altered. A C-5B Galaxy faltered after takeoff and belly-landed short of the Dover Air Base runway. "It is a miracle. Absolutely a miracle," said Lt. Col. Mark Ruse, commander of the base's 436th Air Wing Civil Engineering squadron.

This may sound innocent enough but the statement by our good Lt. Ruse that this was a miracle, and further that it absolutely was a miracle is in fact absolutely 100% false. What it was, it was a plane crash in which fortunately there were no fatalities. A miracle would be something like a giant hand coming out of the sky, catching the plane, moving it backward through the air and setting it back down at its starting point.

That is a rather important distinction. One deals with reality in a rational way, the other falsely conjures up a Divine intervention where non exists and jams a primitive idea of God into our daily lives. The point is that had Lt. Ruse issued a regular statement that was 100% false he would be in hot water, but it is so commonplace to sling bullshit when it comes to religion that nobody thinks much of anything about it.

I am doing my best to get off the religion angle but it is difficult. Last night I accidentally caught the last ten minutes of the hour-long show Charlie Rose. This is unquestionably one of the best shows on the air or cable. Bill Moyers was filling in for Charlie and the guest was author and philosopher Daniel C. Dennett. His book is Breaking the Spell. What little I heard was a lot like listening to myself here.

He is concerned about some of the negative consequences of what religion is doing such as: the enforced ignorance of the young; doctrines that demand that adults not think for themselves but blindly follow their religious leaders; followers being deluded and fleeced by morally degenerate con-artists; and by what he calls the hypocrisy trap. All members of Congress must pretend that they believe in the man in the sky or they will not be reelected, and things of that nature.

He made the point that no one knows any of the answers to the fundamental questions. Theists believe in God but cannot prove it. Atheists believe that there is no God but cannot prove it. Agnostics basically throw up their hands and say, no one knows and neither do I.

Long ago some one wise explained the differences in the beliefs of man about God by saying that it was like several blind men in a room with an elephant. One feels the trunk, another the leg, another the tusk or tail, and someone else other parts of the body. They all are describing the same thing in good faith but none can agree.

That sounds reasonable to me. Why kill each other over it? Why say that if you don't believe what I believe in, you are going to burn in hell? Good grief Charlie Brown!

Dennett made the interesting point that of the hundreds if not thousands of gods that people on the planet still believe in, the most religious of fanatics believe only in their God and are atheists concerning all of the others. An atheist is simply one who doesn't believe in the same gods that you don't believe in, like Baal, Sol, Vishnu, Thor etc., plus one more...yours! Breaking the Spell naturally refers to ending the mass trance that followers are put into by these religious organizations.

At this point you must be convinced of at least one thing, if only one thing, that I do not believe in Divine intervention. Not necessarily so. Divine intervention would manifest itself in the acts of man. If someone runs into a burning building and saves a child, I'll take that as Divine intervention in that the omnipotent, omnipresent, and omniscient field of pure potentiality that we call God sleeps in the rocks, awakens in the plants, walks in the animals, and is conscious in man.

God created all of Creation. Is that not enough? Why do you think that he should have to listen to you whine and plead? Sure, you want God to make house calls, especially to your home, but you know what? It doesn't work that way. Get a grip, observe reality, stop studying the millennia old scribbling of uninformed tribal nomads, and get with the program. Observe

God's real laws both spiritual and those that science studies; and use your head. Be part of the solution instead of adding your weight to the problem.

People often get hung up on fairness, as though the Universe owed them that. Unfairness abounds: a tree falls on their house and they bemoan the unfairness of it. A young child gets cancer, a church collapses on a wedding ceremony killing the bride, and so on.

Mother Nature is unfair. Was it fair to the dinosaurs sixty-five million years ago when that asteroid hit the Yucatan peninsula, it is known as the K-T or Cretaceous-Tertiary Mass Extinction event, and pretty much wiped them out along with about 70% of all the species then living on the Earth? No it wasn't fair to Dino but it was our big break, little shrew like critters that we were. Now we didn't have to worry about being stepped on like ants all the time and could start to really develop.

Fairness is a concept of mankind, or at least mammals. Fairness, peace and harmony in this Earthly realm will be achieved, not by heaving virgins into volcanoes, or praying to a God who has less interest in our personal crap then we have in the love life of a particular ant; fairness is enhanced by following the Golden Rule and development of ethical standards in all that we do as human beings. Fairness is not something for some mythical Judgment Day. Every day is Judgment Day.

Imagine for a moment what you would consider to be a perfect world. One in which all of our hard won treasure that goes into weapons of mass destruction and defense spending by all the people on the globe was instead able to be used toward attaining the common positive goals of humanity. A world that had all of its priorities in order, with population reduction as the number one goal, in order to begin to heal the planet, its life forms and ourselves.

No, I am not advocating unilateral disarmament at this time. It is a dangerous world that we live in. I have great respect for our honorable military and those who serve in it at all levels. But that is not to say one should blindly and unthinkingly support any and all things military. No less a military man than Dwight David 'Ike' Eisenhower, Supreme Allied Commander of WW II made a point in his farewell speech of warning the American people about the potential overgrowth and dominance of the military-industrial complex.

Ike had made a priority of giving us our Interstate Highway System as a way of diverting military spending to civilian use. He got the idea from the Autobahn in Germany. We built ours about the same way but unfortunately only half as thick. This was a splendid and lasting case of living the old swords into plowshares admonition. The Interstate system then went on to transform the United States and our way of life. It also has great military benefit.

It is so easy to say, out of habit, that 'the Interstate system transformed America', but all the residents of all the countries in North, Central, and South America are and consider themselves to be Americans. They rightfully resent our having hijacked that name exclusively for ourselves.

The point here is to imagine not a perfect world, that would be Hell, but an ideal world. Then look at the mess that we have today. The obvious thing to then do is to begin moving from the train wreck about to happen scenario that we are currently in, towards that model world, and the faster the better as time is running out. Are we doing that? Are our leaders leading us there? Hardly, and that is the problem, that is why we need to begin to take matters into our own hands.

I want to be very clear that by saying we should take matters into our own hands, I do not mean for some screwball to take a shot at the Pope or any other insane or criminal act. There are already plenty of organizations such as Greenpeace International that you can apply your time, energy and spare funds to. [www.greenpeace.org/international/] I have no private knowledge of this group other than the fact that the last time I was in Amsterdam, I happened to walk by their headquarters at about 3 AM and there were a few of them busily loading a van. That struck me as real dedication.

Many of our leaders are doing their best to enrich themselves by drilling holes in the hull of our ship. The Earth is our spaceship and we, you may recall, are traveling way over a million mph toward our future. If you were on a boat in a lake going 100 mph you would be quite frightened. Well…be afraid, be very afraid.

We need to wake up, think rationally, and act appropriately. If I were a religious leader I might be exhorting you to slaughter some of your fellow humans. Yes, I know that is a very cheap shot. But it is totally outdated, ancient, and now self-defeating religions as much if not more than anything else that have us in a trance, under a spell, sleepwalking through our ever so precious time on this marvelous planet…as we barrel headlong into a massive human die-off, loss of enumerable fantastic species, and tremendous planetary harm.

Plagues have accomplished several major human die-offs in the past when elevated populations have overburdened their ecosystems. Letting loose the planet's nuclear arsenals would handily do the job right now, taking out billions in one episode.

It is said that California has all kinds of plans for coping with disaster related societal collapse. It is also said that the Arizona plan is to get every gun they have on the California border and to shoot anyone heading their way. It does sound like a joke but what else could they do? The millions who live in large cities are dependent for food, water, and on other products, all of which are being brought in. If that supply were cut off to any major degree it would not take long for all hell to break loose. Witness the recent scene in New Orleans.

I would imagine that the slaughter of almost a million Tutsis by Hutus resulted from economic pressures due to overpopulation relative to available resources. Even a fairly small asteroid hitting our planet could start the ball rolling. Picture millions and billions scrambling for severely limited resources in a frantic attempt to maintain their lives and those of their family. The more overpopulated that we are, the more any mega-disaster of any kind will be aggravated, just as an overloaded boat will magnify all threats to it.

The most frightening aspect of nuclear bombs that practically nobody on the street is aware of is their beneficial effects. Yes they actually have over time some wonderful effects. In fact they rejuvenate and replenish the soil…once the radiation cools down. It has been described as being as if the Sun came down and kissed the Earth.

In the evet of a worldwide collapse, the ruling elite would need to somehow eliminate the rampaging hordes and preserve their own families' lives. Well now, if they had large underground shelters capable of sustaining life fairly comfortably for a very long time, they could nuke the rest of us. Then when the radiation cooled they could come out of their shelters to a newly enriched world. One divested of all those pesky peasants and rabble.

But of course those large underground, under-mountain shelters have existed for quite some time now. They have the latest in communications and satellite surveillance capability. There is all manner of neat stuff there. Trust me…there is always a backup plan.

Item: 04-05-06 Wednesday—A Deputy Press Secretary for the U.S. Department of Homeland Security was arrested for online sex solicitation of what he thought was a female minor. I know I should leave this one alone. But all this talk about sexual perverts and whatnot is just another example of the lack of forthrightness, and the political manipulation in our society.

The simple facts are that whether you are dealing with men, primates, or many other mammals, alpha males are attractive to females of all ages. Further, the older a man gets, the younger his eyes get…that is biological. The Romans thought nothing of old men having sex with young girls. The Roman man also had the legal right to execute his wife and children as he saw fit. He also had slaves. I am not at all endorsing any of that or condoning the molestation of underage youth…far from it.

Most of these adult men who are going after youngsters are not unnatural creatures or monsters. The fact that it is natural is what makes it so difficult and prevalent. Like most criminals they have poor impulse control and are egocentric. Absolutely they need to be stopped. The problem, particularly now that we have the Internet culture, is growing rapidly. They can be tried and shot for all I care, but let's keep it real.

Every day, all day long, 'respectable' businessmen fly from developed Western Countries to places like Thailand and Latin America on sex tours in order to have sex with minors. Or note the Dateline NBC TV show, 'To Catch a Predator' that has been setting up these stings for older men looking for underage girls. They are pulling in schoolteachers, religious leaders, and government employees, a veritable cross section of the community.

Rather than nabbing vicious, murderous predators, they are reeling in pathetic, lonely, socially inept sad sacks. They all get busted when they leave the sting set. It is wrong, very wrong but it is not unnatural. That is why it is such a problem and a growing one.

There are of course a few real monsters out there that actually do rape and murder children and they really should be caught, tried, convicted, sentenced to death, and given the spike.

NOVA had an interesting show last night on the Cassini-Huygens probe of Titan, the largest of nineteen known moons of Saturn and the second largest moon in our Solar System. The largest moon is Jupiter's Ganymede. The original Voyager had raised more questions than it answered. There are only four solid bodies in our Solar System that have atmospheres.

Like the Goldilocks story, Venus is too hot, Mars is too cold, and our Earth is just right. The fourth is Titan. Titan is one half the size of our Earth and has an atmosphere ten times as dense, mostly methane. The way they got the Huygens lander to Saturn was spectacular. In order to save fuel they launched Cassini in such a way that it gained speed by being 'slingshot' around planets four different times, allowing it to travel over two billion miles.

Watching this program I couldn't help but think how all of this science flies in the face of that nonsense of Creationism that the Universe appeared in an abracadabra only six thousand years ago. Think about those poor children who are being mentally crippled by that big lie being planted into their vulnerable little heads.

Then I realized why the big lie. Because the Bible clearly states that the world was created in six days, six thousand years ago. If it is supposed to be the word of God, what choice do they have? God either lies to us, the Bible is not the word of God, or all the evidence in Creation is wrong. These people are so imprinted beyond reason that the Bible is the word of God, despite all evidence to the contrary, that they have no choice but to deny reason and their senses, and take the position that all of the evidence in Creation is wrong. The poor deluded devils.

Sure young people may need stories, fables, fairy tales and such. We give them Santa Claus, the Tooth Fairy, the Easter Bunny, witches and goblins, the boogieman, and others; but after the age of reason, about seven years of age or probably younger now in our culture, they learn the truth. We acknowledge that they were all made up. But not so with the invisible man in the sky…that is where we lose it.

Yes, but we need the threat of hellfire to keep the wild men in line. No you don't, we have long since known that positive reinforcement is far more effective than negative. This is true whether you are dealing with people, retarded children, dogs, chimps, seals, killer whales, or any other mammal.

I recall as a child how it struck me when I realized that they were trying to tell me that if I failed to go to mass on a Sunday, that I would be committing a mortal sin and I would burn in hell forever for that. I knew then that either they were crazy or that they thought I was.

Young men are a handful no matter what you do. That is one reason for warfare. The French and English had the Hundred

Years War that lasted I think 116 years, and not much came of it! Meanwhile the French, English, and other Kings of Europe and Russia continued with their endless feasting and exchange of family members in marriage.

But they did get rid of a whole lot of testosterone raging young scamps. Those guys who cause so much trouble for society and are constantly disrupting law and order. And of course those involved in the war industry made wagonloads of money. On top of that you now had all those extra young women to be preyed upon by those old bastards, the ones who wanted the war but did not actually fight in it themselves.

Even in The Great War, now known as WW I, they slaughtered millions of young men for years over a frontline that barely ever moved at all. When it was all over, all they accomplished was to set up WW II by the harshness of the Treaty of Versailles. That Palace of Versailles is something else; don't miss it if you are ever nearby.

I want to finish with religion right here but realize that I cannot. We will be forced to go back to it time and again. It is no longer adults with immunity from reason telling weird stuff and terror inducing lies to our children; it is the very survival of civilization that is at stake. This is not to say they are solely responsible. Religious leaders are the modern day witch doctors and our political leaders have the executive authority of the old chief. They have always been in cahoots and always will be.

But like artistic ability, we all have God's gift of understanding. Again, you don't have to be Einstein to understand when you see the captain's crew scuttling your ship, that they need to be stopped and that something needs to be done before all is lost.

Globalization is a big part of where we are today with all of this. The April 2006 issue of Scientific American has an interesting chart on page 87. The graph shows the number of people living on less than $1 per day from 1981 to 2001.

Represented on this display are: China, India, Sub-Saharan Africa, South Asia excluding India, East Asia excluding China, Latin America with the Caribbean, the Middle East and North Africa, Eastern Europe and Central Asia, and a composite of all of the above.

Those areas that are improving are: China, India, South Asia, and East Asia. Those areas where it is not getting better are Sub-Saharan Africa, the Middle East and North Africa, Eastern Europe and Central Asia, and Latin America with the Caribbean.

Those that are improving can have hope, those that are not improving are reasonable in assuming that globalization will only make matters worse for them.

South and Central America have much more reason to hope than do Africa and the Middle East. Attitude and customs naturally play important roles. If you are determined to keep the female half of your population uneducated and in the home the battle is already probably lost.

Item: Beware of Pick Pocket signs had to be taken down because the incidence of pick pocketing doubled after they were put up. Why? Because when the signs were read, the reader would automatically touch their valuables with their hand to make sure they that still had them. The pick pockets stationed nearby then knew exactly who was carrying and exactly where the valuables were located.

Human overpopulation is the single root cause of virtually all of the major problems on our planet today. That is a very broad statement but quite true. This global warming that is reaching the front burner in the minds of concerned people all over the world is fueled by people. By people driving cars, using power, consuming more and more; and by all the power plants and factories needed to supply these people. Now we hear that automotive demand in China alone is going to reach fifteen million units per year by 2008.

In Amsterdam almost everybody rides bicycles. In the train station parking lot you see tens of thousands of bicycles. In Copenhagen so many people use bicycles as their means of transportation that the intersections have two sets of traffic signals; the larger ones are for cars and the smaller ones are for bicycles.

The Chinese used to use mostly bicycles and had a good thing going there but now they want to be more modern and comfortable like the people in the West. If you have never seen how traffic flows in China you have really missed out. The following is something I wrote when I returned from a trip there in 2003:

The roads are filled with trucks, mostly baby blue, buses, cars, bikes, mopeds, scooters, small motorcycles, but piled to the sky with boxes, propane tanks, chicken cages, and everything imaginable and then some, rickshaws i.e. three-wheeled bike affairs, every conceivable hybrid of the above, and pedestrians.

The only right-of-way the pedestrian has is to be run down right a way. Crosswalks are rare and mean absolutely nothing. To cross, people simply head across the street and the vehicles try not to hit them. No one ever changes lanes…you just cut off the guy beside you, endlessly.

Do the bicycles stay in the slow lane? Nope. They could come shooting across perpendicular to the traffic flow. If you stop to think about it, you could fit three cars into two lanes…this is done routinely. Vehicles think nothing of going over the centerline and driving right against traffic.

Normally I am too cheap to pay for a taxi but they were so inexpensive that we took them constantly. Disney and Universal Studious have nothing that compares with a ride in a taxi in China.

One man specialized in passing on the right shoulder, another the left. They love to go around blind curves on the wrong side of the road. Every second was a near miss of one kind or another.

I have had cars whose horns I probably never blew. There the horns are used non-stop. The vehicles talk with their horns using all manner and permutations of rhythm, length, pattern and loudness. At first I kept waiting for the inevitable collisions and then I began to look for accidents. Never saw even one.

They seemed to have eyes in back of their heads. Days later I realized that the cars were not even dented. And many were new cars like Chinese VWs, real nice Chinese Buicks, Chinese BMWs and Benzes. They all drove this way. The windows were often so heavily tinted that little triangles of clear glass were left so as to see out to the side mirrors.

The West is left-brain dominant as shown and reinforced by our writing which is a linear stringing of twenty-six letters. The height of this is German that also strings words. In the East they use characters. They are clearly right-brain dominant and that is also where spatial relationships reside. Our traffic is a linear progression with people staying in their lanes and so forth.

Theirs is a self-orchestrated symphony of harmonious spatial events. It was just unbelievable to me.

Once when out taxi missed a girl on a bike by a few inches and blew his horn when he was closest to her, I made a point of looking at her face as we passed. In the U.S. the girl would have been out of her skin with the closest call of her life. There she was looking the other way, totally bored. It was just amazing how they all work together like that.

The above may seem like a diversion from expounding on world overpopulation but it shows just how quickly, in a couple of decades, a country can go from almost all bicycles to full-fledged ten lane automobile traffic. One day we were going to visit the Ming Tombs and ran into a massive total gridlock. This is no exaggeration; traffic had expanded out on both sides of a wide highway and come to a total and complete stop that lasted for untold hours. We managed to take at my insistence the last right turn out of that mess. The driver had never been down that road before but we eventually returned to known territory.

The starvation in the world is certainly caused by overpopulation. We use very few people to produce the food that we do. If there were still the two billion people as when I was born, food would be no problem at all.

People everywhere talk about how there were so many fish in the 1940's that you could almost walk across water on their backs. Now all the fisheries are in big trouble. They farm fish like so-called Atlantic salmon in large pens near the shore but I could go on and on about the problems with that.

Sardines are very good for you and I was diligently eating them once a week until I stumbled onto the fact that they weren't even sardines at all. About forty years or so ago when the sardines were fished out, the industry got our splendid Congress to pass a law allowing non-sardines to be labeled and sold as sardines. Now I have them shipped in from Portugal.

The rainforests that most certainly contain numerous plants with amazing medicinal value, unseen species, and all manner of life forms to be treasured, are being daily slashed and burned by ever-burgeoning populations. Of course the burning just adds more to the CO_2 emissions, while the loss of the forests lowers oxygen production.

Whenever you overly compress people bad things happen like increasing crime, easier disease transmission, and aberrant behavior of all sorts...up to and including genocide. War, Famine, Pestilence and Death, what more could you ask for...if you were Satan and running the show.

If overpopulation is the root cause of all the problems on Earth, why do we give a tax credit for each child? Shouldn't that at least be a tax penalty after the first child? We use tax policy to alter behavior, why encourage children at this point? Sure it would be politically difficult to eliminate a tax credit for each child but we could at least create tax incentives for not having children. The gay community ought to like that. Extra tax credits should be given to people who adopt children. Let's take care of the children that are already here.

The Chinese instituted a one child per family goal as a way of reducing the population to a manageable amount. Many religious people and world leaders condemn them for it. In fact, our right wing does its damnedest to stymie birth control all over the planet. The deluded and violent are induced to murder doctors at abortion clinics to stop the killing of fetuses while tens of thousands of actual living people are starving to death on a daily basis. Meanwhile those urging them on have the unmitigated gall to spout and sputter about the sanctity of life. A rock has more morality than that.

Just how precious does Mother Nature or God view each possibility of life? Many fish produce 500,000 or more eggs at a time. These eggs are fertilized and eventually after all the eating that goes on is over, a few fish may grow to maturity.

Human reproduction follows the same scale, 2.5—3.5 ml of seminal fluid has a composition averaging about 200–300 million sperm, one of which may or may not fertilize an egg under optimum conditions. The rest all die, each and every time ejaculation occurs. Each and every sperm is one half of a potential human being. In other words less than one sperm in a billion becomes a human being! Does that look like the design of an architect who would be terribly upset if every potential human being didn't materialize on an already overcrowded planet? Those are unvarnished facts of life…reality, not delusion.

Item: 04-6-06 Thursday—Jury Finds Merck Liable for Heart Attack Cases—Lawyer Robert Gordon states that this is, "a victory for 100,000 Americans who had heart attacks from VIOXX. This is a victory for the tens of thousands of doctors who were lied to by Merck about the dangers of VIOXX." I wonder why none of these murdering bastards are being sent to prison? Minorities are being jailed daily for boosting underwear from SEARS.

We are being lied to more and more. I watched the Congressional hearings in April of 1994 where they had the corporate heads of all the major cigarette companies before the investigating subcommittee. They included: William Campbell, President & CEO, Philip Morris, USA; James W. Johnston, Chairman and CEO, RJR Tobacco Company; Joseph Taddeo,

President, U.S. Tobacco Company; Andrew H. Tisch, Chairman and CEO, Lorillard Tobacco Company; Edward A. Horrigan, Chairman and CEO, Liggett Group Inc.; Thomas E. Sandefur, Chairman and CEO, Brown and Williamson Tobacco Corp.; and Donald S. Johnston, President and CEO, American Tobacco Company.

The Hearing of the House Energy and Commerce Committee Subcommittee on Health and the Environment was chaired by: Henry Waxman, D-CA

Representative Waxman: The meeting of the subcommittee will come to order. I'd like to ask our guests to please take your seats. This is an historic hearing. For the first time ever, the chief executive officers of our nation's tobacco companies are testifying together before the United States Congress. They are here because this subcommittee has legislative jurisdiction over those issues that affect our health. And no health issue is as important as cigarette smoking.

It is sometimes easier to invent fiction than to face the truth. The truth is that cigarettes are the single most dangerous consumer product ever sold. Nearly a half million Americans die every year as a result of tobacco. This is an astounding, almost incomprehensible statistic.

Imagine our nation's outrage if two fully loaded jumbo jets crashed each day, killing all aboard. Yet that's the same number of Americans that cigarettes kill every 24 hours. Sadly, this deadly habit begins with our kids. Each day three thousand children will begin smoking. In many cases, they become hooked quickly and develop a lifelong addiction that is nearly impossible to break.

I watched and listened spellbound as these men sat there and lied flat out. They denied spiking their products with nicotine among other things.

I go to some length above because this is a good example of what goes on in society every day. These are all wealthy, powerful men. They are pillars of their communities. No doubt they belong to all the right clubs, they shop in the best stores, wear the right clothes, their offspring went to the right schools, and they attend church services regularly or should I say religiously, sitting in the best seats.

It is easy for the common man to assume that those holding lofty positions are high-minded people who know what is true and are doing the right things for the public good. What do we know about the above gentlemen? They are merchants of death. They strive to hook our kids and our grand kids on a worthless product that causes illness and death. It also now carries in this country a severe social opprobrium. Adults who don't smoke are not apt to take up such an expensive, deadly and nasty habit.

They have to hook the kids. That is why they invented Joe Camel and other cartoons to appeal to our youngsters. They get ever more subtle and sophisticated about it as scrutiny on them mounts, but they still have to hook the kids. I ask you, what could possibly be more vile, more reprehensible then educated men doing their best to slowly kill our children and make them pay for their own suffering; just to make a buck? Just one more case of greedy old men lusting for more wealth and power.

The ads that get my goat now are the ones by Philip Morris. They sanctimoniously advise you to visit their website www.philipmorris.com/ and seek information about quitting smoking. On that site they proudly boast that they are the world's leading international cigarette business with products sold in 160 countries worldwide. It also notes that on January 27, 2003, the parent company changed its name to Altria Group, Inc. to better clarify its identity as the owner of food and tobacco companies that manage some of the world's most successful brands.

If I were a merchant of death, I'd change my name too. On the surface it all seems like they are acting in an altruistic way. But they know what any Hollywood actor knows, good publicity and bad publicity are both good for you; it is only no publicity that hurts you.

Another ad series that really makes me want to puke are by a big oil company. They ask some airhead on the street what should be done to preserve the planet and whatever the dupe says, the big oil company says that yes, they are already doing that. They are of course doing and researching everything, what matters is the scale on which they are doing these things. The big pharmaceutical ads are all enough to make you sick, perhaps that is their goal.

There is certainly nothing new about keeping the population confused and in the dark. Where the article elle was used by the Romans, when the Empire fell and Latin was divided up into the Romance languages, the Spanish got the first half of elle or el, as in el lobo; while the French got the latter half le as in le plume. Soon the common people of the various countries could no longer understand one another. The ruling classes and professionals had to communicate and so the doctors and lawyers were taught Latin, the now dead language. Doctors and lawyers are still using Latin in the U.S. to this very day.

At the turn of the Twentieth Century there was a movement by One Worlders to create a common language for the planet so that common people could communicate and have the possibility of exerting more control over their world. The language Esperanto was created in simplified, easy to learn form and the effort was made to promulgate it. Naturally practically no one bothered to learn it. Today we have computer driven translators both handheld and online that get better ever year. That plus the Internet could make some of the dreams of those thoughtful people of a century earlier realizable.

Item: 04-07-06 Friday—Young Adults, Minorities Leading Cellular Way—The revolution is being lead by those 18-29 and minorities that are more likely to use their phones as personal computers, digital music players, cameras, and more, an AP-AOL-PEW poll found.

Item: Judas Iscariot, reviled as the worst betrayer of all time, was in fact Jesus' best friend and the only one who understood him. This according to a long lost 300 AD document that lay hidden in the Egyptian desert and was revealed Thursday by the National Geographic Society.

This document is in Coptic and is a copy of the original that was written in Greek about 140 years after Jesus and Judas died. It had been written by the Gnostics. The Gnostics believed in knowledge, gnosis, and were interested in spiritual knowledge, the essential oneness of the inner self with God.

Naturally the document had been declared heretical by early church leaders. The demonizing of Judas was part of a deliberate campaign by St. Augustine to vilify the Jews and spread the flames of anti-Semitism. Some passages from this authenticated document in which Jesus is speaking to Judas are:

You will exceed all of them. For you will sacrifice the man that clothes me.

Step away from the others and I shall tell you the mysteries of the kingdom. It is possible for you to reach it, but you will grieve a great deal.

You will be cursed by the other generations…and you will come to rule over them.

Why were the Gnostic texts banned from the Bible? What was deemed so dangerous about them? Or was it mostly because they believed, as did the Prophets like Moses, Jesus, and Mohammed; in dealing directly with their Creator and those earning their living as middle-men didn't like that.

Item: President Bush and VP Dick Cheney are shown to be at the heart of the outing of covert CIA operative Valerie Plame. This was done to retaliate against her husband, former Ambassador Joseph Wilson who had discredited false Administration WMD claims re Iraq.

Charlie Rose was missing again last night but Brian Williams was on. I caught part of the show with Jon Meacham the managing editor of Newsweek. He has a new book out called *American Gospel*. He mentioned that the wall between church and state is a low one.

Another tidbit was the saying, "The unexamined faith isn't worth having." He said something about how religion is the most pervasive and least understood force in society or something to that effect. He also mentioned James Madison in connection with his writing, *Memorial and Remonstrance Against Religious Assessments*, and also *The Federalist No. 10—The Utility of the Union as a Safeguard Against Domestic Faction and Insurrection*—Daily Advertiser—Thursday, November 22, 1787. I have expanded slightly the former below. The full-length documents are worth reading.

To the Honorable the General Assembly of the Commonwealth of Virginia—*A Memorial and Remonstrance Against Religious Assessments*—James Madison—1785

"We the subscribers, citizens of the said Commonwealth, having taken into serious consideration, a Bill printed by order of the last Session of General Assembly, entitled 'A Bill establishing a provision for Teachers of the Christian Religion,' and conceiving that the same if finally armed with the sanctions of a law, will be a dangerous abuse of power, are bound as faithful members of a free State to remonstrate against it, and to declare the reasons by which we are determined. We remonstrate against the said Bill…"

Item: Today I received in the mail a solicitation from The Wilderness Society. They state that in his first term President Bush pushed for drilling in the pristine Arctic National Wildlife Refuge; worked to weaken America's clean air regulations, and unilaterally withdrew the U.S. from the Kyoto Protocol on global warming…that had been signed by 55 other industrialized nations.

According to these folks, the Bush Administration now wants to eliminate vital protection for the last remaining road-less acres in our national forests consisting of 58.5 million wild acres that are home to 220 endangered species. They state, that these acres "are targeted for 'asset management,' which is just double talk for giving away these ecological jewels to timber, oil, and mining interests. These precious wildlands belong to you and me…and to future generations of Americans. The Bush Administration has no right to sell out our nations natural heritage."

They say a whole lot more and I don't want to get political. I have not investigated this and do realize that some logging is preferable to losing this timber to wildfires. On the other hand, what's the use of having ecologically sensitive lands set aside for protection…if the oil and coal companies are still allowed to go in and to rip up these last wild places?

Item: Newsweek April 10 Page 18—David Friedman of the Union of Concerned Scientists criticized as inadequate, the new rules issued last week that raises slightly the mileage requirements for SUVs, pickups, and minivans. "To me, it defies logic." He said.

Item: MIT's Technology Review April 2006 — Cover — Advances in biotechnology have put bio-weapons within the reach of terrorists and offer governments new opportunities for violence and repression.

Once again the First Friday's Art Walk has me prowling downtown Bremo and as usual I ended up at the Westside Burrito Connection. A Burmese artist from Seattle, Nyein Aung was visiting and working out front. A lot of his art was on display on the walls inside. I really liked Nyein and picked up two of his creations.

Senator Joe Biden was on Bill Maher tonight and somewhere it was revealed that our own Department of Defense stated in a report issued two years ago that the number one threat to the security of the United States of America was global warming. Senator Biden plans to run for president in 2008.

Also on the program from a remote location was Kevin Phillips who recently authored *American Theocracy*. He states that this is the first time ever that a religious party has been in power in this country. Churchgoers are increasingly members of the

Republican Party and secularists now join the Democrats. There was discussion about these End-Timers, those who literally believe in the Apocalypse and Armageddon and think that the time is soon, and how dangerous they may be. Many are actually looking forward to the end of the world; much like the harebrained Marshall 'Do' Applewhite and his Be-Bopp Comet. The word Apocalypse actually simply means 'to reveal'.

He also detailed some common signs exhibited by empires shortly before their demise and how the U.S. is now displaying those very signs. Such things as overreaching and piling on enormous debt.

Saturday morning I awoke having forgotten all about the monthly meeting of my biker gang, the notorious VERMIN. I suited up in ten minutes and hit the highway. The ride back was in the rain the whole way, but it was quite enjoyable nonetheless.

More from the fact is stranger than fiction department. I was doing my daily turn on a stationary bicycle listening to the end of Car Talk on NPR. The show ended and the next item up concerned a man who was operating a facility that fed homeless people. He said he could put a good meal together for 38 cents. He fed six thousand people and had an annual budget of $50 thousand. The problem arose because he was operating under the name of Love Thy Neighbor. The good old Golden Rule, Love Thy Neighbor as Thyself.

It hit the fan when a lady minister sued him, stating that she had been using the name Love Thy Neighbor before he did, and she had trademarked it. How anyone could trademark the Golden Rule is quite beyond me but apparently she had. The first gentleman has been forced to send her money and hire attorneys and whatnot and all of these expenditures are coming straight out of the mouths of the homeless that he is attempting to feed. Love Thy Neighbor indeed!

Item: 04-08-06 Saturday — Baby-Killing Mom Found Insane — A Mother charged with murder for cutting off her baby daughter's arms in 2004 in what her lawyers portrayed as a religious frenzy was found not guilty by reason of insanity Friday by a judge. Sort of gives religious frenzy a bad name, doesn't it?

Item: Tacoma — Police Attempt to Remove Gold Dental Work — The U.S. District Court case of Flenard T. Neal Jr. and Donald Jamar Lewis, charged with several drug and weapons violations, took an alarming turn when the defendants were taken Tuesday from the Federal Detention center to the U.S. Marshall's Office where they were told that the government had a warrant to seize their grills or grillz, i.e. gold dental work. Before being put in a van to be taken to a dentist in Seattle, they called their lawyers who were able to halt the seizure of the grills that were permanently bonded to their teeth.

04-09-06 Sunday — I began reading *Breaking the Spell* by Daniel C. Dennett at 4 AM this morning. No rest for the wicked. The book is well worth reading and has some really great quotes. I just have to steal one of them here:

"Philosophy is questions that may never be answered. Religion is answers that may never be questioned." — Anonymous

Item: Fossil is Missing Link From Sea to Land Animals — Scientists have discovered fossils of a 375-million-year-old fish, a large scaly creature not seen before, that they say is a long-sought missing link in the evolution of some fishes from water to a life walking on four limbs on land.

A team of scientists led by Neil Shubin of the University of Chicago say that they have uncovered several well-preserved skeletons of this fossil fish in sediments of former streambeds in the Canadian Arctic, six hundred miles from the North Pole.

The skeletons have the fins, scales and other attributes of a giant fish, four to nine feet long. But on closer examination, the scientists found telling anatomical traits of a transitional creature, a fish that is still a fish but has changes that anticipate the emergence of land animals, and is thus a predecessor of amphibians, reptiles and dinosaurs, mammals and eventually humans.

In the fishes' forward fins, the scientists found evidence of limbs in the making. There are the beginnings of digits, proto-wrists, elbows and shoulders. The fish also had a flat skull resembling a crocodile's, a neck, ribs and other parts that were similar to four-legged land animals known as tetrapods.

Other scientists said that the fossils were a powerful rebuttal to religious Creationists, who have long argued that the absence of such transitional creatures is a serious weakness in Darwin's theory. Dr. Shubin, an evolutionary biologist, let himself go. "It's a really amazing, remarkable intermediate fossil," he said. "It's like, Holy Cow!"

H. Richard Lane, director of paleobiology at the National Science Foundation, said, "These exciting discoveries are providing fossil 'Rosetta Stones' for a deeper understanding of this evolutionary milestone, fish to land-roaming tetrapods."

Michael J. Novacek, a paleontologist at the American Museum of Natural History in Manhattan, said: "A good fossil cuts through a lot of scientific argument."

Dr. Shubin's team played down the fossil's significance in the raging debate over Darwinian theory, which is opposed by some conservative Christians in this country, but other scientists were not so reticent. They said that this should undercut the argument that there is no evidence in the fossil record of one kind of creature becoming another kind.

When you live in pollution you become unconscious of it, just like a fish stops seeing water and we don't see air. When Tommy and I lived in Baja, we were amazed to realize how different it was to be in a clean environment. Occasionally we would hear voices and think some people were in our compound, only to find out that they were perhaps a quarter of a mile away.

Smells that would travel only thirty yards in Los Angeles would be detectable for a mile or more. You could put a CB radio that was good for a few miles and by placing it near the surface of the sea; you could pick up Texas hundreds of miles away.

We live in a sea of noise, odors, radio waves, microwaves, TV signals, air and water pollution, and more relevant to this writing; we live in an ocean of misinformation.

We are inundated with SPAM and junk mail. Did you ever try going to the U.S. Post Office and telling them that you don't want anything but First Class mail, and to please withhold the junk? They will not do it. You must get the junk. It is the law!

We are bombarded with bad news from around the globe on a minute-by-minute basis. Programs we want to watch are interrupted by News Alerts consisting of yet more bad news. Armies of people are employed to put a spin on the data coming to us in furtherance of their own ends.

The advertising industry uses every known allowable trick or device to motivate us to buy products that we don't need, are bad for us, or both. Telemarketers and scam artists call us on the telephone to fleece or swindle us. Flaky charities and stock market touts hound us relentlessly. It seems everyone has an axe to grind at our expense.

I caught a little bit of the movie Kinsey a couple of nights ago. They showed some of the material that was in marriage manuals and the like, just a few decades ago and it was so laughable because it was obviously so ridiculously false.

But really there is nothing funny about how those in authority think so little about lying outright to those that follow their lead. These pamphlets would authoritatively declare that masturbation would lead to blindness, epilepsy and death. How the loss of one ounce of seminal fluid was the equivalent of losing forty ounces of blood, and other utter nonsense!

About a thousand years ago some monks in China got the notion, that since seminal fluid contained the human seed and that since it was the life force dating back to the beginning, that perhaps if they were able to prevent this life giving fluid from leaving the body…then maybe they would lead very long lives and have exceptionally healthy ones.

They proceeded to do so and thus tested that grand hypothesis that must have looked really good on rice paper. But rather than long healthy lives, what they reaped was a higher incidence of testicular and prostate cancer and other negative consequences. What they were doing was defying the natural law that says, use it or lose it.

Now we have these deranged people claiming that sex is strictly for procreation and not recreation. I see, so that would mean that if we all had one child in order to reduce the planet's overpopulation we should all have sexual intercourse ideally, once in our lifetime. This when the reality is that whatever you use develops and remains healthy, and what you do not use atrophies, sickens and dies. It is difficult to believe that these mellonheads ever received any schooling at all.

How can we trust that are leaders are looking out for us? I recall some years ago when the San Francisco police force went out on strike. It wasn't but a few days before it became known that the crime rate had gone down after the strike began. It wasn't long after that when the strike came to a screeching halt.

People in our cities are so harried and busy that they often only meet their neighbors through some type of conflict. Rage crimes are increasing and occurring over such trivial matters as cell phones and toilet paper. I have yet to see the Academy Award winning film *crash*, but understand that one aspect of it is that people are so alienated from one another that there are those who will literally crash their car into another in order to meet someone.

Item: A New York Times article by Seymour Hirsh claims that a high level official 'leaked' to him that stepped up plans are being made by the U.S. to attack Iran using tactical nuclear weapons.

I go downtown and eat at the newly opened Anthony's Homeport Restaurant. Yesterday was the opening but they had a $150 per plate fundraiser for Olympic College on Friday night that was sold out long ago. The view was superb and the food was first rate. I had the all you can eat crab and almost had to be wheeled out of there.

Walking back to my vehicle I picked up a free Seattle rag, *The Strangler*. I had not seen this newspaper for over three years. I opened it and there was a notice for a book signing for the following Monday morning. The synchronicity that is happening with what has become an involuntary writing project for me startles me once again. Friday night on Bill Maher I saw his remote interview with Kevin Phillips whose latest literary work is *American Theocracy*. The Strangler notice shows that Kevin Phillips will be doing a book signing mañana in Seattle at the landmark Elliott Bay Book Company at the unusual hour of 8 AM. I commit myself to going.

Later channel surfing I stop at a Government Access channel. There is a four-hour religious program on from 7-11 PM. I watch for maybe twenty minutes. It appears that the gentleman is bashing all religions except Christianity or some segment of Christianity. He confirms that indeed the Mormons believe that if you have ten wives, when you go to heaven you will be made a God of your very own planet! There you can have spirit babies and do whatever you want with these planetary inhabitants.

He says that when Mormons profess to believe in one God they actually mean, one God per planet. He said that Mormons believe that, "As man is, God once was. As God is man may become." He says that Mormons believe that Jesus was a lesser God. He said that the head of the Mormon Church claims to be God's mouthpiece when uttering dogma and therefore infallible, just like the Pope's claim.

A few channels later I hit KWDK, a Christian station owned by Daystar Communications, broadcasting out of Tacoma, WA. I was then subjected to *The Hal Lindsey Report*. He was a straight up End-Timer. He was spewing forth this Apocalypse, Armageddon, and the Last Days of the Book of Daniel claptrap exactly like he was delivering the evening news. His theme was that the year 1948 was the *Hinge of History*. That was the year that modern Israel came into being, the year that the World Council of Churches began the attempt to bring all religions into harmony, and whatever. He repeatedly stated that the generation that he was speaking to was the last one before the End-Time.

While harmonizing the world's religions strikes me as an eminently desirable goal, to Hal Lindsey this was obviously a pet project of none other than the Antichrist himself. In that regard he went on to slam Bishop William Swing and The United Religions Initiative or URI. I Googled the URI and came up with an anti-URI site. The following is a partial rendering:

The United Nations seems a likely tool the Antichrist will use to establish his nefarious one-world government. The Antichrist's false prophet could benefit from a global religious entity in establishing the evil world religion. Mystery Babylon does not have to start from scratch. The United Religions Initiative, URI, is a global religious body designed to be a 'United Nations of religion.' In fact, in March of 2001, the URI became an official Non-Governmental Organization, NGO affiliated with the UN.

The brainchild of Bishop William Swing of San Francisco, the URI is now made up of about 170 'Cooperation Circles'. Each cooperation circle is made up of at least seven members, and represents at least three different religious beliefs. The URI is lead by the Global Council. The GC is made up of members elected from the eight geographic regions. Every two years the URI conducts a conference known as the 'General Assembly'. According to the preamble of the URI Charter, the URI's purpose is "to promote enduring daily interfaith cooperation, to end religiously motivated violence and to create cultures of peace, justice and healing for the Earth and all living beings."

There are 21 principles that make up the URI Charter. In reading the charter, one gets the impression that this body truly exists for a noble cause. However, three of the principles contain language that could tie the hands and gag the mouths of Evangelical Christians.

Principle two states, "We respect the sacred wisdom of each religion, spiritual expression, and indigenous tradition."

Principle seven states, "We seek and welcome the gift of diversity and model practices that do not discriminate."

Finally, principle 21: "Members of the URI shall not be coerced to participate in any ritual or be proselytized."

The more I read about the URI, the better it sounds to me! We are all one and are all different manifestations of the same Creation. When we hate and fight each other we are really only hating and fighting ourselves. Along with that, it is commonly known that what we hate most in others is our own flaws reflected there.

The Hal Lindsey Report ended with Hal Lindsey asking one and all to send money to him in Palm Desert, California. Palm Desert…I wonder if Hal Lindsey plays a lot of golf?

Economic dependence on the audience effects the shaping of the message away from long-term consideration of issues and needs, toward a message addressed to the immediately perceived desires of the audience. Many broadcasters conduct regular market research to learn which aspects of the Christian message will evoke the greater responses from their audiences.

Most of the current broadcasters see no contradiction between such methods and the traditional Christian faith. Jim Bakker, host of the 'PTL Club' openly adopts marketing analogies: "We have a better product than soap or automobiles. We have eternal life!" he once stated.

04-10-06—I take the ferry to Seattle and attend the book signing and lecture. *American Theocracy* by Kevin Phillips is a must read. He is an erudite scholar who has written many books. Mr. Phillips is a Republican who worked for Nixon, supported Reagan with some reservations, and is aghast at what is going on with the Bush Administration. The subtitle of the book is: *The Peril and Politics of Radical Religion, Oil, and Borrowed Money in the 21ˢᵗ Century.*

The Dutch were a major power utilizing wind and waterpower. They were supplanted by the British who used a newer energy source, namely coal. We replaced the British by exploiting an even newer energy source, oil. The Twentieth Century was the Century of America and Oil. But the oil is running out. It remains to be seen if we can make the energy switch from oil to a better, more plentiful source.

In the above regard I think of China that is now perfecting replicable Lego style safe pebble-bed nuclear power generating plants for dispersal throughout that vast country and their contemplation of widespread hydrogen fueled vehicles.

I have only begun to read this book but understand that among other things it examines how our country is heading toward a Theocracy as the Republican Party is being taken over by conservatives of several religions and most dangerously by Christian Fundamentalists.

These End-Timers who have swallowed the Armageddon, Rapture, Tribulation yarn, hook line and sinker, actually look forward to the Final Conflict and the end of our world. Only of course because they have been told that they are God's chosen ones. Interesting how the Jews believe that they are the chosen people, Christians believe that they have been chosen, and

Muslims think they are God's chosen favorites. Actually, almost all religions use this technique as who would join a group that stated that they were not numero uno?

President Bush has made many alarming statements, such as that his policy is directed by God. He reportedly told the Amish in Lancaster County, PA that God talks to him and that he couldn't do his job without that contact. He has said that he doesn't get advice from his earthly father, number 41, but from his Higher Father. He told the Palestinians that God told him to invade Afghanistan and Iraq.

The more I work on this report, the more radicalized I am becoming. On the one hand I have to question the sincerity of our President's religious views. What are the odds of an alcoholic cocaine user, who becomes born-again just as his failed oil industry career runs headlong into the collapsing oil market of 1985, actually believing that baloney? Especially since he was well aware of the mechanics of his father's loss of the Presidency and the growing power of the Christian Coalition.

On the other hand, can we possibly dare to allow someone who states that God is talking to him to have his hands on the nuclear button? Should he not be whisked out of that office based on mental incompetence, if not certifiable insanity?

This End-Timers baloney has been going on for two millennia, at least since the end of the First Century A.D. approached, and every century thereafter. Over and over one cult leader or another will give an exact date when the world will come to an end and Jesus will drop by for another visit. The leader derives his authority from the prediction until the date finally arrives and nothing happens. Interestingly enough, the members that are away from the cult when the big day comes and goes will usually snap out of it, but those that are with the charlatan will continue to believe as the groups mass hypnosis is reenergized, reinforced and continues on, often with a hastily calculated new date.

Item: Lt Gen Gregory Newbold is the third high ranking retired U.S. General to come out in the past week calling for the resignation of Donald Rumsfeld, U.S. Secretary of Defense.

Item: Immigration rallies sweep the U.S. — Tens of thousands of people rallied in U.S. cities. Some have compared this national protest day to the 1960s' civil rights movement. Up to 20,000 rallied outside NYC City Hall, one of over sixty cities where rallies were being held, under the theme 'We are America'. Thousands marched through Washington to gather near Congress. Immigrant rights groups provided buses to bring in protesters. 40,000 people flooded the streets of Atlanta. In Phoenix, more than 50,000 turned out. In Houston, thousands marched chanting 'USA, USA, USA'. About 10,000 protesters marched through Boston singing and chanting, about 8,000 rallied in Omaha, and 25,000 locally in Seattle.

There are estimated to be eleven to twelve million illegal immigrants living in the United States, according to the Pew Hispanic Center. Houston television reported that flyers had been distributed in the industrial suburb of Pasadena urging people to burn down the homes of illegal immigrants!

Item: The TV had a commercial against steroids by DrugFree.com where they were calling for a drug free America. What a joke. All day long they show ads for drugs. Americans are now on billions of dollars worth of drugs and our government has now committed us to paying tens of trillions of dollars in Medicare drug payments. One ad that really gets me is for a drug to take if you are allergic to your pet. The side effects are liver damage and death among others. Would anyone in their right mind put such a needless drug into their body on a daily unending basis?

Item: 04-11-06 Tuesday—The Today Show reports that doctors in Texas think some children born today will live to be 150 years old. This information struck many people as wild and perhaps exaggerated. But if you stop to ponder it you may decide that it is more probably wildly underestimated. Children born today who would naturally live to be 100 would reach the year 2106.

With our knowledge doubling every few years and since we are on the brink of the most fundamental breakthroughs at this time, it is unimaginable today what man maybe capable of in 2106, and long before that time. That is if we do not self-destruct before first. Returning to our cousins the rats, we are already successfully experimenting with altering genes in rodents for the purpose of prolonging life.

A child born today would not have to wait 100 years for a breakthrough but would have life-enhancing means available to him or her throughout their entire lifetime. Once their life expectancy was on track to live 150 years, that would take them to the year 2156. By then there should be no problem with artificial organs, grown in lab factories, and who knows what else. Would it not be much more realistic to assume that once you reached that realm, that you could live 500 years? If so that would take you to 2506. Would you not by then, barring accidental death, be able to live more or less forever?

The issue is, how does this longevity square with the human overpopulation of the Earth? I know that some world population projections indicate a possible leveling off around 2050 but do you know how many more people will be here by then? We already have at least forty thousand perishing daily unnecessarily.

Today I found the following on the front page of [www.overpopulation.org/]

March 20, 2006—The Battle to Ban Birth Control—Mary Worthington regards contraception as immoral and dangerous. This month she launched 'No Room for Contraception', a clearinghouse for arguments and personal testimonials on this subject.

NRFC joins others on an anti-contraception web. NRFC doesn't even address abortion; its sole purpose is to 'prove' that the pill and the IUD cause health problems and destroy women's fertility and condoms lead to the spread of STDs by making people believe that sex can be safe, that contraception destroys marriages by rendering sex an act of pleasure rather than one of procreation.

The vast majority of Americans support access to birth control: even 80% of anti-choice Americans support women's access to contraception. With the exception of a dwindling number of Catholics, a majority of American women have used or regularly use some form of contraception.

Supporters have pressured insurance companies to refuse coverage of contraception and are redefining the very meaning of pregnancy to classify contraceptive methods as abortion. Although its medical arguments are thinly veiled moral and religious arguments, the rising anti-contraception movement, echoed by the Catholic Church, is making significant inroads.

After Roe v. Wade was decided, debate focused on abortion but for anti-choicers they are not separate issues. The National Right to Life affiliates have opposed legislation that would provide insurance coverage for contraception. Iowa Right to Life lists birth control methods, including the pill, the IUD, Norplant and Depo-Provera, as abortifacients.

Contraception lessens the number of abortions. But once one understands what the true agenda of activists like Worthington is, and their attitude toward sexuality, the contradictions vanish. For them, sex should always be about procreation, since contraception prevents conception it is therefore immoral.

They believe that women's biological destiny is to be mothers. Sex and the role of women are linked because "If you can separate sex from procreation, you have given women the ability to participate in society on an equal basis with men."

The anti-birth-control movement has seized recent headlines about emergency contraception to put forth its view that emergency contraception. is tantamount to abortion. Anti-choice activists don't bother to distinguish between RU-486, the 'abortion pill', which terminates an early pregnancy, and E.C. which helps prevent pregnancy.

The American Medical Association defines pregnancy as the moment when implantation occurs; the anti-choice movement, completely ignoring scientific fact, is attempting to redefine pregnancy as the moment when sperm and egg meet.

Once a fertilized egg is considered a human life, it's just a hop to concluding that the standard birth-control pill is an abortifacient. According to the National Conference of State Legislatures, at least fifteen states have fetal homicide laws. That means that one can be convicted of manslaughter or murder for destroying a fertilized egg.

The National Institutes of Health convened experts to evaluate the condom's effectiveness at preventing the spread of sexually transmitted diseases and they concluded that correct condom use definitively protected against the spread of HIV and gonorrhea, and there was a strong probability of condom effectiveness for other STDs, including human papillomavirus, HPV.

The findings were used to declare that condoms don't protect against HPV a wild misappropriation of fact that has nonetheless become a big part of the anti-choice argument against the condom's efficacy. Such subtle shifts have helped anti-choice activists to argue that condoms help spread STDs by giving users a false sense of security.

One reason for the new push to restrict birth control may have to do with changes in the Catholic Church although many anti-contraception campaigners insist this has nothing to do with Catholicism.

NRFC is filled with discussions of Catholic texts and Bible Study documents. Like the Catholic Church, NRFC opposes the use of contraception even within marriage as it leads to promiscuity and furthers the idea the sex has nothing to do with childbearing or commitment.

Contraception has given women the freedom to put off marriage, to go to college in greater numbers, to bring more wanted children into the world, and to find good jobs and thus bring more wealth into their families; and banning contraception would turn back that clock.

Item: Though more than two-thirds of the planet is covered with water, only a small fraction, around 0.3 percent is available for human use and reuse. And no more of this renewable fresh water is available today than existed at the dawn of human civilization.

World population, currently at 6.5 billion, is growing by another 76 million people per year. According to the United Nations the world will add another 2.6 billion people by 2050. That is more than the total world population when I was born! Rapid population growth has placed incredible stress on Earth's resources.

Global demand for water has tripled since the 1950s, but the supply of fresh drinking water has been declining because of over-pumping and contamination. Half a billion people live in water-stressed or water-scarce countries, and by 2025 that number will grow to three billion. In the last 50 years, cropland has been reduced by 13% and pastureland by 4%.

Item: "I am officially announcing that Iran has joined the group of those countries which have nuclear technology. This is the result of the Iranian nation's resistance," Iranian President Mahmoud Ahmadinejad said in a televised address.

Looks like these guys are begging for it…playing right into the hands of the Bush Administration. All smoke and mirrors aside, we are involved in the Middle East for one real reason and one reason alone, oil. They know it and all of us should know it. Iraq has the oil most easily produced and may have resources greater than even Saudi Arabia.

If you want all the detail and history on this, read *American Theocracy*. The unreal reason is this Biblical End-Time rubbish that is required to energize the Christian Fundamentalist base of the Republican Party.

Most oil importing countries were encouraged by the break-up of the former Soviet Union and the subsequent independence of the Central Asian Republics, CARs, because a huge portion of the region contains vast deposits of crude oil, natural gas and coal. The break-up posed an opportunity for the energy importers to exploit CAR's natural resources. Afghanistan is in a key location for a pipeline from the CARs.

We were dealing with the Taliban in that regard until they became too unstable. Many believe that they knew or believed that the U.S. was going to attack them and they decided to strike first with the 9-11 attack on the World Trade Center in NY.

If that is true, they are even dumber than we might think. Had we attacked them first and then they hit the Twin Towers, despite the horror and civilian casualties, they would have had the grudging admiration from many around the world; instead of the near universal opprobrium that they received.

The frightening thing is, on one side we have the Muslim Fundamentalists who want nothing more than a Holy War with all of Islam pitted against Christianity. On the other side we have the Christian Fundamentalists who also want a Holy War against Islam in order to fulfill what they consider to be Bible prophesy authored by God. Naturally they expect to be among the few chosen to survive the scorched Earth scenario.

None of this makes any sense whatsoever unless you are confident that you and your family will make it to the long-term underground nuclear shelters. There you and your future generations while away the time, perfecting longevity techniques until your descendents are practically immortal. When the Earth cools, they emerge into a Garden of Eden for a thousand years of good times, and the Bible prophecy is fulfilled.

The rest of us six billion people are of course...toast. But these are devout Christians that have been chosen by God, they won't have a problem with our charred and smoldering remains.

I just returned from the monthly Navy League luncheon at SubBase Bangor. Our military have got to be comprised of the politest people anywhere. The program had to do with recruitment in general and the possibility of a NASCAR track here in Kitsap County in particular. The Navy is 100% in favor of that and deems NASCAR fans to be the most patriotic of all. I got my hands on quite a bit of slick literature on the NASCAR proposal.

04-12-06 Wednesday—I take the day off and visit a friend on Whidbey Island who has had a stroke. Tom O'Connor has lost the use of his right hand and cannot speak except to say "Yes-Yes". He can hobble along with his right leg in a brace. Tom was in the building trades and built his own extended dream cabin in the woods over many years of struggle.

Relatives and a neighbor allegedly colluded to strip him of his home after the stroke and litigation is ongoing. Tom loved to sketch and paint, often in watercolors. He has learned to paint with his left hand. I took pictures of his new body of work for posting and sale online.

The driving, the ferry crossings between Port Townsend and Keystone, and the time spent with Tom added up to fourteen hours. It was time well spent and a good break for Tom, but at some level it must have been emotionally exhausting because I slept far longer than normal.

Item: 04-13-06 Thursday—On Tuesday a Muslim suicide bomber killed at least 47 and injured over 100 when he blew himself up in Karachi at a massive gathering to celebrate the birthday of the Prophet Muhammad. What can I say?

Apropos of absolutely nothing, the newspaper reports that Cheeta, of Tarzan Movie Fame, Turns 74. Despite being a diabetic, Cheeta is the world's oldest living chimpanzee.

I was able to read some of *American Theocracy* yesterday while waiting for and riding the ferries that made the crossing of the Straight of Juan de Fuca between the Olympic Peninsula and Whidbey Island. I have been hardest on the Catholic Church because I am most familiar with it. The many statistics and deep research that went into *American Theocracy* clearly show that the conservative Protestant denominations like the Evangelicals and Pentecostals are far worse in regard to establishing a Theocracy in the United States.

To quote but one statistic, in answer to the question: Should religious leaders try to influence politicians' positions on the issues? White conservative evangelicals said Yes 62% of the time, whereas Catholics said No 65% of the time.

An October 1999 Newsweek Poll asked: Will the world end in an Armageddon battle between Jesus Christ and the Antichrist? Evangelical Protestants responded, Yes 71%; other Protestants, No 54%; and Catholics, No 57%.

This book goes into great detail on the huge debt that we are piling on at every level including personal debt, to the extent that Financial Services have now passed Manufacturing as the greater source of U.S. Corporate Profits. This is put into historical perspective and is just one more major sign of five critical symptoms of decline that have indicated the beginning of the end for a global power such as Spain, Holland, Britain, and now us.

I admit to taking a perverse pleasure in another observation by Kevin Phillips that in red-states like Texas, where the lawmakers are the most opposed to recognizing the obviousness of Evolution, that the farmers there are having the most trouble with pests that are posing enormous problems as they constantly evolve immunity to various pesticides.

My trip to Bangor with its nuclear subs got me thinking about our next major shift to a new energy source as a nation. Also I have nuclear aircraft carriers docked in view below my ridge-top home. We do have decades of experience with nuclear power and should be able to make whatever transitions are necessary. The twin nuke powered aircraft carriers can operate for twenty years on one fueling!

We also are supposed to have enough cornhusks alone to produce enough ethanol to replace all of the oil that we import. Henry Ford said in 1930 that we ought to be burning ethanol in our automobiles. It has been estimated that we could switch to ethanol in five years and be energy independent like Brazil but the oil companies are unwilling to release the stranglehold in which they have us. FORD 'F' stock is down to $7 and is paying a 5.5% dividend. They are also rapidly turning out vehicles capable of running on ethanol.

There is a caveat to be aware of with ethanol. We have a very strong Corn Lobby and it is naturally pushing for corn-based ethanol. The Brazilians use sugar-based ethanol. Sugar based ethanol is reportedly as much as eight times better than that of corn-based ethanol that requires a lot more energy to produce. Wouldn't it be great if we could stop ingesting all of that sugar that is making us obese and diabetic and burn it in our vehicles instead?

My views do not align with either the far left or the extreme right. On this subject I have observed over the years that people who have the most conservative views often lead the most liberal personal lives, such as these brimstone preachers who time and again get caught with fourth-rate hookers in flea bag motels; and many with the most liberal political views, often lead the most conservative personal lives.

Here is an old investigators tip. In fact, this will probably seem unbelievable to you but just test it out for yourself. The easiest way to do this is by watching the body language of talking heads on TV. People who are unbalanced to the right will have heads that lean to their left. Those unbalanced to the left have heads that lean to their right. Therefore looking at your TV it works directly, heads leaning to your left are leftist and heads leaning to your right reveal rightists.

I guarantee you that you will be simply amazed at the extreme degree to which many heads will lean in one direction or another. Heads that go back and force indicated a thoughtful well balanced person...Brother Ray Charles took that to an extreme, but what soul the man had!

Some people will catch themselves with their head leaned way over and snap it upright but soon it will give them away again. Yes, there are a few right-wingers pretending to be leftist and vice versa. It goes back to the old wisdom of commenting on whether an individual had their head on straight or not...or the one referring to a person as being level headed.

Stand in front of a mirror and relax. Does you head tend to lean more comfortably in one direction or the other? If so, you know what to do. Balance is what you want. More important than whether your legs are big or small is that they are balanced. If you have one large strong leg and one short weak one, you have a problem. You will either walk around in circles to the left or to the right, either way you won't get very far. You want them to be the same, in balance

Back to the mirror, if your head is leaning to your right, forget the mirror, if your actual head is leaning to your right, you are liberal leaning and would do well to strengthen your masculine or left-brain side. If your head is leaning to your left, you need to strengthen your feminine or right brain side. It is no different than if you are right handed and play basketball. The more you practice shooting with your left hand, the more balanced you will become and the better you will shoot with your right hand as well.

Does might make right? Does Manifest Destiny justify our having invaded Iraq? As far as I am concerned we had a legal right to do so because of Saddam's violations of the cease-fire agreements from 1991. The West has been invading Iraq over oil for over a century, there is nothing new going on here. We are not the only ones who covet that oil. The Russians and the Chinese among others would have made even more moves for it than they did, if they had thought that they could get away with it.

If we can sustain ourselves long enough to make the scientific breakthroughs that could be mankind's salvation, we must do that. People who are into whacking off heads and lining human beings up in order to chop off hands during soccer game intermissions at stadiums filled with citizens, they are certainly not mankind's best hope.

But I would sure feel a lot better about it if we had continued to pursue strict energy conservation means and methods rather than to instead embark on an SUV craze. Arrogance and hubris seldom lead to good ends. If we were acting in a high-minded way and coming from a position of moral authority, everything would be so much more palatable.

And then to have some kid from Texas write a paper setting up a purported justification for U.S. Government torture, and be rewarded by being made the U.S. Attorney General. What was that? There must have been tens of thousands of attorneys far more qualified. Wasn't Ashcroft and his asinine clothing of statutes enough for us to have to swallow? Didn't that make us the laughingstock of the entire civilized world?

Despite repeated warnings we set-up Iraq's National Museum and Library for looting and destruction. Many of the items removed had been previously identified and found their way into the hands of collectors from the U.S., Japan, and elsewhere. A tradition of war is, to the victor go the spoils, but raping the conquered women is also a common practice. Are we going to allow that as well?

The damage that we did to ourselves with the Abu Ghraib prison abuse scandal is incalculable. I understand that sometimes you do have to fight fire with fire, but just because we are up against barbarians doesn't mean that we should act like that. That was shortsighted and stupid in the extreme. The Abu Ghraib scandal was let out of the bag by the youngsters using the new technology. They took pictures with their cell phones and emailed them to their friends worldwide via the Internet. The older generation that was in charge was not ready for that.

The National Museum was the greatest storehouse of artifacts from ancient Mesopotamia and many other ancient civilizations and cultures. It held the tablets with the world's first formal laws, the Code of Hammurabi! The National Library's reading rooms and stacks were reduced to smoking ruins. Our troops had shown up to stop the looting very early on but were then ordered out. We did of course totally protect the Oil Ministry and all it contained.

Item: 04-14-06 Friday—Two more respected retired U.S. Generals have gone public calling for Secretary Rumsfeld to resign. This brings the total to at least six this month! This is most unusual.

Bill O'Reilly was on his hobbyhorse again last night about what he calls the left's war against Christianity. I don't see it as an effort against Christianity, but as a secular movement against all delusional and dangerous religious misinformation emanating from any religion.

Item: The Today Show had a piece on TFAs, trans fatty acids, used in frying foods. Because they are so harmful to your health they are banned in Europe but are still widely used in the U.S. McDonalds is not allowed to use them in Europe but continues to use them here.

McDonalds spends close to one and a half billion dollars in worldwide advertising for its products. Pepsi spends over a billion. Children are exposed to about ten thousand advertisements yearly of which 95% are pushing sugar products and other junk food. Cartoon characters, promotions, games and toys are all used to entice children to consume what they should be shunning.

Wouldn't it be nice if the major sport, music, and movie stars were encouraging our youth to eat fruits, vegetables, and other healthy foods? Most young kids have no idea who George Washington was, or who George W. Bush is, but they sure as hell know who Ronald McDonald is.

Item: The port of Bremo is to receive $3 million from the Feds EDA, Economic Development Administration, to enlarge the waterfront marina. The $22.9 million dollar project will expand the visitor slips from 45 to 352. Twenty-five slips will be allocated to the Harborside Condominiums that are now under construction.

Item: Iraq's beauty Queen Fears for Her Life—She has gone into hiding from Islamic militants who have threatened to kill other contestants. The original contest winner and two runner-ups have already bowed out after being threatened with death.

What a shame to think that God hates beauty. Lies and delusions are harmful. It may seem that the notion of the traditional Heaven is a comfort but it is a two-edged sword like everything else. Once you have people believing in that, it is a hop-skip-and a jump to telling them that God has 72 virgins waiting for them if they will just strap on high explosives and blow up a bunch of innocent civilians of all ages.

How ridiculous is that? A God that disapproves of beauty contestants but hands out virgins in six-dozen lots to mass murderers! That is the problem, once you enter the delusion and allow yourself to be controlled from the outside, anything goes, absolutely anything. If religious people believe that Satan exists and is actively operating on Earth, I ask you, what better cover and shield is there to work behind than that of religion?

Item: Good old Bill Cosby was in New Orleans giving the Black Community there a piece of his mind. That is exactly what is needed. I hope he is listened to and joined by others. A lot of house cleaning is in order.

Muslim religious psycho stabs six Christian Copts in Church on Good Friday, killing one.

Item: 04-15-06 Saturday—The fastest growing churches in the U.S. are The Assemblies of God 1.81% to 2.8 million, Mormon 1.74% to 6 million, and Roman Catholic 0.83% to 67.8 million.

Item: 04-16-06 Sunday—Puget Sound Orcas share their food with other pod members. Puget Sound Chinook salmon, an Orcas favorite are more contaminated with PCBs than other Chinook leading to why Puget Sound Orcas have some of the highest levels of contamination in the world. Banned chemicals like PCBs and DDT still show up in lesser amounts but toxic flame retardants are building up. Chinook are now only one half the size that they were in the 1950s!

Item: 04-17-06 Monday—Here is a lovely story from the Newsweek April 17th issue. A four-man squad of U.S. Navy SEALS was ambushed in Afghanistan by the Taliban. One wounded SEAL escaped. Before the Taliban could find him, an Afghan named Mohammad Gulab, who was foraging for edible wild plants, found him and saved him.

He did this knowing that he, his wife and six kids would be marked for death. He lost his home, his little lumber business, his truck, and his brother was shot in the chest. After all that he states that he has no regrets and that Pashtunwali, the tribal mountain code of honor, demands that it is a sacred duty to help those in need. He is a handsome man who looks like he just stepped off a Hollywood Biblical movie set.

There seems to be a common understanding that man is so evil that unless he is threatened with eternal hellfire on a regular basis, he will commit terrible crimes. But the evidence contradicts this. The Germans, the Japanese, the Koreans, the Vietnamese, the Afghans, and Iraqis are basically good people. Folks just want to take care of their families and avoid trouble. It is the people with high concentrations of power that start the trouble, whether it is purely political or religious power. Power corrupts and absolute power corrupts absolutely, some things never change. Beware the rich, greedy old men lusting for more money and power.

Item: 04-18-06 Tuesday—South Kitsap Home Prices are up 40%—The median price in overall Kitsap was up 14% in March.

NOVA was about Sun Dimming. The amount of solar radiation reaching the earth's surface has been dropping dramatically for the past half century. Many didn't believe these findings coming first from Israel and later from Germany. Then the Pan Evaporation Rate that has been well documented worldwide for the last 100 years confirmed the findings exactly.

The upshot is that Sun Dimming is making the planet cooler and that is cutting the global warming in half. In other words Global Warming is twice as bad as we thought but being masked by the Sun Dimming. The latter being caused by pollution that is both blocking sunshine and turning the clouds into giant mirrors.

The three days after 9-11 when all U.S. planes were grounded allowed measurements to be made for the first time. The result was a startling improvement in air quality and a startling immediate increase in solar radiation reaching the ground due to the absence of jet contrails.

Our improvement in visible pollution by means of scrubbers, catalytic converters, and so on will only cause Global Warming to accelerate rapidly. Many already think that we have at best, ten years to reverse the present trends. The pollution generated by the developed nations caused a climatic shift that caused the decades long draughts in places like Ethiopia that killed millions. Actually the horror story is far worse than I have time to relate here.

Item: 04-19-06 Wednesday—Chinese President Hu Jintao arrived yesterday and begins a Seattle tour. About 100 attended the dinner at the Gates' home hosted by Washington Governor Christine Gregoire. Today it was reported that President Hu told Boeing employees that China will need thousands more of their planes in the future. Well, there goes the environment. Meanwhile Microsoft would really like to get paid for its programs being distributed in China but it is still a pirate's game.

Today I received a solicitation from Greenpeace that states, "If you hate what they are doing to our world...you will love what Greenpeace is doing to stop them." And "The first step to making the world greener is seeing red."

Item: AARP Bulletin—April—Every year Americans throw away billions of dollars worth of prescription drugs due to bogus expiration dates.

Phase I of this three-phase report is approaching its conclusion. Phase II is scheduled to begin on May 02, 2006.

Item: 04-20-06 Thursday—Toluca, Mexico—A Mexican priest confessed to strangling his pregnant lover after Easter Mass, cutting off her head, and hacking her body to pieces with a kitchen knife. He loaded the pieces into bags, put them into a pickup truck and dumped them in a nearby cemetery. She had asked him for money to deal with the pregnancy. Okay...but isn't Easter all about fertilizing eggs?

A Cal Thomas article states that it is Time to Get Serious About Energy. If JFK could get us to the moon from scratch in eight years, why aren't we running a crash program to free ourselves form Middle Eastern oil? He says that it is our own oil money that is being funneled by the Islamic Banks to fund the very terrorists that we are fighting! Thus American citizens are paying for both sides of this War against Terror.

I spent most of the day on a special private tour of the Seattle Coast Guard's VTS, Vessel Traffic Service, installation. They have a 3,500 square mile territory in which they control the shipping coming and going from Puget Sound, mostly through the Strait of Juan de Fuca. The border with Canada runs smack down the middle of that Strait, so they work very closely with the Canadian CVTS.

This is Homeland Security's frontline of defense with respect to our waterways. The control room and capability was amazing but in the interest of national security I will leave it at that.

Item: 04-21-06 Friday—Central Kitsap High School received the top national honor in the State by being awarded the Siemens Foundation's one per state recognition for its AP math and science program.

Drug Cartel beheads former police commander along with some other fellow. He had resigned days earlier due to death threats. He, or I should say his head, was accompanied by a message that read, "So that you learn to respect." Oh yeah, sure thing…we all have the utmost respect for that. Now we have beheadings in North America.

Item: A young boy looked up two local Registered Sex Offenders, whose names and addresses are posted online, and murdered them. He killed himself when cornered by authorities. The crime of one of the 'Sex Offenders' was to have had sex with his 16-year-old girlfriend when he was 19 years old. In other words he was perfectly normal and in no way a sexual pervert of any kind.

This is one of the current scare campaigns. Obviously the violent sexual predators should be dealt with harshly but now we are branding as many people as possible. Some years back the same scare tactics were used with missing children. For as long as they could get away with it, we were told that tens of thousands of children were being kidnapped in the U.S. annually. Eventually it came out that something like over 99% of these were kids with their own, non-custodial, parent.

In the 80's and 90's we were told that thousands of kids were sexually abused by hundreds of day care workers in the U.S. and Great Britain. Many were arrested and ruined financially and otherwise. The young children were led and cajoled into bearing false testimony. The children that were strong enough to withstand this pressure and kept denying that anything happened...they were offered as more proof; the authorities claimed that the denials were really evidence of just how badly they had been abused.

Almost all of these charges turned out to be bogus. Eventually, after all the damage was done, this madness ended and we were subjected to a newer batch of scare tactics. Keep everyone scared and hating and fearing one another, and those in power can get away with just about anything.

Item: Two guys named Tim LaHaye and Jerry B. Jenkins have been pumping out books on the Apocalypse, Armageddon, the Rapture and the whole nine-yards of this crapola. They have people jumping into their SUVs to head for the hills to avoid the End-Time earthquakes and all that malarkey.

It is extremely difficult for an author to sell a few hundred thousand books. So how popular is the *Left Behind* series? At the last count that I have, the *Left Behind* series has exceeded 63 million books in sales, making it the best-selling Christian fiction series in history. *Left Behind* was voted one of the top 10 books of the 20th century on barnesandnoble.com and ivillage.com. *The Indwelling*, book #7, *The Mark*, book #8, *Desecration*, book #9, *The Remnant*, book #10, *Armageddon*, book #11, and *Glorious Appearing*, book #12, have all reached #1 on The New York Times bestseller list.

Has anyone detected any concern in these words yet? You are damn right that I am concerned, and getting more concerned the more I put this inflow of information together. Is anyone doing anything about all of this? The people who are supposed to protect ordinary citizens from creeping Theocracy, governmental abuses of power, and the trampling of our human rights are the A.C.L.U.

So that means the A.C.L.U. should be very busy these days, right? Oh they are busy all right. Busy giving the right-wing maniacs all of the most perfect ammunition that they could ever possibly wish for. The A.C.L.U. is defending NAMBLA, the group openly dedicated to pedophilia, they are attacking Christmas, the Boy Scouts…oh it is just too sad and outrageous to go on. Either the A.C.L.U. has been secretly taken over by Pat Robertson, or it is being run by imbeciles.

Gasoline is hitting as high as $3 and even $4 a gallon today. Meanwhile back at the ranch; for 13 years as chairman and chief executive, Lee R. Raymond propelled Exxon, the successor to John D. Rockefeller's Standard Oil Trust, to the pinnacle of the oil world.

Shareholders benefited handsomely on Mr. Raymond's watch. The price of Exxon's shares rose by an average of 13 percent a year. The company, now known as Exxon-Mobil, paid $67 billion in total dividends.

For his efforts, Mr. Raymond, who retired in December, was compensated more than $686 million from 1993 to 2005, according to an analysis done for by Brian Foley, an independent compensation consultant. That is $144,573 for each day he spent leading Exxon's 'God Pod' as the executive suite at the company's headquarters in Texas is known.

Despite the company's performance, some Exxon shareholders, academics, corporate governance experts and consumer groups were taken aback this week when they learned the details of Mr. Raymond's total compensation package, including the more than $400 million he received in his final year at the company.

Meanwhile, despite record profits, the world's largest oil company has yet to pay a single penny in the damages they owe to the Alaskan fishermen whose livelihoods were destroyed by the 1989 Exxon Valdez oil spill. The 9th U.S. Circuit Court of Appeals will hear oral arguments about whether the 30,000 plaintiffs affected by the spill will get the $4.5 billion in punitive damages that was awarded to them...but never paid. Around three thousand plaintiffs have already died while waiting sixteen years for Exxon-Mobil to pay punitive damages that amount to small change for that company.

This debate precedes record-breaking annual profits by Exxon-Mobil. Last year they had net profits around thirty-six billion and are on track to beat that this year. This quarter looks like it will be coming in just under eight and a half billion. Coupled with last quarter's eleven billion that makes about nineteen billion for the past half year.

Meanwhile documents are leaking that reveal Exxon-Mobil's deliberate unconscionable decision and strategy to muddy the waters on Global Warming by falsely attacking the science concerning this major world threat. Once again we have old men of limitless greed, consumed by power lust.

Item: 04-22-06 Saturday—Today is Earth Day. According to Bill Maher last night, "When Glacier National Park opened there were 150 glaciers, today there are 26 left." Speaking of Mr. Maher, ticket sales opened today for his appearance in Seattle on July 21. I did manage to get tickets, only because I caught the announcement in the *Seattle Weekly* when I took the ferry to Seattle Thursday to tour the Coast Guard installation.

Another item from the Bill Maher show: Only one major U.S. building project in Iraq is on schedule and on budget. The American embassy compound is slated to cost $592 million and cover 104 acres or about the size of 80 football fields. It is being built by 900 non-Iraqi foreign workers who are under the supervision of a Kuwaiti contractor. According to the special inspector general's office, 25% of nearly $21 billion for Iraq reconstruction has been diverted to pay for security.

I attended the 60th Anniversary celebration of the PSNBA, Puget Sound Naval Bases Association at Olympic College. The Keynote Speaker, U.S. Congressman Norm Dicks was introduced by U.S. Senator Maria Cantwell. It was a fine evening indeed.

Item: Colton Simpson's autobiography, *Inside the Crips: Life Inside L.A.'s Most Notorious Gang* impressed the critics. It also impressed the D.A. who may put him away for life using the book as evidence. It has already been ruled admissible in his trial.

The Washington State Ferry System, the country's largest, is the number one target for maritime terrorists according to the Justice Department.

Item: U.S. Army suicide rate in 2003—60; 2004—67; 2005—83. Four more are under investigation for 2005. This despite the Army's having been making a growing effort to detect and prevent suicides.

On the subject of suicide here is another tip for you. Not from an old investigator but from an old philosopher this time. Just as anomalies are instructive in peeking behind the veil of the image of reality that our minds produce, paradoxes are far more instructive. Keeping with the Biblical theme, here is one that if you figure it out, I guarantee that you will evolve your consciousness and understanding of reality to a higher plane, or more accurately, to a larger sphere.

According to the Bible suicide is the one unforgivable sin. When you understand this paradox, you will agree with that statement. What makes it a paradox is when you run scenarios. Suppose man X murders and tortures and rapes twelve children and then he repents, confesses and atones. This man may go to Heaven. Man Y leads an exemplary life but eventually commits suicide. He may never enter the Pearly Gates.

That seems so wrong on the surface. One would think that man X would have been a much nicer fellow if he had killed himself rather than doing all the evil that he did. That is the paradox. Understanding that at the deepest level will greatly expand your mind. Don't bother to Google it, I just did and as usual everyone has a contradictory view and nothing that I saw there even came close…they were not even in the right ballpark. Just more inane superficial religious blather.

Item: Local Bremo elementary school teacher named Washington State Science and Engineering Fair Mary Haviland Teacher of the Year.

The ancient practice of tithing as described in the Bible is particularly strong in the Black Community. According to a 2002 IRS study, religious institutions garnered three out of every four dollars of charitable giving. A case in point is the Greater Mount Nebo African Methodist Episcopal Church. Eighteen years ago when Reverend Jonathan Weaver took over the congregation, it had 65 members and less than 1% tithed. Today of the more than 2,000 members, more than 75% tithe.

"Some people have a sense that pastors are heavy-handed in the use of the Scripture to insist that people tithe," he said. "But we are not encouraging people to give us 10%. We want them to be effective managers of the other 90%. God wants us to be effective managers of what He has entrusted us with."

Thank you Reverend Weaver! By Jove that just may be my missing link. The Bible is everywhere because it is the Word of God telling all people to give 10% of their income to tax exempt religious institutions. For all I know Reverend Jonathan Weaver may be a saint. He may live frugally and give all this income to the poor.

But let's look at the numbers for a moment. He has been motivated to expand his followers from 65 to 2,000. He has managed to Bible-slap them until he went from less than 1% tithing to over 75% doing so. That means that from 1,500 people he gets 10% of each income or the full income of 150 people. If he averages only half of that from the other 50 he gets the equivalent of the income from another 25 people. This is the same as the full income of 175 people and it is tax exempt! That makes it worth the income from perhaps 200 people.

One man now receives the income of two hundred! Do you see the tremendous pressure to expand and increase the revenue from your base? To get to this enviable position he preaches a sermon to them every Sunday wherein he works them over with the Word of God until the fear of damnation is greater than the love and need of their money. It takes a lot to make people part with their money when they don't have to and ostensibly get nothing for it but more Bible-beatings. Are they God-fearing people or is it the good pastor that they fear?

Once again I am not trying to rag on Reverend Jonathan Weaver. He certainly knows how to motivate people and perhaps his congregation is far better off under his supervision then they were before they met him. I do know one thing though; you probably won't find me in his church. If I want or need to communicate with God, I will do it in a quiet setting under a nice tree, something that God made.

It does make sense that sheep need a Shepard but in the words of bunko artists the world over, "Sheep were meant to be shorn." Must human beings act like sheep?

In China wedding guests are honor-bound to give the newlyweds money. The Chonngqing Morning Post last reported that the residents of thriving Wenzhou gave nearly 11% of their income on wedding gifts; this was reportedly the highest rate in China. I would rather do that and consider the money better spent than had I given it to a Bible-thumper.

Back in the early '60s when I was a repo-man for GM I would occasionally strike it rich at a certain Jazz Club in New Haven, perhaps on Dixwell Avenue. Once a year or so they had a preachers' convention there. Virtually every car that showed up was a Cadillac and all were from the Deep South. I would copy down all the license numbers and then run them through the G-MAC offices of the various States. Once I had learned which ones had past-due accounts, I would pull those cars about 3 AM in a blitzkrieg. You may be sure that the Lord's name was invoked quite heavily after that.

Item: The Smithsonian April issue—The Young and the Restless—Saudi Arabia's baby boomers, born after the '73 oil embargo, are redefining the kingdom's relationship with the modern world. It states that Saudi Arabia is one of the world's youngest countries with 60% of the population under 21, 75% under age 30, and 33% under 14. Between these youngsters and the Internet, this extremely conservative society is beginning to open up.

There is an interesting story about a religious young man who did everything right, memorized the Quoran by heart, fasted, and so on, but was hit by a car on the way home from evening prayers. After a three month coma, a year of rehab and a lot of reading of liberal Arabs and Western philosophy he came out of his religious trance and began putting it all together.

This article has a picture of a McDonalds showing different ordering lines for men and women. A closer look reveals two women properly clothed and covered but waiting in the shorter men's line. Good for them!

Item: 04-23-06 Sunday—New Bin Laden audiotape states that, "The West is at War with Islam". No, it is all about oil and oil has no religion.

Item: Iran says that its nuke program is 'Irreversible'. It would have to be wouldn't it? If all a country has to export is oil, and the oil will run out, what else could it do for energy other than nuclear energy? This is the great Persian Civilization we are talking about. But they sure are going about it in absolutely the worst possible way at the worst possible time.

We are meticulously planning air strikes on about 1,500 targets that will set them quite a way back. This educated and intelligent country is in the grip of these fascistic mullahs that in the last election disqualified something like 1,300 candidates from running because they knew that the people wanted to elect these moderate or progressive individuals to represent them and to govern them.

Item: A gorgeous summer-like day had me on the *Yellow Dragon*. I made a quick stop in Poulsbo at the Central Market. An elderly lady was standing there collecting signatures on a petition to require local utilities to get at least 15% of their energy from sources other that hydrocarbons.

Item: 04-24-06 Monday—The Today Show had a clip of Dan Brown, author of the *Da Vinci Code*, saying something to the effect that, "Science and religion are partners. They are two different languages attempting to tell the same story." Brown is relaxed about the controversy and revels in the discussion. "Controversy and dialogue are healthy for religion as a whole," he says on his website. "Religion has only one true enemy...apathy...and passionate debate is a superb antidote."

He takes cover from the flak by adopting the "but I was only asking" defense. "We are all trying to decipher life's big mysteries", he writes, "and we're each following our own paths of enlightenment. I consider myself a student of many religions. The more I learn, the more questions I have. For me, the spiritual quest will be a life-long work in progress."

Item: 04-25-06 Tuesday—The Today Show had a segment on operations performed on the wrong body part, such as the wrong knee or ear or whatever. 84 cases reported last year and the estimate was that only 1% are reported. That would make the total 8,400 for 2005. I doubt that it is that high but make a big red X on the right spot anyway. The stat given for other surgery errors was 1 in 30.

A decision has been made that the two Seawolf-class fast-attack submarines that are to be shifted to the West Coast will be based not at Bangor but at Bremo, according to Congressman Norm Dicks. They will move here from Groton, CT in the summer of 2007.

Item: If your car was as efficient as a Black Hole, you would get about a billion miles per gallon. Looks like God doesn't have to worry about us catching up to him anytime soon.

Fox News—Tens of thousands of rescue and cleanup workers from the Twin Towers 9-11 site are and will become gravely ill due to toxic waste that they were exposed to. Doctors say the 2,700 who died that day were the tip of the iceberg. A detective on the broadcast has months to live and has a drug bill of $7 thousand monthly. The government is not helping them. He is facing a choice, if he switches to Medicare part D for the drug benefit, the rest of his family will loose the drug coverage that they now have.

Item: Iran hints at pulling out of the Nuclear Nonproliferation Treaty if the U.N. Atomic Energy Agency tries to stop them from enriching uranium.

Item: Israel successfully launched today a highly accurate imaging satellite enhancing its ability to spy on Iran. Israeli Defense Minister Shaul Mofaz said that Iran's nuclear program was the most serious threat faced by Jews since the Nazi Holocaust. The Eros B satellite has a camera that can decipher objects on the ground as small as 70 centimeters across. It orbits the Earth in a polar orbit, across the rotation, and can monitor changes on the ground on a daily basis.

The satellite covers every square kilometer worldwide, including Iran. It was launched from the Svobodny Cosmodrome in the Russian Far East using a Russian Start-1 rocket. The United States accuses Iran of seeking to build nuclear bombs and has refused to rule out military options if diplomacy fails. Iran says its nuclear program is peaceful and aimed at generating electricity.

Item: Senate Hearings on Bush, Now — In this Vanity Fair.com exclusive, a Watergate veteran and Vanity Fair contributor calls for bipartisan hearings investigating the Bush Presidency. Should Republicans on the Hill take the high road and save themselves come November? — By Carl Bernstein

Worse than Watergate? High crimes and misdemeanors justifying the impeachment of George W. Bush, as increasing numbers of Democrats in Washington hope, and, sotto voce, increasing numbers of Republicans...including some of the president's top lieutenants...now fear. Leaders of both parties are acutely aware of the vehemence of anti-Bush sentiment in the country, expressed especially in the increasing number of Americans, nearing fifty percent in some polls, who say they would favor impeachment if the president were proved to have deliberately lied to justify going to war in Iraq.

Item: Two Columbine type plots were uncovered this week. The first involved five Kansas teenagers at Riverton Kansas High School who allegedly planned to mark the seventh anniversary of the Columbine High School massacre in Colorado with a shooting spree of their own.

Two days later six seventh-graders at the North Pole Middle School in Alaska were arrested and accused of planning to kill both fellow students and teachers.

Item: 04-26-06 Wednesday—A Toledo, Ohio priest is standing trial for the murder of a nun, just before Easter twenty-six years ago. Father Robinson is charged with strangling and stabbing Sister Margaret Ann Pahl at the hospital where they worked. The body was found in the chapel of Mercy Hospital draped in altar cloth and surrounded by candles. The elderly nun had been strangled and stabbed about thirty-two times with a letter opener.

Police suspected Robinson at the time but didn't have enough evidence. Two years ago the cold case squad got a big break. An ongoing investigation into allegations of sex abuse by priests brought forward a woman who claimed that she'd been victimized during Satanic rituals involving Father Robinson. Detectives took a new look at the evidence using CSI-type blood spatter technology that enabled them to zero in on both the murder weapon and Father Robinson. What is this with murdering priests and Easter?

Item: Georgia plans to teach Bible classes in schools, while five other states consider doing the same. The National Council for Bible Curriculum in Public schools is backed by many conservative sects, Evangelicals and Pat Robinson. It states that its curriculum is already in 353 school districts. The Georgia move would be the first time that a state has officially endorsed a Bible study program, according to the May 01 issue of Newsweek.

Item: Another Newsweek article by Michael Hirsh—Stuck in the Hot Zone—Describes how our armed Predator drones flying in Baghdad are being piloted remotely from Las Vegas, Nevada. It also describes one of out four super-bases being built in Iraq, namely Balad Air Base. Currently Ballad has 27,500 takeoffs and landings monthly making it second only to London's Heathrow in traffic volume.

Item: The NPR program Fresh Air tonight interviewed Bart D. Ehrman who has a book out, *Peter, Paul, and Mary Magdalene*: The Followers of Jesus in History and Legend. The readers who rated it on Amazon.com have given it five stars.

He covers a lot of ground but for our purposes his depiction of Jesus as an Apocalyptic Jew is telling. He shows that Jesus believed that his generation would be around for the coming of God and the establishment of eternal life on a utopian Earth. This was a resurrection of actual bodies, not a matter of souls going to Heaven. Heaven was to be in the here and now. Later when he was allegedly resurrected, his followers thought that he was merely the first and they all would be on their way shortly. Of course it never happened.

He has studied the Gnostic gospels that were never included in the Bible and are therefore non-canonical. The early Christian beliefs were extremely diverse. After Jesus' death Peter took over the leadership and performed all kinds of miracles. Like any 'fish story' with time these miracles grew more and more numerous and frankly absurd. At one point they reportedly would just lay out rows of sick people and all it took was the falling of Peter's shadow on someone to cure whatever ailed them. Another story is that when Peter was preaching in Rome about the resurrection of Jesus and the crowd was skeptical, Peter went over to a fish stall, grabbed a smoked tuna fish and threw it in some water bringing it back to life.

Item: 04-27-06 Thursday—The first major genocide of the 21st Century has and is going on in Darfur, the western side of the Sudan. Perhaps as many as 400,000 have already been slaughtered and millions are homeless. What has been the world's response to this? What have the world's political and religious leaders done?

I don't know. What I do know is that George Clooney, Angelina Jolie and Brad Pitt, and Oprah are out front trying to raise awareness and urging everyone to contact their political leaders. Imagine that! If it weren't for a few movie actors and a TV icon, most of us wouldn't even know about it. That is certainly a splendid example of citizens taking matters into their own hands. But what a shame it is upon the world's power structure that they have to. How much does it cost to run the United Nations each year…over ten billion dollars?

Here is a moral question for those religious judgmental types who take such pleasure in condemning others. Angelina is pregnant with Brad's baby even though they are not married. Do you consider her to be immoral? Ms. Jolie has adopted children from Cambodia and Ethiopia. While very far along with her pregnancy, she is living in Africa doing everything she can to help these children and is urging all nations to mandate schooling for all children. What are you doing?

Brad Pitt and Angelina Jolie and the kids were recently named 'The World's Most Beautiful Family'. That is exactly what we are so sorely in need of, people who live by ethical principals and not by dogmatic religious hooey.

Item: A book published by Globe Pequot Press, *Gardenwalks of the Pacific Northwest* features five gardens on the Olympic Peninsular. Of these five gardens, four are in Kitsap County. They are the Bainbridge Public Library Gardens, the Bloedel Reserve, the Little and Lewis Garden Gallery, and the Heronswood Nursery Ltd.

Item: Religious Leaders from all over the world met yesterday at Georgetown University. The two-day International Prayer for Peace included, Eastern Orthodox Christians, Jews, Menno- nites, Methodists, Muslims, Roman Catholics, and Shintoists.

Item: 04-28-06 Friday—The Today Show had George Clooney and his 72-year-old father, a reporter, speaking about Darfur. They had just returned and were calling for a worldwide uprising of the people to stop this genocide. The Sudan Government is supporting and arming the Muslim African Arab militias who are robbing, raping, and killing the Muslim African Blacks, and driving them out of the country into Chad.

Two out of six million have already lost everything and are in refugee camps where they are still being attacked. Villagers who must go forth daily to survive have to choose between sending out their men who will be killed or women who will be raped. As in Bosnia, the wholesale raping is meant to destroy the soul of a society. The Sudanese government in Khartoum is apparently being protected by China, France, and Russia. For the latter it is all about Sudanese oil.

Meanwhile, back at the ranch, Kitsap County plans two more Softball Fields in South Kitsap.

Item: Last night NOVA was *Ancient Refuge in the Holy Land*. Remote caves in the most inhospitable desert of Israel, formerly Judea, were explored that had apparently been used by rebels both at the time of the destruction of the Temple in 66 AD and again in 132 AD when the Romans got really cranky and slaughtered a few more hundred thousand Jews.

This *Cave of Letters* was very interesting and in the same neighborhood where the eleven caves containing the 800 Dead Sea Scrolls were found. Only one of those scrolls was on copper.

That one told of sixty-four locations where sacred objects from the Temple were hidden before its destruction. This program had me convinced that the 'Cave of Letters' was one of those sixty-four locations and items recovered from it were buried as described in the copper scroll and therefore from the Temple.

But like the *Da Vinci Code*, for me it all adds up to a big nothing as far as God is concerned. Sure it is interesting that these artifacts were once used to slaughter animals as a sacrifice to God and even had pagan symbols on them. But the fact remains that sacrificing animals to God is no more effective than tossing virgins into volcanoes. All it does is reveal your ignorance. God sacrifices a gazillion critters per nanosecond…do you really think that he needs your goat?

Item: Randall L. McCloy Jr. the sole surviving minor who now lives on Miracle Road has just written a letter to the families of those who died in the mine. In it he states that four of the survival air-packs didn't even work and there were not enough to go around. Pretty shabby doings for a Divine intervention.

I would think that more reliance should be placed on the company's stocking the mine with more emergency equipment and air-packs that work. It is also coming out that the rescue effort was delayed an intolerable eleven hours! What that tells me is that without that unconscionable delay and sufficient air-packs, that all these brave hardworking men would have survived. According to McCloy, they stuck together, shared what air that they had, recited the 'Sinners Prayer' together and went out as the real mensch that they were. Praise the Lord but pass the ammunition.

Item: A NOW program on KCTS featured a story out of Lancaster, Ohio. A conservative Evangelical Senior Pastor named Russell Johnson is apparently violating IRS rules of separation of church and state by actively campaigning for a fellow conservative Christian named Ken Blackwell. Pastor Johnson takes the Bible literally, states that you should act on your beliefs, and preaches that Evolution is a fiction and Creationism is a fact.

He has established the 'Ohio Restoration Project' and publishes a newspaper. All are tools in his political efforts. He is associated with the Arlington Group, also known as the American Taliban.

The Arlington Group is composed of virulent so-called pro-lifers and is attempting the passage of a marriage amendment. Three of Arlington's hatchet-men are: Focus on the Family's Dr. James Dobson; Chairman of the Free Congress Foundation, Paul Weyrich; and last but not least, Jerry Falwell, a prominent Southern Baptist wing-nut who is famous for making false and wildly outrageous statements followed by retractions and sham apologies. This group has many other far right pieces of work like Don Wildmon, President of the American Family Association.

Looking at Senior Pastor Russell Johnson I had to wonder if this self-righteous pasty-faced milquetoast guy actually believed what he was putting out or if he is a wolf in sheep's clothing. To my mind, where he gave himself away was when the reporter braced him with some telling questions. He was so smooth and slick when parrying those questions that you could see the fast mind working behind the placid facade. He could not possible be the saintly dimwit that he pretends to be.

The History Channel had a Modern Marvels program on Paint. One detail was the fact that the first known use of paint dates back thirty-four thousand years to cave paintings in France. Now as soon as you misinform children that the Universe is only six thousand years old, you have put their minds in an irreconcilable position with respect to nothing less than reality. How schizoid is that? And as mentioned earlier, I have traced my own DNA back seventy thousand years to Africa.

Item: 04-29-06 Saturday—Bremo and the port city of Yantai, China are to become sister cities. Yantai has a population of 6.5 million and is also located on a peninsula; Bremo is on the Kitsap Peninsula. Yantai is situated south of Beijing where the Bohai Sea meets the Yellow Sea.

Item: Nashville—Southern Baptist Activists are urging members to remove their children from public schools so they won't learn the science of Evolutionary reality but rather be home schooled where they will be brainwashed with the myth of Creationism.

Item: Linda Schrenko, the first woman elected to a Georgia statewide political office is about to stand trial in U.S. District Court. As the Superintendent of State Schools and a conservative Republican Christian she pushed for Bible Studies in the schools and the teaching of Creationism. Although married, Schrenko took her Deputy Superintendent on as a lover and according to the complaint, as a partner in crime.

She stands accused of embezzling $614,000 in Federal Department of Education funds. Some of this money was allegedly used for such things as her failed run for the Governorship, a face-lift, a computer, a TV, and the down payment on an automobile. Her lover has already pled guilty and is expected to "Turn State's Evidence" against her.

Now isn't that something! If a woman can push Creationism into schools Statewide and make a run for Governor, while lying, fornicating, and thieving...it looks like we had better open up that 'Greedy Old Rich Men Lusting for More Power Club' to women.

I rode the *Yellow Dragon* 7-8 hours in rain to and from Cape Disappointment for a Navy League Tour of the U.S. Coast Guard Station there. Cape Disappointment is located in the southwest corner of the Olympic Peninsula at the mouth of the Columbia River and across from Astoria, Oregon.

The USCG personnel were just great. We went up to the lookout point and down to the boats. The standard boats are the 47' aluminum rescue craft powered by twin V6 turbo charged diesels, but the special boat, one of only four ever made, was the *Triumph*, a 52' steel beauty powered by twin inline 6 Detroit Diesels. It can go out to sea when nothing else can.

The highlight of these tours is 'crossing the bar' as the rough water is called where the river empties into the Pacific Ocean. When the tide rises and the ocean water wants to come in against the river's outflow the rough water can make for a very interesting ride.

I can't say that riding the bike in what eventually became a rare downpour was delightful but it was still enjoyable. Riding a bike is like sex or pizza, when it is good it is great and when it is bad...it is still pretty good.

Item: 04-30-06 Sunday—The SEED Project, Sustainable Energy and Economic Development, was endorsed by the Kitsap Economical Development Council. It will be built near the Bremo National Airport on 72 acres. The energy efficient stand-alone buildings will generate their own electricity and not require water or sewer hook-ups.

World-renowned economist and Harvard professor John Kenneth Galbraith died yesterday at age 97 in Cambridge, MA. His many books included *The Affluent Society* in 1958 and *The New Industrial State* in 1967. He argued that the free market economy had become a myth as our economy and life have become dominated by the top one thousand U.S. corporations.

May 2006

Item: 05-01-06 Monday—This is Day 90 and the last day for Phase I—The Bremo Memo. I truly hate to end it on the following note but the facts compel me to do so.

Item: Regarding the Duke University Lacrosse Team scandal, the Black Panthers have entered the fray and are marching at Duke declaring the players guilty before trial. This is sadly so perfectly on point with my earlier observations.

I don't recall hearing about the Black Panthers in decades. It is as if they have been waiting all this time for the worst possible cause to get behind. Their cause celeb this time is a stripper. One who was not hired from a Striping Service but rather from an Escort Service, and we all know what that means. The woman was found passed out drunk and taken to a drug rehab and mental health location by police. It was only after all that had happened that she first alleged that she was raped by three lacrosse players. At first her co-stripper stated that she did not believe it. The DNA test from the players all came back negative. She has made contradictory statements.

This accuser had once before in her life accused three people of having raped her. Her own father said he didn't believe her that time. Charges were never filed. She accused an ex-husband of dragging her into the woods to kill her. He denied the charge and she never showed up in court. She has had mental breakdowns and been in therapy. She is deep in debt. She has a record of being caught driving a stolen car. She stated that one of the rapists had a mustache but none of the players have one. One of the two players charged seems to have an airtight alibi. What a mess!

Now of course she could be correct. None of us are in a position to prejudge this without more evidence. But if anyone should respect the notion of innocent until proven guilty it should be the Black Panthers. How many great causes have come and gone in the past thirty years? Yet they wait for this can of worms! They have totally destroyed their image and reason for existence in my eyes. Back in the 60s I had respect for Huey Newton, Bobby Seale and the Black Panther Party for Self-Defense. They did good things for the Oakland Black Community and showed real courage. But this march on Duke chanting 'Guilty' was nothing more than blatant ignorance on parade. What a shame.

Suppose the team players were Black and there was a drunken White stripper/hooker with a police record making the accusations. What if the KKK was marching declaring the Black men guilty before trial? If turn around is fair play, what would the Black Community think of that?

Item: Bill O'Reilly had engaged Ex Sex Crimes Prosecutor Wendy Murphy, a strident female gunslinger to honcho his drive against child molesters. But now he must realize that she is several fries short of a Happy Meal. She was on last night commenting on the above Duke Scandal and she defended the Black Panthers stating that she sees no need for the presumption of innocence outside of the courtroom either. Then she stepped all over Bill's lines. What is this world coming to when your own hired gun turns on you? Hilarious!

Final Item: The illegal immigrants' boycott is on today across the nation. The word I have from Los Angeles is that the freeway traffic is so light that people are zipping to work in ten minutes. Careful, this alone could cause a boycott backfire if commuters get the notion that life would in fact be a lot easier without the undocumented workers. That reminds me of the very politically incorrect joke about the two Mexican families that were submitted to the *Guinness Book of World Records*. One had an only child and the other one had automobile insurance. Lo siento mucho mis amigos. Perdonarme por favor!

Well that should do it. If I have somehow failed to insult any group that you may belong to, take heart, there is always Phase II and Phase III. Please send all concerns and hate mail to: tom@flymonster.com

The time is up and we have all we need and more to fully complete Phase I. A major omen has made an appearance. That money clip that I lost on February 01 has reappeared in a glove. Apparently what happened at the body shop was that I did toss the clipped money into my backpack. Chance had it fly completely into a glove. When I arrived home, the first thing I did was to remove those gloves and put them in a closet. After that, all the searching and backtracking that I did was doomed to failure.

What this planet needs and all life on it, above the insects, is for mankind to conduct his life within a rational and ethical framework. The major religions have gone so far off the track that instead of aiding that pursuit and being the solution, they have become in large measure one of the most intractable parts of the problem.

Which religions are the worst you might ask? It is not a matter of religion generally but of Fundamentalism. It is those people going through life backwards with blinders firmly on. Instead of focusing on the future and its needs, they are rooted in books centuries old, and deny the reality all around themselves. Of the three main people of the Book that we have concentrated on, the Jewish orthodox seem to cause the least trouble, and with their full beards, long black overcoats, and odd hats…you can at least see them coming.

The fascist Muslims are raising hell but are in a tight spot, mostly of their own making, and have little real power other than a willingness to blow themselves up. It is hard to win a war of attrition with that technique, and if they do manage to get WMDs and use them, our response will surely be to annialate them all. Make no mistake about that. Even with tactical nukes and radiation-clean neutrino bombs, the fallout is not realistically calculable.

The regular Christians that are the most zealous and loony seem to be the Pentecostals and the Evangelicals. These people are really scary. They have power and are irrational. Another group that really bears watching are the Mormons. I do not personally consider them Christians. They have wandered totally off that reservation. Their beliefs seem to be based on nothing even remotely grounded in reality of any kind.

They are extremely united and disciplined and function in a fascistic way. Whereas most churches collect money from their parishioners and then forward some up to their hierarchies, all monies collected by each Mormon church goes directly to Salt Lake City. Salt Lake then decides how much to send back to each church! Those at the top have everyone by the short hairs.

They have global aims and with their missionary programs they are carrying them out. I am perhaps painting them as devils in disguise. The majority of the individual members are really some of the nicest people you could hope to meet and as kind and honest as the day is long. But it is a fascist organization running a Theocracy in one of our States and they are making a successful effort to infiltrate all levels of governmental power on a national basis.

Already there is talk of Governor Mitt Romney of Massachusetts running for President of the United States in 2008. What I want to know is how in the world did a Michigan Republican Mormon became Governor of a staunchly Democratic State like Massachusetts in the first place? Be afraid…be very afraid.

I should add that I personally have no knowledge of Governor Romney. He may be the greatest guy ever. He has to be extremely talented to have gotten where he is. He is behind the plan to see that almost all Massachusetts residents are covered by health insurance. That seems like a good thing and long overdue. Or is that the 'bait' to try for a successful run at the Presidency?

I don't doubt but that Mormons are efficient. Fascists are very efficient, at least in the short run. The trouble with 100% efficiency is that it allows for 0% creativity. To understand 100% efficiency we only have to look at such beings as ants or termites. They are so efficient that if a comrade expires, they stop and eat him. The thing is, ants and termites are doing exactly the same thing today that they were doing hundreds of millions of years ago…and will be doing hundreds of millions of years from now. That is not what human beings are all about. It is learning from our errors and mistakes that lifts us up.

I mentioned above some elitist Fundamentalist Orthodox Jews being comfortable ripping off goyim. There are a significant number of Mormons who feel the same way whether it be outright scams, welfare fraud especially by the polygamists, or dubious MLM schemes. They even have a name for the welfare fraud; they call it 'Bleeding the Beast'. The American taxpayers being the Beast.

You don't have to look any further than the Mafia to find overtly religious Christian criminals

A friend in a position to know who is generally aware of what I am into with this has advised me that a real sicko named Warren Steed Jeffs will soon become a national household name. It seems that Mr. Jeffs is a 'living god' prophet of a huge outlaw Mormon polygamous sect. His history and practices are alleged to be enough to turn any stomach.

Of course there are criminals of every stripe but when you pretend to be highly religious and God's chosen ones and are thieving, I think that warrants special exposure and condemnation for the blatant hypocrisy that it represents. The elitism angle is a significant one. This is a big appeal for people who perhaps have feelings of inferiority. For these people to be able to psychologically negate those internal feelings by joining a belief system that tells them that they are superior to all others…that is very attractive to them and creates an almost unbreakable bond.

Should fate decide that this document be widely circulated, you can be sure that there will be those who will labor to refute and dismiss it. It should not be difficult to nitpick it. I am mostly recording this in a cold vehicle, in a cramped position, at night in the dark. To find a little error here and a number that is a bit off over there…that should be easy to do. That will be your clue that you are being subjected to yet another snow job. A snow job inundates you with so many little facts, true or otherwise, that you end up not being able to see the forest for the trees.

I am not a trained scholar. I am just a Joe six-pack who is an avid reader. The figures I am using may not always be precise but they should all be in the ballpark and not off by any order of magnitude. The breakdown of the estimated of 30 to 40 thousand daily deaths due to extreme poverty are not exact. They represent a total due mostly to outright starvation but also to those caused by what should be easily remedied medical conditions such as diarrhea.

What I am giving you is an overview with many pieces of the puzzle. Imagine you are in the International Space Station orbiting our Earth. This gives you an almost God-like view and perspective on the planet. You have a monitor in front of you that allows you to zoom in and out anywhere that you want as the globe rotates beneath you.

You can literally see the rainforest being diminished, the ice sheets melting, the new cities of humans springing up every few days, the pollution billowing forth in the air and running into the seas, and unfortunately you can zoom in and observe the tens of thousands of people starving to death on a daily basis.

Above, the U.S. Congress likened the deaths in this country caused by cigarette smoking to be the equivalent of two fully loaded jumbo jets crashing each day. Using that same scale, forty thousand daily needless deaths would amount to more than thirty jumbo jets crashing each and every day or about eleven thousand crashes per year. Of course these people don't ride on jumbo jets...they walk.

You have to wonder why all on the planet are not scurrying to alleviate this dire, horrifying situation. Then you eventually determine that in fact, many in positions of influence and authority are deliberately making the situation worse. It is a fact that the more fear and division that exists, the easier it is to rule the populations. What are you to do? Here is one piece of advice:

The powers that be often persecute those who sound the alarm, not those who set or are fanning the fire.

Mankind has come so far. We are literally on the verge of understanding and dealing with so many aspects of Creation at the most fundamental levels. We have mapped the human genome and are studying the parts of it. We are refining our abilities to handle nuclear fission and particularly fusion. Our capabilities with chemistry, engineering, sub-atomic physics and all manner of sciences are enhanced and improved daily if not hourly. The possibilities with nano-technology are mind-boggling.

The May 2006 issue of Scientific American has an article on page 34 where they describe recreating the first few microseconds of the Big Bang at Brookhaven National Laboratory on Long Island. They are crashing opposing gold nuclei at nearly the speed of light and creating temperature in the trillions of degrees. The next article is about DNA computers that could give rise to machines so small that could speak directly to living cells.

Given the above, why would we risk it all by basing our actions on the early attempts of simple, uninformed, tribal, nomadic, desert folk hundreds and thousands of years ago as they strove to understand their world? We don't live or think like they did. We don't live in the shelters that they did. We don't get around on donkeys or camels like they did. We don't dress like they did. One would be hard pressed to come up with anything that they did that we value enough to be copying them today.

So why in the name of God would we blindly follow their lead in matters of our understanding of reality? Why would rational people even consider acting so when the changing times have made doing so harmful to us, to the planet, and to all future generations? Why...habit?

The American people do not yet fully understand 9-11, what happened that day and why. When they do, and they will…sooner rather than later, I would wish that you would reread this document, recalling that a cornerstone of civilization is human sacrifice.

Here are some quotes from that marvelous human being and Founding Father of our country, Benjamin Franklin:

I conceive that the great part of the miseries of mankind are brought upon them by false estimates they have made of the value of things.

Hear reason, or she'll make you feel her.

He that's secure is not safe.

An investment in knowledge pays the best interest.

A small leak will sink a great ship.

The following quote is just too timely to leave out:

"Fascism should more appropriately be called Corporatism because it is a merger of state and corporate power"

The above was delivered by none other than Benito Mussolini, way back in 1925!

The future is unwritten. The one we get is up to us.

Allow me to end with a quote from what else, the Bible—John 8:32.

"And ye shall know the truth and the truth shall make you free." Jesus of Nazareth

* * * * *

So you have reached the end of Phase 1 of the Bremo Beacon and you complain that you still do not have a clue as to what in the hell is really going on here!

I feel your pain, really I do. Here is a clue: Powerful outside forces want Bremo to soar like the eagle that she is…but the triggering impetus must come from within. Are we happy now?

The fact that sixty percent of blighted Bremo is comprised of rental units will make the task much easier than earlier supposed, but it is certainly no walk in the park. Phase II of this report, that begins mañana on May 02, 2006, will hopefully make everything quite clear.

Meanwhile let me leave you with one last thought: Never let your dog guard your lunch.

CPSIA information can be obtained at www.ICGtesting.com
261569BV00001B/16/P

9 781424 167319